MW00652336

Understanding Modern Japan

Understanding Modern Japan

A Political Economy of Development, Culture and Global Power

P.W. Preston

SAGE Publications
London • Thousand Oaks • New Delhi

© P.W. Preston 2000

First published 2000

All rights reserved. No part of this publication may be
reproduced, stored in a retrieval system, transmitted or
utilized in any form or by any means, electronic, mechanical,
photocopying, recording or otherwise, without permission in
writing from the Publishers.

SAGE Publications Ltd
6 Bonhill Street
London EC2A 4PU

SAGE Publications Inc
2455 Teller Road
Thousand Oaks, California 91320

SAGE Publications India Pvt Ltd
32, M-Block Market
Greater Kailash – I
New Delhi 110 048

British Library Cataloguing in Publication data

A catalogue record for this book is available
from the British Library

ISBN 0 7619 6195 X
ISBN 0 7619 6196 8 (pbk)

Library of Congress catalog card number 99–75740

Typeset by Mayhew Typesetting, Rhayader, Powys
Printed in Great Britain by Athenaeum Press, Gateshead

CONTENTS

PREFACE

In the wake of the end of the Cold War there has been a rise in concern among scholars, policy analysts and political commentators with the overall dynamics of the global system. In the context of a newly prominent concern for 'geo-economics', the emergence of an increasingly integrated and distinctive Pacific-Asian region is of considerable interest. The core economy of the region is Japan. The text looks at the development history of Japan and considers the exchanges of Japan with the countries of the Pacific-Asian region, and thereafter the wider global system, where each distinctive phase is informed by a particular Japanese political-cultural project.

The text is intellectually grounded in the classical European tradition of social theorizing with its broad concern to elucidate the dynamics of complex political-economic, social-institutional and cultural change within the developing global industrial-capitalist system.

I hope that the book will provide a useful introduction to those who are new to the study of Japan and will be of some interest to established scholars who are concerned with the role of Japan within the dynamic Pacific-Asian region.

ACKNOWLEDGEMENTS

The present text took its preliminary form while I was Canon Foundation Research Fellow in the Faculty for Comparative Culture of Sophia University, Tokyo. I should like to thank the director of the foundation Mr Richard Burke and his colleague Ms Corrie Siahaya-Van Nierop for their help. In Tokyo I was given assistance by very many kind people and I should like to thank Professor Saadollah Ghaussy, Professor Radha Sinha, Professor John Clammer, Professor Richard Gardner, Professor Kate Nakai, Professor Linda Grove, Father Maurice Bairy, Mrs Ueda, Mrs Hamabata, Mrs Fujisaki and my groups of summer-school students. The text has been completed in the rather different surroundings of the Department of Political Science and International Studies at the University of Birmingham, England, and I should like to thank my colleagues and students for their congenial and positive company. I should also like to thank Professor Glenn Hook, Professor Ian Neary and an anonymous reader who commented most encouragingly on my early manuscript proposal. Lucy Robinson has been my editor at Sage and I am happy to record my thanks to her. Professor Hook kindly read the completed manuscript, as did my colleague in the University of Birmingham Japan Centre, Dr Julie Gilson, and I am grateful for their sympathetic and acute criticism.

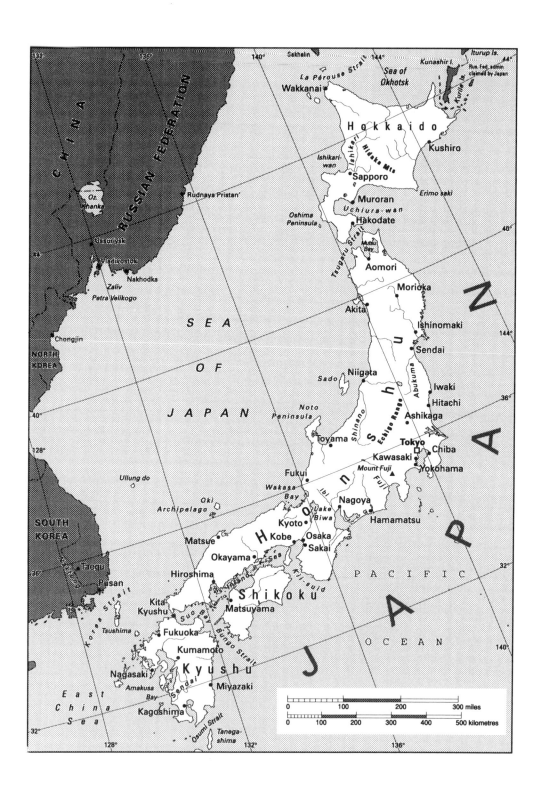

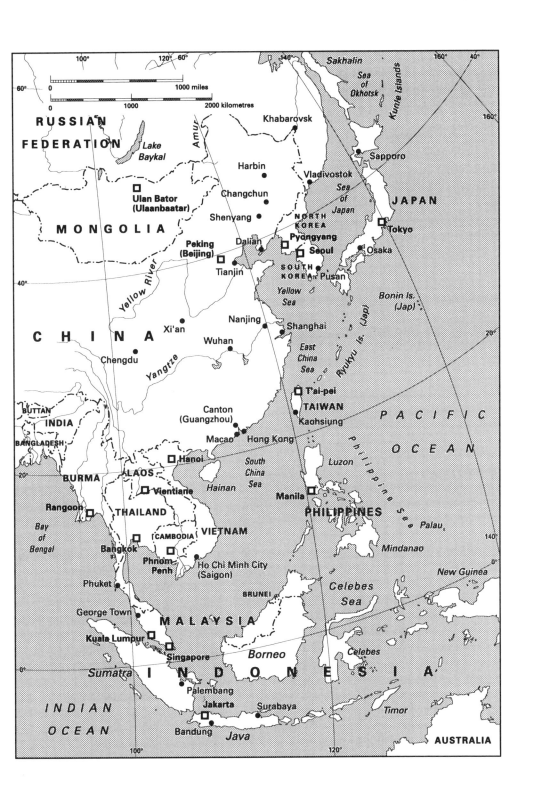

1

THE HISTORICAL DEVELOPMENT EXPERIENCE OF JAPAN

This study is concerned with the historical development experience of Japan in the context of its relations with the countries of Pacific Asia and the wider global system. As will become clear in this text, one cannot identify a 'region' on the basis of simple geography. In social scientific terms a region is an historically constituted sphere which comprises, in some measure or other, an extensive economic network, significant social linkages and deep cultural resources that enable the elites and masses of the region to understand themselves in terms of a broadly common identity. In this way we can speak of North Americans, Europeans and Asians. The term Pacific Asia identifies those Asian countries which border the Pacific Ocean – Japan, North Korea, South Korea, China, Taiwan, Hong Kong, Vietnam, Laos, Cambodia, Thailand, Burma, the Philippines, Malaysia, Brunei, Singapore, Indonesia and Papua New Guinea. It is a 'contested region' as membership, character and future lines of development are all disputed. It might be noted that Pacific Asia is not the same as Asia-Pacific, a term which reduces the Pacific Ocean to the status of an American lake and locks the economies and futures of the countries of Asia to those of the USA. The more familiar terms for the countries dealt with here would be Southeast and East Asia. The term Pacific Asia is preferred in order to call attention to the region's role within the wider global system (see Preston, 1998a).

This chapter will introduce the intellectual approach adopted, outline the substantive material to be addressed and note a series of issues which will run throughout the text. In brief, first, the discussion will be grounded in the classical European tradition of social theorizing which is concerned with the elucidation of the dynamics of complex change in the ongoing process of the shift to the modern world. It is possible, using these theoretical materials, to characterize the patterns of structural constraint and opportunity within which agents pursue their political-cultural projects. In this context, second, the substantive development history of Japan can be analysed as a series of phases, characterized by particular political-cultural projects, which together embrace the long period from the nineteenth century, with the concern for development and security associated with the Meiji Restoration, through to current discussions of contemporary regional dynamics, which are centred upon the idea of Pacific Asia. Finally, the chapter will introduce a series of more particular interrelated issues which will be pursued throughout the text:

1 The contested nature of the development history of Japan, where there are scholarly and politically occasioned debates about the country, the region and their dynamics.
2 The extent to which it is possible to speak of a distinctively Japanese (and, thereafter, Pacific-Asian) model of industrial-capitalist development.
3 The implications of the rise of Japan and the region for European and American social theorists, policy analysts and political commentators.

Approaches to the analysis of Japan

This text is grounded in the classical European tradition of social theorizing (Preston, 1996). It is a distinctive tradition whose central concern is with the elucidation of the dynamics of complex change in the ongoing shift to the modern world. It is the tradition which the author inhabits. It is also different from the more familiar realm of American and American-influenced work, with its characteristically discipline-based concern for putatively technical analyses of industrial society. It is also quite different from indigenous Japanese traditions of systematic reflection upon the social world (Dale, 1986; Yoshino, 1992; Clammer, 1995).

In dealing with the social sciences it is generally possible to identify the ways in which particular contexts shape intellectual enquiry. One might assert that social scientists are not exempt from the action of those social forces which they study (Hawthorn, 1971) or, more strongly, that social scientists are inevitably embedded within received cultural traditions which provide the necessary materials for formal critical reflection (Gadamer, 1960; Habermas, 1989). In this context, it is clear that in the years following the end of World War II the USA attained a broad hegemony (that is, economic, military/diplomatic and cultural dominance) within the territories of the West. The influence of the work of American social scientists throughout the West in the post-World War II period flowed from this hegemonic position. For a brief period of time what counted, generally, as social science, its methods and substantive concerns, was established by the particular intellectual traditions of the community of scholars in the USA and the period was dominated by the naturalistic study of industrial society (Giddens, 1979).

The social science which produced the theories of industrial society was lodged firmly within the American intellectual and institutional context, with its characteristic, early twentieth-century, naturalism, professionalization and disciplinization (Giddens, 1979; Swedberg, 1987).

The generic methods of social science were taken to follow, in outline, those which were understood to be typical of the natural sciences, a mixture of induction and realism, such that scientific enquiry was understood to centre on the pursuit of accurate descriptions of what there was in reality. The work was positivistic in both intellectual conception and practical intent (Fay, 1975, 1987). Social science, thereafter, was split into specialist disciplines (economics, sociology, political science, international relations, etc.) and in turn these disciplines were separated into sub-disciplines. Each of these disciplines had its own place in the institutions of learning and each defended its own territory. Finally, American work tended to adopt an applied empirical approach as each discipline took itself to be competing within an intellectual/ institutional marketplace and it had to stand out in order to prosper (Mills, 1959). Each discipline laid claim to a particular body of knowledge and an accumulated spread of technical expertise which might be deployed by consumers in the knowledge marketplace to secure practical ends. The general object of enquiry was conceived as that form of industrial society which had first evolved in the seventeenth to nineteenth centuries, the early modern period, in Europe and America.

In the period of American intellectual hegemony the general object of enquiry, industrial society, formed an element of a wider package of ideas:

1 Industrialism: the system was driven by an underlying logic of industrialism (Kerr, 1973).
2 Convergence: the First and Second Worlds would converge on a single model, not capitalism and not socialism but a common model driven by the common logic of industrialism.
3 Modernization: whereby the Third World could catch up and join in with the industrial world.
4 The end of ideology: as general affluence became the norm debates about alternative types of society would fade away into irrelevance.

The wider package expressed the view that the global system as a whole was moving in the direction of the model of the developed West.[1] The package has found recent reaffirmation in the guise of theories of globalization/postmodernism where the same ineluctable logic of the market-based industrial system is presented once again as entailing convergence. As before, these arguments, which work to assimilate the diverse forms of life within the global system to the historical experience of the USA, are sharply different from those made within the classical European tradition.

Against this version of social science there has been a recent rediscovery of European social theory which, in contrast to the American approach, is concerned with the analysis of the dynamics of complex change in the ongoing shift to the modern world (Winch, 1958; Giddens,

1979, 1982; Bauman, 1987; Habermas, 1989). This conception of social scientific enquiry is also a part of a wider package of ideas, in this case, the pursuit of the modernist project (Pollard, 1971). The notion of modernity is lodged deeply within European culture and expresses a set of ideas about the place of reason in human life. The modernist project celebrates the power of human reason and looks to its extension to all areas of life – thus natural science, the rational ordering of society, and the rational collective decision making of democratic systems of government. This project is taken to be ongoing. The familiar form in which all this is expressed is as a belief in progress.[2] Overall, the classical European tradition of social theorizing is the key (inevitable) resource of this text. It will provide the materials for the articulation of a distinctively European approach and the framework for a routine endeavour to dialogically appropriate the work of Japanese scholars.

Classical European tradition of social theorizing

The widest context for the approach taken in this text is the European modernist project with its extensive and profound celebration of reason. Within this broad context there is a more specific context, that of formal social theorizing, where we can say that the core of the European tradition of social theorizing is the attempt to elucidate the business of complex change in the process of the ongoing shift to the modern world with a view to rendering it amenable to human will. In simple terms, the work of the European tradition finds expression in three sorts of activity:

1 Politics, where analysis and evaluation feed directly into the political public sphere.
2 Policy analysis, where systematic enquiry is presented in a technical fashion as policy science.
3 Scholarship, where enquiry both acknowledges a general concern for dispassionate truth and a particular role for social scientific work, which can be characterized, after the style of Jurgen Habermas, as the provision of emancipatory arguments on behalf of humankind (Habermas, 1971; Holub, 1991).

The classical tradition of European social theorizing deploys a repertoire of key strategies of analysis:

1 The political-economic analysis of economic structures.
2 The social-institutional analysis of social structures.
3 The culture-critical analysis of the ways in which agents understand and act within enfolding structures (Preston, 1996).

All these strategies were considered, initially, within the context of debates within social philosophy. There was no simple borrowing from the model of the natural sciences. Social scientific enquiry was taken to be interpretive and critical rather than descriptive and found its useful-ness in public debate rather than technical expert action. European social theory has been less concerned with disciplinary specialisms (although of course it does have them). It has often pursued work in an intel-lectually catholic fashion, borrowing useful ideas from anywhere. While the work has been routinely practical, it has often proceeded in a distinctly theoretical fashion (Hawthorn, 1971; Giddens, 1987). There-after, it is around the core concern for change, with its characteristic macro strategies of analysis, that a series of more specialist areas of micro analysis cluster, using a variety of strategies of description and analysis (which can be presented as technical expert social science):

(a) economic life;
(b) political life;
(c) social life;
(d) culture.

Legislation and interpretation

The intellectual character of the classical European tradition of social theorizing was shaped by the context within which it was produced. As the context has slowly changed over the years, so too has the articulation of the concerns of the classical tradition. Bauman (1987) has argued that as the countries of Europe developed through the eighteenth and nine-teenth centuries, the European tradition underwent a series of changes and the original alliances of progressive social groups and intellectuals, which had generated the optimistic modernist project, were dissolved. As the new ruling elites became more firmly established in power, their interest in optimistic interpretive work became muted. In the nineteenth-century phase of the high tide of European development and overseas expansion, the available notions of social science tended to be positiv-istic, unreflexive and disposed to 'legislation' (Bauman, 1987). It was supposed that a social scientific analysis of the social world, which would in broad outline rehearse the successes of nineteenth-century natural science, was in process of construction. The multiple confidences of the period in respect of the civilization of the Europeans, the power of their science and the progressive nature of their vigorous commerce combined to produce an approach to the analysis of the social world which was deeply Eurocentric. The experiences of the denizens of other forms of life were measured according to the standards of Europeans.

The scholarship of the period reflected these assumptions of the priority of the Europeans. The various characterizations of the social world offered at this time have entered the commonsense of Europeans and have been transmitted down the generations. The culture which contemporary Europeans inhabit has been in part shaped by these cultural resources. It is clear that this opens up a series of problems for contemporary scholarship. First, we have to acknowledge that the contemporary world, for all its increasing interconnectedness, is home to diverse voices, to different ways of reading the intermingled common history of humanity. Relatedly, we have to acknowledge that we face similar problems in reconstructing a plausible narrative of the intermingled history of the development of the modern world. We can no longer take the historical experience of the West as a model of the historical experience of all peoples, or as a universal model to which all peoples must necessarily defer. Bauman (1987) argues that reflections of this sort point to a reconsidered role for scholarship, a renewal of the notion of 'interpretation'.

It is clear, following Bauman (1987), that the work of the classical tradition can be read reflexively; which is to say that the strategies of analysis can themselves be located within those broad processes which they endeavour to elucidate, and thus can we acknowledge the ways in which the process of the social construction of knowledge shapes those knowledge claims we would make. The classical European tradition of social theorizing represents the materials which theorists and commentators in Europe deployed in formulating. ordering and responding to the shift to the modern world. An approach to analysing complex change which is intellectually plausible according to the tenets of the classical European tradition must be sceptical, dialogic and routinely open to debate and revision (Preston, 1985, 1996).

Overall, for the classical tradition of European social theorizing, the key theoretical terms are these:

1 Emancipatory engagement: a particular value engagement which celebrates the power of rational human beings self-consciously and collectively to order their activities.
2 Elucidatory intention: a particular conception of the nature and possibilities of social science which avoids claims to technical expert positive knowledge in favour of more sceptical and piecemeal contributions to the general ways in which society understands a given issue.
3 A concern for social dynamics: a focus upon the active and changing processes which underlie/constitute the social world we inhabit/observe (Giddens, 1984).
4 A concern for complex change: the making and remaking of whole social systems (economic, social, political and cultural), which set of interlinked processes necessarily involves the social theorist (Gellner, 1964).
5 A concern for the ongoing development of the modern world: the ideal model lodged in these strategies of analysis and first formulated

by the classical European theorists of the nineteenth century is an image of a rational world, an ideal of progress achieved (Pollard, 1971).

Phases, breaks and political-cultural projects in the development history of Japan[3]

In recent years the ideas of globalization and postmodernism have been presented as a way of grasping a series of interlinked processes of liberal market centred economic, social and cultural change which together are taken to be uniquely problematical for contemporary polities. The theorists of globalization and postmodernity argue that a new system has emerged whose fundamental economic, social and cultural logic centres upon marketplace vehicled expressive consumption. As a consequence, the politics of states, nations and publics are redundant. But this is an implausible line of argument, not only in respect of the flaws in the argument machineries (Hirst and Thompson, 1996), but also because in the broad sweep of history it is clear that agents have always had to deal with structural change. Against the dramatic claims of the proponents of globalization and postmodernism it can be asserted that the industrial-capitalist system is always in flux and agents are always adjusting.

Structural change and agent response

The process of long-term change can be analysed in a number of ways, but matters have recently been cast in terms of the dynamics of structural change and agent response. Strange (1988) identifies four key structures – production, finance, security and knowledge – which provide the context for action on the part of agents. In a related way, if we consider systemic change in a broad historical perspective, then it is clear that the trajectory of industrial-capitalist development is not smooth, but is marked by discontinuities, reconfigurations and relatively stable phases. All these are intrinsic to the process of industrial-capitalist intensification and expansion. A series of responses by elite groups to changing historical structural circumstances can be identified. The two lines of reflection allow us to speak of a series of discrete interlinked discontinuous routes to the modern world (Moore, 1966).

Any elite group must read enfolding structural change, formulate a response (identify a route to the future) and order appropriately its population. As the circumstances which constrain the patterns of action of relevant agents change, then agents must respond. These responses will be both necessary, flowing from simple recognition of change, and contingent, as agents self-consciously identify new routes to novel futures. The core set of understandings, intentions and expectations will constitute a distinctive political-cultural project. The way in which elite

groups read and react to enfolding patterns of structural change shapes
both the domestic political-cultural project and, thereafter, wider patterns
of regional and global change.

In this context, it is clear that there have been a series of discrete
phases in the historical development experience of Japan and the region
of Pacific Asia.

Phases in historical development experiences

The idea of phases points to the discontinuous nature of development for
any particular area. Within the frame of any one phase we would expect
to find a specific and continuing pattern of economic, social and cultural
life, a more or less settled way of doing things. The settled form of life
could be characterized both in terms of its internal dynamics and the
linkages which it had with the relevant wider system. The notion of
phases applies generally. It is not restricted to pre-modern times and
runs up to the present day.

If we reflect upon the broad sweep of history then we can point to a
series of fairly typical episodes. After the patterns of change of the pre-
modern period the business of a territory being taken up into the
developing global industrial-capitalist system was not an evolutionary
process or sequence of incremental changes. The shift to the modern
world entailed an interrelated set of discontinuities as economies,
societies and cultures were more or less extensively remade. Thereafter
one might point to the similarly problematical era of formal decolonization. But these are only the broadest of changes. As we pull back from
schematic discussions to attend to the detail of actual cases then we find
that the development experience of any particular area will be determined by shifting global/regional structures and the ways in which local
agent groups read and react to these changing structures in order to plot
routes to the future.

What we should note in all this is that within the parameters of a
particular historical developmental phase there is a specific political-
economic, social-institutional and cultural pattern within the territory
and definite patterns of linkages with the wider global system. It is
within the confines of these broad frameworks that the people of the
territory make their ordinary lives, pursue their several projects and
elaborate their cultural self-understandings. It is also true that when
these settled patterns are disturbed, either as a result of the logics of
internally secured advance, or as the enfolding global structural pattern
shifts with consequent internal implications, then the business of orches-
trating coherent responses is very complex and the resultant period of
complex change can be traumatic for the elite and the general population
alike.

In the case of Japan it is clear that the country has experienced long
periods of relative stability as extant patterns of life persisted down the

years. In this fashion we can point to the period before the late nine-teenth-century arrival of the West when the country saw the rise and fall of a succession of political patterns within the frame of an agrarian political economy (Bowring and Kornicki, 1993). Thereafter the country was drawn into the Western system. The oligarchic rulers of the Meiji Restoration extensively reconstructed the country in line with the demands of the expanding global industrial-capitalist economy and quickly joined the modern world (Beasley, 1990; Iriye, 1997). The early part of the twentieth century saw further Japanese development and regional expansion. The years following the Pacific War saw the wide-spread post-colonial pursuit of national development among the countries of the region and a process of Japanese reconstruction in the context of their Cold War alliance with the USA. In recent years a new regionally ordered pattern has developed around the core economy of Japan.[4]

Breaks in the historical development experiences

The original historical occasion of capitalism has been widely debated and Brenner (1977) has pointed to the pattern of circumstances in late feudal Europe which linked the early development of natural scientific knowledge, and thus the possibility of increasing absolute levels of production, with a pattern of class alliances which allowed existing merchants within agrarian societies to advance their own interests against the established power holders of monarchy and church. It was out of this fortuitous pattern of circumstances that a system developed which required enterprise level technical and organizational innovation and the system as a whole prospered. It is clear that the innovative dynamic of capitalism was not restricted to the intensification of capitalistic activity within any localized domestic sphere but similarly encouraged geographical expansion. In the sixteenth, seventeenth, eighteenth and nineteenth centuries the capitalist system which had been initiated within Europe spread to encompass large areas of the globe. It is therefore clear that for many cultures the impetus to radical change came with shifting patterns within the global system. Change has been impressed upon many cultures. The routes to the modern world taken by non-European territories have depended upon the ways in which local elites have read and reacted to shifting patterns within the enfolding global industrial-capitalist system.

The process of the expansion of global industrial capitalism has made shifting demands on particular territories whose histories will therefore be recorded as a series of discrete phases. The movement from one phase to the next will be discontinuous. It will not be an evolutionary movement. It will be a break, as one pattern is set aside and another developed. It is clear that discontinuous change can place a considerable strain upon existing patterns of social order. An episode of more or less complex change implies that there will be some groups who are 'winners'

and others who are 'losers'. It is at this point that we might begin to
speak of political responses within territories:

1 The shifts and changes initiated by elite groups, which might include
   resistance, accommodation or supercession (Gellner, 1983).
2 The responses of the general population within a territory, which
   again might involve a range of responses (Scott, 1985).
3 The patterns of action of a spread of minority groups (ethnic, religious
   or economic for example).

It is clear that the ways in which the internal dynamics of response to
shifting enfolding patterns are resolved and local political projects
inaugurated will effect the overall trajectory of the shift to the modern
world achieved by the territory.

   In the case of Japan it is clear that the country has experienced a series
of fairly abrupt breaks within its overall historical development experience, ranging from the decline of the earliest unified Yamato state into
the period of medieval civil wars, the assertion of Tokugawa authority
around 1600 and, from 1868, in broad terms, the process of the acceptance and indigenization of the demands of the global industrial-capitalist
system. The earliest contacts made by the West within the region as a
whole were in Southeast Asia where the demands of the incoming
traders were initially supportable within the confines of extant patterns
of life. However, as the pace of economic advance within the metropolitan core accelerated, the demands made upon the territories of
Southeast Asia increased. In the absence of any coherent overall response
by local elites, these areas eventually came to experience a process of
absorption within colonial systems and consequent extensive economic,
social and cultural reconstruction. A little later the ruling elites of China
made the mistake of underestimating the dynamism of the capitalist
system which supported the Western traders coming to Chinese ports
and over the latter part of the nineteenth century China was absorbed as
a quasi-colony. In Japan, the Tokugawa elite was displaced in the Meiji
Restoration, whose leaders, thereafter, contrived a coherent progressive
response to the novel demands placed upon them and by the end of the
century the country had joined the ranks of the Western powers as an
industrial-capitalist society.

Agent's projects in the historical development experience

If we turn to the agent level, we are looking at the various manoeuvres of
the various agents who animate the overall tale. The key players will be
state-regimes, industrial, commercial and financial organizations and the
various groups of ordinary people involved in the region (the newly
prosperous, the newly poor, the marginals, the weak and so on; Moore,
1966; Scott, 1985).

It might be noted that the state should not be seen as a solid bounded unit, enclosing a nation, operating within an overall system comprised of a collectivity of similarly bounded nationstate units, in pursuit of familiar market-liberal goals, but rather as a membrane whereby trans-state, political-economic flows within the global industrial-capitalist system are ordered by specific groupings of class elements. States are transmission mechanisms; that is, formal machineries for the integration of a given population or territory into a wider system (Tivey, 1981; Jessop, 1990). States thereafter invent nations and nationalisms to buttress their control (Anderson, 1983; Gellner, 1983). The resultant general pattern of these complex and historically specific dynamics of structures and agents could be termed, after the style of Overbeek (1990) and Jessop (1988), a 'state-form'.

It is clear that the notions of state, nation and nationstate have to be seen as cultural artefacts created over time and deployed to make sense of the present day. Such ideas are neither fixed in terms of meaning, nor are they deployed in a politically neutral fashion, rather powerful groups deploy these ideas to legitimate and order given class-fissured circumstances. The pattern of ideas promulgated in respect of state, nation and nationstate will flow from extant circumstances; that is, the way the territory fits into and deals with the surrounding system. The institutional and organizational expression of these sets of ideas, the vehicles for the translation of theory into practice, are also social constructs. They too are historically contingent expressions of global political-economic dynamics. So too, finally, will be the ways in which elite promulgated ideas are read into routine social practice, the sphere of political-cultural identity (Preston, 1987; Billig, 1995). Any extant state-form will represent the way in which local agents have read and reacted to these trans-state patterns of power.

The political sociology of nationstatehood can be formally unpacked as an elaborate vocabulary of concepts. The ideas of state, nation and nationstate are familiar. The animating agents can be characterized as a state-regime, the elite group able to control and deploy the machineries of the state. The ways in which agent groups read and react to the shifting play of the structural patterns which enfold them will be varied, including (schematically): incomprehension (as with the Qing dynasty confronted by the West); vacillation (as with the Tokugawa rulers faced with the same demands); and rational action designed to secure a specific route to the future (as with the oligarchic rulers of the Meiji Restoration) where the mix of elite action, institutional ordering and popular mobilization can be embraced in the notion of a political-cultural project (Preston, 1997).

In the process of the shift to the modern world effected in the territories of Pacific Asia it is clear that the key players were the incoming Western traders, manufacturers, financiers and subsequently the whole apparatus of colonialism. The place of indigenous elites was marginal, except for the case of Japan, and everywhere, as Worsley (1984) has noted, the ordinary people saw their lives remade over the generations. However, the expansion of the Western industrial-capitalist system generated the intellectual and political means whereby the formal colonial system could be resisted and in the confusions attendant upon the Pacific War indigenous nationalist groups attained a measure of influence and eventually secured independence for their countries. In contemporary Pacific Asia it is clear that the key players in recent years have been the state-regimes of the various countries, the regions multinational corporations (MNCs) and certain international and regional organizations.

Japan in the modern world

The historical development experience of a particular territory can be described directly, that is, as a history of that territory, but these individual patterns of development are always lodged within the contexts offered by the wider system. The dynamics of change within territories will not be equivalent. Against the modernization theory inspired expectations of a single logic of industrialization repeating itself in diverse contexts, such that all territories might expect equal advance in the absence of accidental inhibitions to progress, the structural international political economy line of argument carries within it a recognition of the fundamentally uneven nature of progress. The patterns made by global structures of power are not regular and different territories will advance or retreat, relative to the fundamental expectations of progress lodged within the classical European tradition of social theorizing, at different rates, as local elites read and react (in the light of shifting domestic opinion and patterns of power) to the enfolding patterns of structural change. It is clear that there will be shifts in patterns of development within a region as particular areas advance (or retreat) relative to others. In a similar way, it is clear that there will be shifts in the patterns of relationships between a particular region and the wider developing global system as patterns of development advance unevenly at the global system level. In the case of Pacific Asia it is clear both that the region has undergone a recent period of rapid relative advance within the global system and that within this general pattern of advance particular countries in the region have advanced more rapidly than others. At the present time the region has a core economy in Japan.

Analysing Japan through the framework of the European tradition of social theorizing focuses attention on the way in which Japan shifted into the modern world and how contemporary Japan exhibits the characteristics of modernity. The process of the ongoing shift of Japan to the modern world can be dealt with in terms of a series of phases whereby each phase represents a particular way in which the Japanese polity was lodged within the wider global system.

In the first phase, the Tokugawa period saw a sophisticated hierarchical polity underpinned by an agricultural economy. A mixture of internal decay – as the polity failed to accommodate to the slowly developing economy – and external shock – in the guise of the demands of the Western traders – lead to the system's political collapse. In the second phase the Meiji period saw a revolution from above which reconstructed the political economy, society and polity over a period of some thirty years. The model of the West was borrowed for a process of top-down social reconstruction. At the end of the period the Japanese state was strong enough to begin establishing a colonial empire in East Asia. In the third phase this pattern of development continued through the Taisho reforms until a mixture of internal problems, when the death of the Meiji oligarchs coupled to the inherent unclarities of the system allowed the military to exert their expansionist views as a solution to the social and economic problems occasioned by the Great Depression, and external pressures, which flowed from overseas reaction to the expansionism of the military in China, occasioned a drift into war and defeat. In the post-World War II period a fourth phase was evident with the developmental capitalist state pursuit of economic expansion at home and overseas. The result has been a mixture of enormous economic success coupled to a relatively low level of living for ordinary Japanese. At home there are pressures for economic and political reform. From overseas there is increasing pressure for economic adjustment. However, expectations of change are relatively modest. Looking to the future, it is possible to identify a possible fifth phase by noting that the links of Japan and Pacific Asia revolve around trade, Official Development Fund (ODA) and Foreign Direct Investment (FDI). It has been suggested that Japan is now the core economy of an increasingly integrated Pacific-Asian region.

Japan, Pacific Asia and the global system

In the wake of the collapse of the bipolar system it has become clear that the global industrial-capitalist system has developed into three broad regions: the Americas, the European Union and Pacific Asia. The current situation within the global system thus displays a mixture of global internationalization and regionalization. The regions have political economic cores and peripheral territories, trade among themselves and evidence distinct varieties of industrial capitalism.

It is not a straightforward matter to identify Pacific Asia as a region. Historically, in the long period prior to the invasive spread of industrial capitalism, it is clear that the region was Sino-centric, and then with the expansion and deepening of the demands of industrial capitalism it was absorbed within colonial empires. In the period of the Pacific War the region formed a part of the Greater East Asian Co-Prosperity Sphere which was centred upon Japan. Thereafter, most recently, it has been

divided by Cold War alliances into a Western sphere, lodged within the
US-centred Bretton Woods system and an inward-looking socialist sphere.
The Western focused group has been subject to the political-economic,
political and cultural hegemony of the USA. The socialist sphere had an
uneasy double centre in Beijing and Moscow. However, the recent end of
the Cold War system has opened up the issue of the delimitation and
future shape of the region (Shibusawa, 1992; Mackerras, 1995; Gamble and
Payne, 1996). The Western focused group is undergoing considerable
change and in brief this may be summarized as the beginnings of a
political-economic and cultural emancipation from the hegemony of the
USA. At the same time the countries of the socialist bloc which had spent
decades following autarchic development trajectories are now opening up
to the Western focused group. The current regional project in Pacific Asia
is contested and a series of variants can be identified.

The position of the USA is still shaped by Cold War security thinking
with a significant relocation of anxieties from geo-strategy to geo-
economics. The region is economically threatening and needs must be
ordered according to US agendas, hence Asia-Pacific Economic Cooperation (APEC). In contrast the Japanese view is ordered around the
image/programme of flying geese, such that the Japanese high technology economy leads the successively lower technology economies of
the region. The newly industrializing countries (NICs) slot in just behind
the leader with their economies growing along with that of Japan and the
Association of South East Asian nations (ASEAN) brings up the rear of
the formation. A related formulation was offered in 1991 by the
Malaysian government, the East Asian Economic Group (EAEG), which
sought at first to embrace the ten Asian countries of the region (it later
became the East Asian Economic Caucus within APEC). The Chinese
view the regional arena within the frame of Greater China, or the China
Circle, where the growing economic power of China is taken to be
expanding and drawing in the other powerful economies of the region.
Finally, the European Union (EU) interest might be characterized as part
of that grouping's slow integration, where one aspect is an increasingly
explicit concern to be represented within the Pacific-Asian region. In
recent years the EU has begun conversations with the Pacific-Asian
countries, particularly in relation to economic issues, under the aegis of
Asia-Europe Meeting (ASEM) (Gilson, 1998a, 1998b). However, overall,
it can be said that regionalism within Pacific Asia is only developing
slowly and will develop in its own fashion, with slow networking rather
than decisive formal institutional shifts. It is also clear that the regional
core economy is Japan.

Scholarly and intellectual implications

The social scientific movement away from received enlightenment claims
to the universality of the European experience, which has been in

progress for several years, finds new practical impetus in the development experience of Japan (and the countries of Pacific Asia). A series of key fundamental issues are represented including the nature of the modernist project, the role of intellectuals and the ways in which economies, societies and cultures are construed and ordered and action thereby proposed and undertaken.

In respect of economies, the historical development experience of Japan (and the countries of Pacific Asia) has occasioned a series of hotly debated issues in economics including:

(a) the nature of the role of the state, where debate revolves around the costs/benefits of such interventions;
(b) the nature of the role of social networks in economic activity to supplement or replace the marketplace (for example, in Japan and among Chinese businessmen);
(c) the role of political elites in the pursuit of economic growth;
(d) the role of politicians, bureaucrats and other strategic groups in the process of economic growth.

It should be noted that these enquiries routinely call into question the plausibility of orthodox market-liberal economics.[5]

In a related way, in respect of societies, the development experience of Japan (and the countries of Pacific Asia) generates a series of issues that are hotly debated by social analysts:

(a) the nature of social discipline, how it is secured and thereafter legitimated;
(b) the relationship of the individual self to key social institutions (family, community, local town and state/country);
(c) the extent to which the state can self-consciously and legitimately order the structure and dynamics of society.

It should be noted that these enquiries routinely call into question European notions of individual and community and are wholly inimical to the expressive individualism of the USA.

Thereafter, the experience of Japan (and the countries of Pacific Asia) generates a series of issues in respect of culture and politics which are hotly debated and include:

(a) the nature of 'great traditions' and the extent to which there can be said to be a discrete package of Asian values;
(b) the nature of 'little traditions' and the extent to which these might be subsumed within developing national cultures;
(c) the extent to which extant cultural resources are being subsumed within a global postmodernist culture;
(d) relatedly, the value of culturalist explanations of success;

e of political legitimacy;
ent to which the notion of democracy has (and might be
.ed to have) purchase.

ild be noted that these enquiries call into question the routine
dis, sition to ethico-political unversalism variously evident in Western
discourse (and US great power interventions (Gray, 1998)).

Finally, within the context of the overall historical shift of Japan to the modern world there are a series of sharply debated areas of key micro-analytical concern. These are:

(a) the nature of economic life (state versus market);
(b) the role of the state (intervention);
(c) the reform of economic life (market opening and consumption);
(d) the lessons of the development experience of Japan;
(e) the nature of social institutions (family, school, work, crime);
(f) the nature of social relationships (gender, groups, authority);
(g) the nature of social conflict and change (order, legitimation);
(h) the role of culture in Japan (strategies of explanation);
(i) the role of images of Japan (strategies of explanation and ideologies).

Policy implications

The historical development experience of Japan (and the countries of Pacific Asia) presents three areas of particular concern for European and American policymakers: first, in respect of economic policy making; second, in the specific matter of trade relations; finally, in regard to security.

In the first place, in respect of economic policymaking, it is clear that the claims to universality of the Western experience are now in question. In the standard market-liberal account, the industrial-capitalist system is ordered by the marketplace and it is through this mechanism that general social benefits are maximized. However, it is clear that in the case of Japan (and the countries of Pacific Asia) the economic system is subject to the routine and extensive control of state-regimes and intra-regional socio-cultural networks (in particular the circuits of Japanese and overseas Chinese capital). It makes no sense whatsoever to speak of 'disembedded' markets in Japan (and the countries of Pacific Asia). The experience of Japan (and the regional countries) offers lessons for policymaking in the areas of economic, social and political management.

Second, the most immediate area of policy concern focuses on trade connections as the region develops and further extends its linkages with America and Europe. This is potentially a thoroughly awkward area. If it is true that the three core regions of the global system evidence different versions of industrial capitalism, then managing their relations becomes much more than applying a simple set of agreed rules. Zysman (1996:

180) comments: 'One implication . . . is that, increasingly, in the years to come, the politics of trade, defined broadly, will be about reconciling differently structured political economies that express different values.' It is clear that trade relationships will have to deal with the ways in which economies are lodged within societies that in turn are lodged in cultures. If there is no simple liberal market inspired set of rules able to govern economic exchanges between various agents, then policy analysts will have to fashion ways of dealing with the substantive differences between versions of industrial capitalism. Zysman (1996: 180) remarks that debate will come to revolve around 'deep market access'. It is clear, Zysman (1996: 181) continues, that the 'notion of competing capitalisms implies at once a rivalry between economic systems, conflicts between governments, and competition between companies from different countries advantaged or handicapped by the market logic of their home bases'.

Third, a key practical area of concern will be with security networks and alliances as the apparatus of the Cold War winds down. There is now a regional arms race and concern to fill the vacuum left by the eclipse of the USSR and the partial disengagement of the USA (Drifte, 1998: 52–4). The area is in process of reconfiguring around an economically strong Japan with renewed links to the USA (Drifte, 1998: 67–75) and an assertive China. The Japanese armed forces are powerful and technologically advanced. The Korean peninsular is heavily militarized as is the island of Taiwan and the countries of ASEAN are rapidly upgrading and moving to position themselves with regard to China.

Political implications

The key implication is that political elites acknowledge the requirement of managing the emergent tripolar system in the new post-Bretton Woods era (Preston, 1998b). This implies work in the areas of security and economics. Thereafter, the issues of regionalism and the intersection of regions with the global system are all central to political activity.

As the tripolar system develops a whole set of multilateral and bilateral exchanges at the state–state level is underway. American theorists are aware of the need to adjust and the stress on geo-economics is evidence of a new position. The organizations NAFTA and APEC are ways of ordering the emergent system to US advantage. Relatedly, the EU is both pursuing its own programme of integration and re-engaging with Pacific Asia after the gradual disengagement of the period of American hegemony.

Conclusion

In the intellectual perspective of the classical European tradition of social theorizing the task of the social scientific analysis of Japan presents itself in broad outline as the business of detailing the dynamics of the ongoing shift to the modern world experienced by Japan. In this perspective the developmental history of Japan is unique to Japan but represents a variation upon a theme – that process of 'the shift to the modern world' which was first experienced in Europe and thereafter by other areas of the world until today we stand (arguably) on the threshold of a global industrial-capitalist system. Against those Japanese nationalist celebrants of the culturally sui generis character of modern Japan (Dale, 1986; Yoshino, 1992), the view from the European perspective is that of one country's shift to the modern world. The development experience is in principle intelligible. The shift to the modern world experienced by Japan has run through a series of familiar phases, has evidenced a series of familiar problems and, as is the case with all other countries, has seen each phase lay down institutional and cultural residues that form the givens for the actions of subsequent generations. As Marx (1852: 1) said, 'Men make their own history, but they do not make it just as they please; they do not make it under circumstances chosen by themselves, but under conditions directly encountered, given and transmitted from the past.' It is in this spirit that the classical European tradition of social theorizing can be deployed to read the historical development experience of Japan.

Notes

1 It is clear now, following the end of the Cold War, that 'the West' was never a simple description of an otherwise constituted territory but was a political rhetorical trope in the service of a particular political-cultural project, that is, the post-World War II US-sponsored liberal market sphere. At the present time this political-cultural project is in relative decline as its convenient 'other', the world of official state socialism, has dissolved and the consequent improvement in intellectual clarity has revealed a nascent tripolar world. The new US political-cultural project, flagged in the terminological shift from geo-strategy to geo-economics, looks to place Washington at the centre of an overlapping trio of liberal free trade areas encompassing the Americas (NAFTA), the Asia-Pacific (APEC) and embracing Europe in the notion of an Atlantic community (OECD, BIS, IMF and IBRD).

2 We should note that this general argument can be extended. The traditions of the USA and Europe cannot exhaust the ways in which social science might be pursued. There have been alternative conceptions in the past, and today new ways of making social scientific arguments are presented. In parts of the Third World there is a commitment by some scholars to using the resources of Islam and commentators have spoken of distinctively 'Asian values'. However, it probably remains the case that the key problem for any social science, however it is assembled, will be the analysis of the ongoing dynamics of the global industrial-capitalist system.

3 A fuller statement of the arguments made in this sub-section can be found in P.W. Preston, *Pacific Asia in the Global System* (Blackwell, Oxford, 1998a, Chapters 1 and 2).

4 The development history of Japan and the Pacific Asia region have intertwined and cross-cut in a practical sense. Thus Japanese trade, FDI and ODA have contributed to the economic development and nascent integration of the region, as has the development model of Japan, with its characteristic 'developmental state' and strategy of 'export oriented industrialisation'. Thereafter, in respect of intellectual reflection, the development experience of Japan has again intertwined with the development experience of the region. In this text the focus is on Japan, but, inevitably, routine reference will be made to the wider Pacific-Asian region (see Preston, 1998a).

5 In this text *market-liberal ideas* (that is, theories, ideologies, policy statements and so on) are distinguished from *liberal-market practices* (that is, patterns of actual real world activity), in order to avoid the error of supposing that familiar Western economic ideas and practices are universal. They are not. There are many ways of theorizing and organizing human livelihoods (see Gudeman, 1986; Appelbaum and Henderson, 1992).

2

JAPAN AND THE SHIFT TO THE MODERN WORLD

Tokugawa, Meiji and the Pursuit of the Project of Modernity

The Tokugawa shogunate ruled Japan from 1603 to 1867 and maintained an inward-looking, agrarian-based hierarchical yet widely successful society. In the late Tokugawa period the restrictive nature of the regime militated against indigenous economic, social and political change until the arrival of the Europeans and Americans. The regime was unable to respond to the internal and external demands placed upon it and collapsed. The subsequent Meiji Restoration was a contested reform from above that inaugurated the pursuit of national development, which in turn secured an extensive ambiguous success (Moore, 1966). In brief, it can be argued that the late nineteenth century saw an effective process of late industrialization and a related programme of late imperialism as Japan became one of the great powers. It is clear that the manner in which Japan came to be a part of the modern world established a dual elite concern for domestic development and international security, in the particular context of Pacific Asia, which has coloured much of the subsequent history of the country.

It is clear that the historical development experience of Japan can be presented in terms of a series of stages. In each stage there is a distinctive mixture of system constraints and agent sponsored lines of response. It is in the period of the earliest exchanges of Japan with the modern, in late Tokugawa and Meiji, that the resources of the past are remade into novel patterns which in subsequently amended forms persist to the present day. The precise nature of the legacies of the past is disputed, but for the moment we can simply follow Hunter (1989: 2) who notes, as do others, that in the shift to the modern world two key episodes have shaped modern Japan – the Meiji Restoration and the US occupation.

In this chapter we will consider the way in which Japan came to be a part of the modern world; however, we can begin with a note on the broad sweep of pre-modern Japanese history.

Pre-modern Japan to Tokugawa

The long history of settlement on the islands of the Japanese archipelago can be summarized in terms of a series of discrete phases:

(a) the pre-history period;
(b) the Yamato-Nara period;
(c) the medieval period.

Pre-history of the Japanese archipelago

The islands of the Japanese archipelago were slowly populated over a long drawn out period. Bowring and Kornicki (1993: 42–62) report that it is likely that the archipelago was first populated while it was a part of the mainland some 30,000 to 50,000 years ago. The timing is disputed as archaeological evidence of occupation prior to 30,000 years ago is slight. The geography of the islands has influenced the population pattern with the heaviest concentrations of peoples down the years being found in the Kanto area around Tokyo Bay and the Kansai region bordering the shores of the Inland Sea (Crisman, 1995: 19).

The earliest clearly demarcated period of history is called the Jomon period (10,000 to 300 BC). The Jomon people seem to have been tribal hunters and gatherers who, unusually, had settled sites and left pottery and tools. The emergence of agriculture is evident in the Yayoi period (300 BC to AD 300). The Yayoi people undertook wet rice cultivation with other grains on higher drier ground. Bowring and Kornicki (1993: 42) record that the Yayoi communities were drawn into tributary relationships with the Chinese Han and Wei dynasties, thereby opening up an early line of cultural influence.

The ancient history of Japan

In the period AD 300 to AD 710 the ancient history of the Japanese archipelago begins to take a recognizable shape. It is at this point, remarks Borthwick (1992: 28), that the early history of Japan emerges from the realms of myth. Bowring and Kornicki (1993: 44) report that archaeological evidence shows a rich agricultural form of life. It is during this period that a series of tribal groups are slowly brought under the control of the Yamato state. In the same period the emperor system is established. The people of Yamato had writing and their court histories are the earliest Japanese literature. The period also saw urbanization with a series of capital cities in the Nara region. There is evidence of significant trade and cultural links with the Paekche kingdom in the Korean peninsular. However, towards the end of the period, in the seventh century, there was a shift of attention towards China as a new source of models of government and civilization. The governmental system was

overhauled in the Taika reform which initiated a legal system, embodied
in the Taisho Code of 701, which served to order an hierarchical society
by closely specifying the social duties of officials and commoners. Subsequently, the Nara period (AD 710–794) saw further administrative
advances, new capitals and denser patterns of communication. Nara
came to rule most of the two main islands, Honshu and Kyushu. The
period saw a rise in independence for temples and the establishment of a
dual authority, secular and divine, both with land as their economic base.
In an agrarian society land was the key resource along with the peasants
to work it (Worsley, 1984).

Medieval Japan

The medieval age encompasses three periods: Heian, 794–1185;
Kamakura, 1192–1333; and Muromachi, 1338–1573.

The *Heian period* is regarded as the flowering of early Japan when for
most of the period government, religious orders, economy and cultural
activities all prospered. However, rivalries continued between landed
families and a system of dual secular power was established which made
the emperor nominal leader but left real power with the landed families.
The religious groups also grew in power. In Kyoto, the capital city, the
court and lords ruled via an elaborate Chinese-inspired bureaucracy. At
the end of the Heian period there were the beginnings of warfare among
powerful landed families and the stability inaugurated by the Yamato
state fell away. A little later, in 1192, Minamoto no Yoritomo appropri-
ated to himself the archaic title of shogun (which had been used in the
Nara period in wars against northern tribes) and established what was in
theory a military dictatorship. This came to be the new central power as
the emperor moved into the background. It is the beginning of the long
period of warrior rule (Borthwick, 1992: 41; Henshall, 1999: 30). The key
trio of political players were the shoguns (nominally representing the
emperor), the landed families and the religious foundations.

The *Kamakura shogunate*, with its bafuku or warrior government, took
the capital to the town of Kamakura. The period saw a series of wars and
power began to drift from the centre to strong regional landed families.
In this period there were also attempted invasions from the Korean
peninsular by the Mongols in 1274 and again in 1281 (Henshall, 1999:
30–6).

In the fourteenth century the *Muromachi shogunate* returned the capital
to Kyoto and the shogunate became more embroiled in court politics
while the regional landed families increased their power. The pattern of
powerful regional lords, daimyo, emerged in the late sixteenth century.
There were about 250 important regional lords. As Henshall (1999: 39)
notes, it was a period of decentralization, ruling group disaggregation
and warfare. The slow advance of earlier epochs was lost in the confusions of more or less continuous warfare.

Overall the medieval age saw:

(a) the disintegration of the ordered polity of Yamato;
(b) a continuing slow population rise along with economic advance;
(c) the rise of important competing land-owning lords as key players in the increasingly fractious polity.

The Tokugawa shogunate, 1603–1867

The sequence of wars through the later medieval period eventually saw the rise of a trio of extraordinarily successful regional lords: Oda Nobunga, Toyotomi Hideyoshi and Tokugawa Ieyasu. The reunification of Japan was begun by Nobunga, continued by Hideyoshi and sustained thereafter by Ieyasu. The brief period of confusion following Hideyoshi's death in 1598 ended in 1600 when Ieyasu defeated the key regional lords at the Battle of Sekigahara. Ieyasu assumed the title of shogun in 1603 and the Tokugawa shogunate ruled Japan until 1867.

The founder of the dynasty, Tokugawa Ieyasu (1542–1616), gradually defeated and brought under control the regional lords, the temples and the peasantry. The capital was established at Edo (Tokyo). It was the first period of peace for some 300 years. The system worked for close on 250 years. In this period Japan was largely closed to the outside world, yet within the confines of the home islands an elaborately ordered, hierarchical, feudal agricultural society was constructed.

The system was successful. In 1600 the population was some 18 million and by 1850 it was 30 million. Yet by the 1850s Hunter (1989: 5) notes: 'The tensions brought about by social, economic and political change were already beginning to pose a serious threat not merely to the rule of the Tokugawa but to the system itself.' The shogunate was limited in the political response which it could make to developing problems. In time a mixture of tensions flowing from socio-economic advance and attendant changes in the social status and life chances of core class groups within the society, together with the direct political shock occasioned by the demands of the European and American trading nations, lead to the collapse of their authority and the subsequent radical reconstruction of the historically particular and successful system which they had constructed over the centuries.

Economy of Tokugawa Japan

Beasley (1990: 9–15) notes that the Tokugawa period saw a series of significant changes in the local economy:

1   There was sustained economic success within the agricultural sphere, evidenced in the growing population.

2   There was significant commercial development. As production began
    to rise above subsistence levels, farmers produced for the market and
    a basic transport and distribution system developed.
3   This resulted in the monetization of the economy and the develop-
    ment of credit facilities.
4   All this found expression in extensive urbanization, such that Edo, for
    example, which had a population of one million in the early 1700s,
    developed a highly sophisticated urban form of life.

   Tokugawa was an agricultural society. Over 80 per cent of the population were peasant farmers, scattered across the country in hundreds of
small villages (Hunter, 1989: 83). The staple crop was rice, grown in
paddy fields which required collective work. In the early years of the
shogunate the economy was mainly subsistence as a result of the
upheavals of decades of civil wars. However, with stability the economy
became successful and output rose, artisanal skill based manufacture
prospered and commercialization slowly spread. A measure of the
success of an agrarian society, in particular the economy that sustains it, is
the level of population and, as noted, during the period of Tokugawa it
more or less doubled.
   Over the period production began to rise above subsistence levels as
technology improved and farmers started to produce for the market. A
basic transport and distribution system developed. Howe (1996: 49–57)
reports that the level of trade within the country increased. Overall,
Henshall (1999: 62) notes that living conditions improved throughout
society.
   A crucial aspect of this long period of relative economic success was
the monetization of the economy. As the development of the economy led
to increasing specialization and exchange, the role of money increased.
Howe (1996: 58–61) reports that the city of Osaka developed an important financial role whereby the surplus of agricultural products could be
translated into money. Henshall (1999: 62) records that the pattern of life
of the regional lords required that they raise money to pay a wide range
of expenses, which also contributed to the development of a money
economy. An important aspect of this process was the extension of credit
facilities whereby the surpluses of the successful sectors of the economy
were recycled by city merchants to underpin the expenses of regional
lords and their warrior-bureaucrat functionaries.
   The economic success of Tokugawa helped to generate an urban
network, originally around castles of lords and warrior-bureaucrats. In
time the importance of the rural agricultural regions slowly declined.
The rise of the urban areas had two important aspects:

1   The developing sophistication of the urban people in manufacturing,
    distribution and the commercial facilities associated with trade (for
    example, financial facilities).

2   The rising importance of the urban areas within the economy as a
    whole, as the basis of political power began to shift away from control
    of land plus peasants towards control of production, distribution and
    exchange.

It was in these prosperous towns that the sophisticated literate urban
culture of the Edo period Japan developed (Ueda, 1994; Clammer, 1997).
    An important aspect of economic growth was the impact of these
processes upon existing class and caste structures (Moore, 1966; Howe,
1996). A new class of powerful merchants emerged. The towns were also
where the samurai warrior-bureaucrats resided. However, the samurai
were losing track of events in a confusion of maladministration and debt
(addressed via forced loans, taxes and the granting of monopolies). As
new classes began to emerge – merchants, richer farmers, artisan craft
producers – the class make-up of the urban economies began to shift and
the samurai emerged as a key group as elements of their number
eventually became progressive reformers.
    Sheridan (1993: 18) argues that the period did contribute to later post-
Meiji success by establishing:

(a) low birth and death rates;
(b) urban growth and commercialization in villages;
(c) ethnic uniformity;
(d) irrigation systems;
(e) commercial and financial systems;
(f) systems of land tenure and taxation.[1]

The level of prosperity rose steadily, if slowly, over the whole period.
Nonetheless, the ordinary people lived hard lives and remained poor.
Sheridan suggests that they developed a 'hard work' ethic. She also notes
what the period did not produce; specifically, no capital for industrialization, no technology for industrialization and no entrepreneurs to
run that type of system. In sum, Sheridan sees a stable and growing
agricultural and craft-based economy that had by pre-Meiji days developed just about as far as it could go.

Social system of Tokugawa Japan

The overall social system was hierarchical. The caste system of Tokugawa
Japan derived from Chinese Confucian models and in intention was rigid:
lord, samurai, farmer, artisan, merchant. The castes were further sub-
divided into an elaborate division of labour encompassing 'hundreds of
occupational divisions' (Howe, 1996: 58). There were also outcast groups
which dealt with ritually unclean tasks. In Tokugawa society each person
in his place owed a duty of allegiance and obedience to their superior.
Hunter (1989: 64) adds:

Throughout the Tokugawa period the lifestyles, customs, work practices and privileges of each caste were minutely regulated by a host of detailed sumptuary laws [regulating private expenditure] and other provisions. Members of each stratum were not expected to deviate from certain prescribed occupations. Within each caste there existed numerous subdivisions, which allotted members a ranking vis-à-vis each other. The hereditary nature of social gradation offered little opportunity for social mobility.

In the end the system was based on control of land and peasants, and force of arms, in particular via the warrior-bureaucrats known as the samurai. However, as will be noted, the system was by no means static and the economic dynamism of the Edo period did eventuate in social or caste change (Moore, 1966; Henshall, 1999).

The society of the elite comprised the shogunate, the emperor, the regional lords and the warrior-bureaucrats. At the apex of the hierarchy, stood the emperor and court nobility, with little real power, whose lives were circumscribed by elaborate prescribed duties (and often by penury). A similar situation obtained in the powerful household of the shogun. Thereafter the pattern was repeated in the households of the regional lords. The samurai warrior-bureaucrats were a subordinate layer of the aristocracy. The status of the samurai group was legitimated in the code of bushido, the Way of the Warrior, which emphasized an ideal of ascetic selfless devotion to one's lord. Hunter (1989: 64) notes: 'The rulers of Japan ... attempted to confirm their dominance by restricting all political, social and economic change in the country to within rigidly defined limits ... a rigid hierarchy of hereditary caste continued to prevail.' Overall, the system was financed by the surplus of agricultural society and the crucial material concern was the control of the land and its peasants.

The society of the common people, the farmers and artisans, centred on the 'continuing family' and thereafter the village. In the continuing family patterns of life were tightly controlled. The family owned property rather than individuals and worked as a group, within which the obligations of individual members were specified. The male head of the household exercised control over the members of the continuing family. A small group of families would constitute a village and one of the family heads would be the village headman. The merchant castes were relegated to the bottom of the social hierarchy with only outcast groups having a lower status. The social system was ordered, therefore, in terms of a series of quite distinct groups, whose particular status locked them into the overall social hierarchy (Moore, 1966: 254–66).

Over the later years of Tokugawa the economic successes of the period began to undermine the class and caste system (Moore, 1966). As the Tokugawa period wore on, the improvement in agricultural production and the rise in the power of the towns began to weaken established patterns. A new class pattern began to develop. The merchants, rich peasants and artisan craft workers all prospered. Some peasants remained poor. The outcasts who performed ritually unclean tasks also remained poor. A crucially important class, the samurai warrior-bureaucrats, experienced downward mobility as their social role began to lose importance and as they fell into debt to the increasingly important merchant traders.

In sum, Tokugawa Japan began as an inward-looking agrarian hierarchical country that prospered within the limits of this framework, which was clearly pre-modern. It began to develop towards the end of the period without, however, coming to the point of making that shift to the modern world that had been contrived over roughly the same period in Europe. The legacies of the Tokugawa era which were transmitted to the next stage of Japanese development, and are residually present in contemporary Japan, are many:

(a) the social routine of obedience to authority;
(b) the bureaucratic character of decision making;
(c) the stress on familial and local relationships;
(d) an appreciation of patterns of craft production and relatedly a concern for food self-sufficiency.

Culture of Tokugawa Japan

The elite of Tokugawa Japan comprised the emperor (and his court), the shogun (and his retainers), the regional lords (with their retainers) and the samurai warrior-bureaucrats. It was within the sphere of elite political life that decisions in respect of economic, social and cultural matters were taken. Thereafter, the lives of the ordinary people were engaged with either the rhythms of the agrarian village or the life of the towns. It was this intermingled set of elements which together comprised the distinctive culture of Tokugawa Japan. The patterns of ideas lodged within these sophisticated social practices were to be the vehicle of response to the demands of the foreign traders whose arrival was in short order to mark the end of Tokugawa.

The high culture of the Tokugawa elite centred on the Confucianism of the period which was selectively borrowed from China and provided a source of legitimation for the shogun, regional lords and samurai. The Chinese Confucian ideal of enlightened rule and social harmony was reworked by the Tokugawa shogunate to serve the interests of an hierarchical, disciplined and military dominated society. The Japanized Confucianism encouraged by the shogunate made a series of significant revisions to the received body of ideas:

1   The ideal of obedience was shifted away from family to the formal political hierarchy.
2   The meritocratic principle did not take root as the ordering principle of the shogunate was one of military control.
3   The broad Confucian ethic of humanism had little place.

In addition, the concern for the sphere of the military found a particular expression in the philosophy affirmed by the samurai (whose original role as soldiers was not directly useful in an era of stability). The model of the Confucian sage was reworked in the code of the warrior, the cultured and austere figure who eschewed the pleasures of ordinary folk in pursuit of the discipline of service (to superiors and hence the social world broadly).

At the same time, the influence of Chinese ideas was resisted by nativist scholars who reached back to the Yamato state period in order to assert the autonomy and vigour of the indigenous traditions of the Japanese, which were traced back to the emperor descended from the sun goddess Amaterasu. The nativist scholars' criticisms of Confucianism were one vehicle for the presentation of doubts about the shogunate and these found further expression in the associated revival of Shintoism. Of course, all these abstract debates were a matter for the elite. Thus, on the other hand, the life of the villages and the rise of the urban culture of the Edo period is the counterpoint to the patterns of life of the elites. The lives of the majority of Japanese were circumscribed by the demands of family-based, caste-structured, agrarian life. The bulk of the population were peasant farmers. Nonetheless, as the economy prospered so too did the sophisticated urban culture of the Edo period, with its literature, arts and popular activities (Ueda, 1994).

One particular strand of cultural development was the slow dissemination of imported Western technical knowledge, in particular in the spheres of military technology and medicine. In the centuries prior to the establishment of the Tokugawa shogunate the Japanese had traded widely in Eastern Asia and there were early and extensive cultural borrowings from China. Yet the arrival of the Portuguese, who brought with them Christian missionaries, provoked anxiety among the shogunal ruling groups in respect of the long-term intention of the foreigners, whom they came to suspect of nursing ambitions to colonize the territory. The response of the elite to these perceived threats was to close Japan to the outside world. There was a long-term policy, from approximately 1663, of closing off Japan. However, one line of communication was kept open at the port of Nagasaki in the south of the country and the Dutch and Chinese were allowed to trade. Some ideas about natural science did filter through and these were passed around somewhat surreptitiously and became quite influential – particularly matters relating to medicine and warfare. In subsequent years the link with the Dutch came to have an important and subtle influence through this import of ideas – known locally as 'Dutch learning'.

In the early nineteenth century the ruling shogunate had to deal with the overtures of the Europeans and Americans and a revised nativism emerged which suggested that the samurai warriors, who had affirmed their readiness to defend their emperor, should organize themselves to resist the foreigners. The nativist ideas contributed to the emergence of a modern-style nationalism – the state would have to organize the entire population to resist the demands of outsiders – and eventually these ideas fed into the emperor-centred politics of the period of the Meiji restoration.

Politics of Tokugawa Japan

Tokugawa was a period of stability. The system is often called feudal although, as Beasly (1990: 1–8) notes, the use of the word 'feudal' in relation to Japan is a matter of debate. It is not clear that the term is correct, as it implies assimilating Japan's history to that of Europe. The pattern of development within Japan evidences a greater political centralization and at the same time a rather more dispersed economy (with the growth of towns) than was the case in Europe. However, all this is a technical debate for historians, which revolves around the nature of relations of power in an agricultural society; what is clear is that this society centred on the control of land and peasants.

In Japan the system derived from medieval wars when territories were carved out by force. It was after Tokugawa Ieyasu was militarily victorious in 1603 that he took the title shogun. There was a ruling group around the shogun that nominally followed the rule of the emperor, who in reality had little power, plus a series of regional lords (daimyo) and a wide spread of nobles, the samurai, and thereafter farmers, artisans, and merchants. The system was known as the bakuhan – a word combining bakufu (warrior rule) and han (rural agricultural domain).

The shogun's people or relatives dominated court life. Court life was ceremonial and without real power. It was strictly regulated – down to dress, marriages, behaviour and pass times. The emperor was a pensioner of the shogun and virtually a prisoner.

In Edo where the shogun ruled the land-owning lords came together. The shogun and his immediate samurai had vast landholdings which funded their government. The office of shogun was in principle absolute and hereditary, but in practice more flexible. The central administration was called the bakufu and this core group were Tokugawa clan. In all, many thousands of officials and administrators lived in Edo.

The feudal lords, the daimyo, ruled landed territories. They were appointed to these territories by the shogun and could be moved around. The lords were ranked in terms of the relation of their family to the shogun. Each domain had its local bureaucracy and derived its wealth from the land. The centre maintained control via a system of 'alternate attendance' which required the regional lord to reside in Edo for alternate years and to leave family in Edo when returning to their domains. In addition there were pledges of allegiance, dynastic marriages, restrictions on local forces (thus castle defences were by permission of the shogun) and so on. Tokugawa was an agricultural society and in the end the shogun controlled the key resource, the distribution of land along with its peasant farmers. The samurai warrior-bureaucrats acted as administrators within the domains of the regional lords.

The system may have brought peace but it had its drawbacks. The shogun's economic power was limited in relation to the obligations of a state. The daimyo often prioritized local interests and the samurai warrior-bureaucrats were inefficient. The system failed to establish a modern-type rational bureaucratic state (because of the inhibitions to reform of an authoritarian and essentially military pattern of rule), or any mechanisms which would routinely draw into the decision-making process the contributions of socially progressive groups (again, a matter of the inhibitions attendant upon the use of a class and caste system of allocation to positions within the economy).

The shogunate proved unable to respond effectively to the economic, social and political tensions which were generated by domestic economic advance. As the agricultural economy matured into an early agrarian-based capitalism, the artisanal and merchant classes increased in importance as the landowners and warrior-bureaucrats declined. The basis of power within the system was shifting (Moore, 1966) and was moving away from the control of land and peasants typical of agrarian systems (Worsley, 1984) towards control of production, distribution and exchange (typical of urban-industrial systems). A little later, in the early nineteenth century, it was clear that the shogunate could not respond to the external demands of European and American traders. At the end of the period the official centre was quite unable to secure change and it was an alliance of southern regional lords, dispossessed samurai and those within the emergent classes, who could see the shape of the future and who came together to overthrow the Tokugawa shogunate in the Meiji Restoration.

Stability, success and conservatism in the Tokugawa shogunate

The route to the modern world undertaken by Japan begins with the Tokugawa period. The economy and society was agrarian, hierarchically ordered and successful, and the success was to prove its undoing:

1 The rural agrarian elite experienced slow relative decline as its finances came under routine pressure.
2 The warrior-bureaucrats experienced sharper relative decline as their stipends paid by the rural elite did not keep pace with the developing economy.
3 The peasants, organized through the system of the continuing family, experienced slowly improving overall circumstances.
4 The artisans improved their position relative to other groups as the economy advanced in terms of technology and levels of activity.
5 The merchants improved their situation relative to other groups as the slow rise of trade offered them new ways of organizing a livelihood.

Relatedly, the politics were hierarchical:

1 The elite revolved around a single imperial family which had an extensive retinue of advisors, courtiers and servants.
2 The local lords operated in a similar fashion.
3 The local area around a town with a spread of farming communities again worked hierarchically.

The system of alternate attendance controlled the lords. The system of class and caste controlled everyone else. However, the system was not static and economic success generated social change.

Overall, as the Tokugawa period developed, economic power slowly drained away from the regional lords and their warrior-bureaucrats towards the merchants and artisans. The merchant group came to have extensive financial influence as the economy advanced and rising political influence as the debts of the elite and their warrior-bureaucrats grew.

In sum the Tokugawa period was:

1 a successful and stable agricultural society;
2 which was unable to respond effectively to change;
3 consequently collapsed when the dynamics of change in the countries of the wider system impinged upon the internal dynamics of Japan. However, Tokugawa left an extensive legacy for subsequent periods.

Tokugawa and the demands of European and American traders

Hunter (1989: 2) argues that two 'epochal events have dominated the history of modern Japan. The revolution of 1868 . . . and the American-dominated Occupation of 1945–52'. The relationship of Japan and the West remains a problematical issue for Japanese political and intellectual elites. Indeed Hunter (1989: 16) argues that there is a fundamental dichotomy in Japanese thought which revolves around the 'simultaneous existence of both "indigenous" and "western" modes of thought and behaviour'.

Early contact and the policy of a closed country

In the centuries prior to the establishment of the Tokugawa shogunate, the Japanese had traded widely in Eastern Asia and there were early and extensive cultural borrowings from China. However, the arrival of the Europeans provoked anxiety among the shogunal ruling groups who came to suspect these foreigners of nursing ambitions to colonize the territory. The shogunate responded in 1633 with the first of a series of five directives which by 1639 together comprised what was later to be called the policy of National Seclusion, whereby Japan was largely closed to the outside world (Kodansha, 1993: 1062).

After the country adopted the policy of National Seclusion or 'closed country', in 1633–9 all trade and links with the outside were tightly controlled. The southern port of Nagasaki was the only point of access for Chinese and Dutch traders. The Korean traders were restricted to Tsushima. Over this long period European ideas did slowly enter Japan, including some natural science, medicine and military technologies. Yet the spread of the 'Dutch learning' was slow and resisted by patriots, who saw it as implicated in the 'moral decline' of the country.

In the seventeenth and eighteenth centuries trading vessels from America and Europe became frequent visitors to Pacific Asia. The Russian empire also made overtures. The European and American movement into the region gathered pace and attained its most vigorous form in the mid-nineteenth century when the Europeans and Americans forced the Chinese government to open up a series of trading ports. A mixture of technological superiority, commercial advantage and actively deployed military force drew China into the modern economic system.

All this was watched by the Japanese government with some anxiety. The Europeans and Americans eventually began to look to Japan. After a series of approaches were rebuffed, the American Commodore Perry obliged the shogunate to accept a treaty, the Treaty of Kanagawa, in March 1854. The British signed a similar treaty in October 1854 and the other European powers followed. These treaties allowed trade, controlled tariffs and guaranteed extra-territorial rights for foreign nationals – the Japanese called them the 'unequal treaties' and regarded them as a national disgrace.

The collapse of Tokugawa

As the European and American powers expanded their trade in the Pacific-Asian region the shogunate came under increasing pressure. In the late eighteenth and early nineteenth centuries a series of attempts were made by Western powers to open trade relations with Japan (Henshall, 1999: 64). In 1853 the US representative Perry began negotiations with the shogunate and returned the following year. The shogunate officials attempted to divert the demands but were slowly obliged to give ground. Perry secured an agreement to open two ports at which ships might call for stores. The foreign traders were sceptical of the value of these facilities but Perry saw them as a first move upon which others could build. The Europeans and Russians followed, as did further Americans, and in 1859 a treaty port system modelled on the one imposed upon China came into being in Japan (Beasley, 1990: 34). Over the period from 1854 to 1867 there was a slow increase in influence of the West with its traders moving into Japan to a very uncertain welcome.

The political elite in Japan was split. Beasley (1990: 32) suggests that while the Tokugawa officials knew that Japan was obliged to give ground to the foreigners, who had, after all, only recently humbled the core country of the East Asian sphere, China, the regional lords and samurai did provide a reservoir of pressure for resistance. The political community of Tokugawa Japan was therefore divided. Indeed there was small-scale violent conflict on several occasions.

A related aspect of the political turmoil was a series of incidents involving foreigners. Eventually the Western powers bombarded the Choshu town of Kagoshima in 1863 and the Shimonoseki Straits forts in 1864. The lesson for the domestic critics of the Shogunate was that more was required than spontaneous minor attacks upon foreigners. A group of southern regional lords and samurai came together to demand that the shogunate be dissolved in favour of a new government, built around the re-established position of the emperor. The resultant political crisis in Japan led to a partial revolution from above known as the Meiji Restoration, which in turn produced a remarkable period of economic, social and political reform.

We might note one political-cultural legacy of this period – a continuing concern for Japan to have the 'wealth and strength' necessary to deal with outsiders from a position of equality. The debates of the pre-revolution period are reprised throughout the Meiji period until in the period of late Meiji in the early twentieth century they come to form an influential line of nationalist ideologizing known as nihonjinron (Dale, 1986; Yoshino, 1992).

Continuing role of the West in Japanese thought

The Japanese exchange with the West has produced a complex and tangled response; a mix of borrowing, incomprehension, rejection and the defensive insistence upon the particularity of the Japanese.

Hunter (1989: 16) remarks that after Japan severed virtually all contact with the West in the early years of the Tokugawa era, the country 'did not stand still during this time . . . [however] the substantial advances that did take place were not influenced by external models of ideas [and this generated] . . . a fundamental dichotomy that has dominated Japan's recent history; the simultaneous existence of both "indigenous" and Western modes of thought and behaviour'.

It has opened up a debate about what is local and what is borrowed and what should be the relationship of these elements. The manner in which Japan was obliged to engage with the West, Hunter (1989: 18) notes, 'seemed calculated to reinforce rather than diminish a sense of separateness and need for security in the face of manifestly unequal treatment'. She points out that:

Japan was both militarily and economically vulnerable and the lack of outside support for her resistance to great power domination reinforced a sense of national isolation which originated in national myth, grew in the seclusion period and was strengthened by an awareness of the cultural divide between Japan and the West (Hunter, 1989: 18).

The Meiji oligarchy made a lengthy study visit to Europe and the USA in 1871–3. The Iwakura mission brought an appreciation of the extent of the technological backwardness of Japan. Hunter notes:

> The result of this realization was a massive programme of change [which] went far beyond the destruction of the old order . . . No single country was taken as the model in implementing change. The degree of eclecticism was considerable, and efforts were made to find the Western model, or the aspects of it, that would be most appropriate to the Japanese situation. (Hunter, 1989: 20)

The shift of Japan into great power status was met with some Western resistance to Japanese gains. The stress on traditional Japan made by some was reinforced. In the 1930s there was a further turning away from the model of the West – another return to traditional roots and resources. Thereafter, the Occupation created a renewed interest in the West in general and the USA in particular. Again the borrowing has been partial and contentious.

Hunter (1989: 35) concludes that as 'Japan is closely integrated into the international economy, an absolute distinction of this kind [between Western technology and Japanese values] is clearly not feasible but the pattern highlights an ongoing dilemma. Japan faces a fundamental problem in reaching an accommodation between those values and practices whose origins are primarily indigenous and those that are broadly termed "Western"'. Yet, contrariwise, it is clear that the business of elites adjusting to shifting structural circumstances, and thereafter mobilizing their populations, is by no means particular to the Japanese. It would seem to be an entirely general historical and political-sociological phenomena. Once again, in respect of the experience of Japan, the particular characteristics of competing strategies of Western analysis can be considered. If the Japanese experience is read through the lens of modernization theory, with its unselfconscious affirmation of the intellectual and global-system priority of the model of the West in general and the USA in particular, then it is clear that the problem Hunter points to is a Japanese problem. However, if these matters are read through the lens of the classical European tradition of social theorizing, then the requirement to adjust to shifting circumstances is everyone's problem. In the case of Japan, as indeed with the USA or European Union, we have a particular attempt by particular theorists to grasp the ongoing shift to the modern world (Preston, 1997).

The early Meiji era, 1868–94

The Meiji Restoration took place in 1868. The episode could be described as a revolution from above and was organized by two southern domains, Choshu and Satsuma. The changes involved the removal of the shogun from power in favour of the nominal restoration of the emperor Meiji. However, in reality, a modernizing oligarchy took real power. Henshall (1999: 70) lists Okubo Toshimichi (1830–78), Saigo Takamori (1827–77) and Matsukata Masayashi (1835–1924) from Satsuma; Kido Koin (1833–77), Inoue Kaoru (1835–1915), Ito Hirobumi (1841–1909) and Yamagata Aritomo (1838–1922) from Choshu. The new ruling group immediately embarked on a far-reaching programme of political, economic, social and cultural reconstruction.

Reforming the polity: towards a rational bureaucratic state and national polity

The politics of revolution involved southern regional lords displacing the shogun in favour of the nominal restoration of the emperor Meiji. However, in reality, this revolution from above was ordered by those who had suffered both economically and politically in the later years of the shogunate and at the same time saw the need for extensive reforms. It can be called a partial revolution as the whole system was not swept away to be replaced by another but was extensively remade, retaining a strong measure of continuity with what had gone before (Sheridan, 1993: 20). The fundamentally hierarchical socio-political ethic of Tokugawa, sometimes called a 'Japanized Confucianism', was carried forward into Meiji and redeployed in pursuit of modern nationstatehood. The new ruling groups involved representatives from the domains which had overthrown the shogunate and thereafter many young samurai with administrative experience; in all, an elite group oriented to pushing through an extensive reform programme.

Having taken power, the new elite faced the task of constructing the basic elements of a modern rational-legal nationstate. The task was accomplished in stages over the next decade as the key economic, social and political elements of the old agrarian feudal society were reordered to establish the basis of a modern rational-legal industrial society.

A new state was constructed by the oligarchic group which made the revolution in the name of the emperor. The project included a series of elements:

1 A modern pattern of central and local government was instituted and the domains of the regional lords were transformed into prefectures within a modern state centred on Tokyo.
2 The caste system was abolished.
3 The daimyo and samurai retainers were paid off.

4   Landownership and taxation were reformed to provide state revenues.
5   A centralized bureaucracy was formed.
6   A standing conscript army was formed.
7   The state theory of Germany and the constitutional law of France were studied in order to write and promulgate in the name of the emperor a new constitution in 1889.
8   A political structure involving emperor, parliament and cabinet was formed and the oligarchy, or genro, remained outside as a group of 'elder statesmen advising the emperor', although in practice they both held all the power and held the system together.
9   Political parties formed.
10   The system of state-shinto which stressed the role of the emperor was inaugurated and Buddhism was repressed.

In all this we should note the construction of the emperor system. The Meiji revolutionaries had justified their coup d'état by arguing that they were restoring the position of the emperor. The episode was legitimated in the Charter Oath of April 1868 which stated the government's intentions to attend to the interests of all Japanese people and to consult widely in order to build national strength. The role of the emperor was further reinforced in the establishment of State Shinto. The emperor came to play both a practical role – as one of the key figures lodged within the new oligarchic system (and the precise active contribution is another matter) – and a symbolic role. The symbolic role offered both a way of abstractly and indirectly legitimating the rule of the oligarchy and a way of legitimating and ordering the very practical task of reorganizing society (Large, 1997). The emperor was presented as the father figure of the Japanese people, the stern father who ruled paternalistically the continuing family which was the totality of the Japanese people, the national polity.

Hunter (1989: 9) notes that the interpretation of the overthrow of the Tokugawa and the establishment of Meiji has long been a matter of controversy:

The term 'restoration' used in English has overtones of a return to the past; the revival of a hallowed Japanese tradition which accorded supreme power to the imperial family. Japan's post-1868 rulers utilized this nationalistic focus and claimed throughout to exercise power in the name of the emperor. Yet the Japanese term normally used for the transfer, ishin, is more correctly translated as 'renovation' – a term which implies not retrospection but a sense of renewal and looking forward. This terminological ambiguity symbolizes a basic contradiction embodied in the whole process of change which followed 1868, a running tension between those who looked back and sought to revive what they saw as the best in Japanese tradition in the face of a Western onslaught, and those who looked to the future and were prepared to accommodate the values and techniques of their competitors, if only to compete effectively with them. (Hunter, 1989: 9)

Hunter also notes that whereas standard popular histories record that the reformers were an integrated united group, the reverse is the case:

History has too often tended to view the leaders of the new regime as a single-minded body of men, united in their commitment to political, economic and social change and the creation of an internationally strong Japan. In fact, the participants in the revolution were far from united – many had little more in common than a desire to end the dominance of the Tokugawa and to secure some of its power for themselves. Right through to the beginning of 1868 the anti-Bakufu forces were riven by disagreements, and disputes within the ruling elite over the nature and role of the state continued for the next two and a half decades. (Hunter, 1989: 164)

Reforming the economy: creation of an industrial-capitalist economy

Sheridan (1993: 5) notes that there is a standard explanation for Japan's historical success which claims that the government intervened in the face of external threats and mobilized a submissive population to secure the benefits of late development. The state corrected market failures. Yet Sheridan thinks this is subtly wrong because the state did not correct market failures, rather it had long been involved in the economy since feudal days, and the Meiji Restoration merely represented a new policy direction based on an established role within the economy. Sheridan (1993: 6) suggests that while the particular policy mix and focus of attention of the state may have changed from time to time, there have been two constants: the political approach to economic matters; and the key role of state planning.

Sheridan (1993: 18) points out that the feudal system had many characteristics favourable to economic growth, including: low birth and death rates, urban growth, commercialization, ethnic uniformity and tenure and tax systems that favoured agricultural productivity. Sheridan (1993: 18) adds that while the system was still feudal, with revenues extracted from the peasantry and passed up the social hierarchy, it did see peasant standards of living rising steadily through the Edo period. Sheridan (1993: 19) notes the absence of entrepreneurs or capital investment. In sum, in the mid-1800s Edo Japan had reached its economic limits. However, in 1868 a new set of possibilities opened up. The Meiji government initiated an economic modernization drive which involved learning the available lessons from the Europeans and Americans in the fields of military technologies, scientific work, industrial and commercial organization, educational provision and legal structures.

As the Meiji elite faced the demands of the outside world they picked up ideas presented in the later years of Edo and these were the basis for a project of national development which included establishing a modern centralized state with tax powers to replace the scattered domains and generating a notion of nationhood to replace the allegiances to family and domain which had typified Edo feudalism. Sheridan (1993: 22–3) discusses the emergence of the slogan 'fukoku-kyohei' (rich country, strong army) and notes it was crucial in the period 1868–85. It was on the basis of this ideology of national development that an interrelated series of initiatives were begun: first, the establishment of a nationstate; second, the securing of public revenues to fund development; third, the start of a novel role for the state in economic development via the establishment of public enterprises.

The reform of public revenues involved:

(a) the establishment of a new currency, the yen, to replace various domain currencies;
(b) an extensive reform of land tax, now payable in currency;
(c) the payment of compensation to expropriated lords and retainers via pensions;
(d) the abolition of clans and establishment of prefectures run by appointed governors (Sheridan, 1993: 23–4).

The state was also active in encouraging economic development. In 1870 the Ministry of Industrial Development was set up and three areas of activity were pursued:

1 Fostering the development of coal, steel, railways and machinery, viewed as crucial to a modern economy, which the Meiji government took over from domain control.
2 The establishment of public model enterprises in key sectors was begun when early expectations of private enterprise were not fulfilled.
3 With the Ministry of Home Affairs, the drive to modernize extended into agriculture and agricultural products such as silk.

The state also encouraged the development of the knowledge and skills necessary to a modern industrial economy through overseas education, the use of temporary foreign experts and the reform of domestic schooling (Sheridan, 1993: 24–8). It might be noted that many of these projects, as with setting up model plants, were unsuccessful in narrowly commercial terms, but their role was to contribute to the inauguration of a new political-cultural project for Japan.

The rise of industry was intimately bound up with the activities of the state. The Meiji government had begun a nationwide search for entrepreneurial talent as early as 1877. These were 'seisho' (merchants by grace of political connections). The direct role of the government slowly subsided as private enterprise grew. The state factories were sold off in the 1880s, slowly turning into the later zaibatsu, and the Ministry of Home Affairs was dissolved. After the sell-offs the new relationship of state and enterprise was one of routine cooperation.

In the early years of the Meiji period the model to which the rulers looked was that of the UK with its legitimating theories of market liberalism. However, the appropriateness of the model to a late industrializing country was debated (Sheridan, 1993: 28). There were two camps – the Enlightenment and the Nationalists. The former group looked to the model of England and the notions of free trade, which favoured certain established textile and light industries, while the latter looked to the German model, which seemed more useful in building up new industries. In 1877 the new Tokyo Imperial University had begun classes that looked to the German Historical School and this pattern was repeated in public universities while private schools looked more to business. The bureaucrats were trained in the public universities and the intellectual disposition to stress national needs over laissez-faire complemented existing patterns of cooperation. The Nationalists eventually won the battle. A key event was the 'Meiji 14th Year Incident' in 1881 when a debate that had been ongoing since the restoration, and indeed with anticipations in debate prior to restoration, between 'enlightenment' and 'nationalists' was settled in favour of the latter as a group of Meiji leaders favouring the former position was ousted. The role of the state within the developing economy was confirmed. The upshot was a burgeoning success and in 1894 the 'unequal treaties' were revised.

Sheridan (1993: 33) argues that the period 1881–1900 covers the Japanese 'take-off'. The key here is establishing a Japanese approach to industrial and national development. Overall, Sheridan notes:

> The Tokugawa efforts at rural-centered industrialization used indigenous economic methods and administrative frameworks. In the 'Enlightenment via Westernization' exercises the Meiji government used a different approach and pursued industrialization more aggressively. In 1881 the drive for industrial progress changed its course once again as it searched for its own Japanese formula . . . By 1900 the government had developed a coherent, public/private, Western/Japanese mode of national economic planning and management, and at some point around 1900 the state economy 'took off' from its previous infantile and formative experimental stage. (Sheridan, 1993: 33)

There is debate about the level of development at the start, but most seem to agree that Japan began from a position that had obtained in the UK approximately a century before. In the early years of Meiji much was achieved, in particular the broad shift away from rural feudalism into the modern world. However, there was dissatisfaction and in 1881 there was a change of direction. A new Minister of Finance, Matsukata Masayashi, inaugurated a deflationary policy which aimed to reorder the financial system. Two key institutional developments were made: a national budget was established; a state bank was created. Sheridan (1993: 36) notes that these financial systems were designed by bureaucrats and were intended to insulate financial management from any day-to-day political involvement.

The Bank of Japan was established in 1882. Originally distinctly independent, after the model of the Belgian national bank, it was quickly integrated more closely into the financial activities of the government than was the case with equivalent Western banks. Other banks had been encouraged and by 1900 there was a national network of specialist banks – post office savings banks, foreign exchange banks and long-term financing banks for firms. All these banks were set up rather in advance of industrial activity and when this took off firms continued to rely on them rather than develop other sources of finance. The influence of the state thus remained quite central (Sheridan, 1993: 37–8).

As the economy began to advance Japan looked to integrate itself into the contemporary global trading system. Sheridan (1993: 39) notes: 'Japan began to take initiatives to integrate herself into the global economy by developing the mechanisms of foreign trade. An important step was the adoption of the gold standard in 1897.' Trade and investment improved – indeed there were two pre-1900 investment booms followed by slowdowns.

The turn of the century picture can be summarized:

1 In Tokugawa 70–80 per cent of the workforce were peasant farmers which by 1900 had fallen to 65 per cent.
2 The shift from village-based industries to modern industry took a series of forms as traditional industries such as silk were modernized and new industries were initiated by the state. By 1900 economic change was translating into social change, for example, in schedules of consumer demand.
3 Structural change began in areas linked to international trade because the development of tradable sectors was important in the growth of the economy in general and was a government priority (silks, ceramics and cottons were important; Sheridan, 1993: 41).

Sheridan (1993: 44) cites Arthur Lewis on the basics of growth (knowledge, capital and economic activity) and notes that the Japanese government was routinely involved from Meiji onwards. It sponsored study missions to gather knowledge and fostered education at home. Both these fed into industrial development, but also established the role of the state in, and focus of education upon, national economic development. It is the role of the government which Sheridan stresses. It was never an addition to a functioning or developing liberal-market economy, but rather was deeply involved in moving Japanese economic activity forwards, from agrarian feudal to industrial capitalist. Sheridan (1993: 46) says: 'The case of Japan may be seen as one in which the government translated the greater portion of its national aims directly into economic terms, and consequently pursued economic development to the maximum extent.' In other words, this is a matter of broad mobilization, the pursuit of a political-cultural project, formulated by the elite and disseminated through the population.

Reforming the society: social demands of national development

The starting point was the legacy of Tokugawa: a period of elite-engineered stability. An hierarchical caste system had been established and buttressed by an ethic of obedience to superiors. The social ethic of Tokugawa derived from Confucianism and stressed loyalty, filial piety, obedience, courage and self-sacrifice. In contrast to the development of the ideals in China, where Confucianism allowed that an incompetent leader could lose the mandate of heaven, the Japanese historical experience of military rule issued in a stress on obedience and loyalty. It produced what Nakane (1970) called a 'vertical society'. The Meiji government reworked the legacies of the Tokugawa period in order to fashion a mobilized corporate society. A series of intermingled lines of reform were pursued: structural, as the feudal caste system was abolished; institutional, as the continuing family was reworked; and cultural/ ideological, as social expectations and mores were refashioned.

The impact of the West caused confusion at elite level, where there were both admirers and critics, yet the caste system was abolished in 1872. However, as Hunter (1989: 66) notes: 'What is indisputable is that the Meiji government, having abolished the official status system of the Tokugawa, tried to impose a permutation of the Tokugawa social ethos, and this ideal sought a fusion of social structure and social morality.' Hunter records:

> In the years after 1868 the new regime attempted to manipulate selected facets of Tokugawa society to impose a uniform social structure and morality which could then be trumpeted as 'traditional' . . . For the cardinal virtues and family structure the Meiji 'tradition' drew on the ethos of the warrior class. In some other respects it relied on centuries of evolution of peasant society. (Hunter, 1989: 66)

A related aspect is that of gender relations and in the domestic sphere the model of Tokugawa elite-class women came to be the model for women in general, a patriarchal mix of childrearing and looking after men.

The continuing family was the vital social organization translating ideals into routine practice. Hunter (1989: 68) notes: 'that the combination of vertical and group ties was such that individuals tended to be viewed by others not as individuals, but as group members, and a network of reciprocal obligations and feelings between group members was the key to the maintenance of social order'.

The sets of social expectations which suffused ordinary life were extensively reworked in the early Meiji period. The inherited cultural resources of the Tokugawa period were revised and put to work in pursuit of the Meiji elites' new political-cultural goals. Hunter notes:

Beginning with the family into which an individual was born, he or she contracted a series of group memberships in quasi-family institutions or groups, such as school, college or company. Within each group each individual had a specific ranking, but now the hierarchy was imposed by convention rather than being formally assigned. The most important and all embracing of these groups was the 'family state', which figured prominently in the official political ideology . . . The structure and ethos of the village community remained pivotal to the whole system . . . The village came to be represented as the source of all the traditional virtues, the heir of the Japanese tradition. (Hunter, 1989: 71)

As the Meiji elite pursued its programmes of reform the masses of the population were carefully drawn into the overall process. Hunter points out:

The official imposition of conventional social forms and norms was achieved largely through the education and legal systems, but its strength lay in its manipulation of existing social values and a long-standing social system which enabled it to be internalized by the average Japanese. Patriotism was added to the warrior virtues of duty, obedience, loyalty and filial piety to become the attributes of morality. (Hunter, 1989: 71)

The continuing family was the key social organization and the model was copied to other social organizations, such as firms and the state. The imperial rescript on education in 1890 backed all this up. So did the new civil code of 1898 which enshrined in law the role of the patriarchal continuing family. At the same time individual social mobility was possible and was pursued – but it was individual change within the prescribed frameworks. Hunter (1989: 75) notes: 'After 1931, and especially after the outbreak of full-scale war with China in 1937, social regimentation in Japan became more obtrusive.'

Legacies of engineered reform in Meiji

In many respects the overall pattern of organization of the modern Japanese economy (large firms served by a mass of smaller firms and all subject to the guidance of the bureaucracy), society (ordered and disciplined), and polity (with power reserved to an elite and the general population not directly involved) were put into place during this period.

The Tokugawa system was successful, but it was not politically responsive. As the economy and society of Japan advanced, the formally specified social and economic order began to break down. As the economic power of the rural elite declined so the economic power of the urban artisans and merchants increased and the system could not produce a political response to the dispersed pattern of tensions brought about by internal dynamics of change. Thereafter the regime was unable to fashion a response to the particular and specific problem of how to respond to demands of the Europeans and Americans for trading rights. In the face of these twin sets of demands the regime collapsed.

The Meiji Restoration was a revolution from above by a group of southern Japanese regional lords with the assistance of a wider spread of disenchanted warrior-bureaucrats. They secured control of the government and thereafter presented their revolution in terms of a restoration of the emperor. The Meiji Restoration shifts power to an oligarchy comprising figures from the key regional domains which quickly moves to put in place those necessary reforms which Tokugawa had been unable to contemplate:

(a) the establishment of a modern rational-bureaucratic state;
(b) the encouragement of a modern industrial-capitalist economy;
(c) the organization of a modern society, including, over a somewhat more drawn-out period, a national democratic polity.

The political reforms included:

1 The restoration of the emperor as a key figure within the polity (practical and ideological).
2 The abolition of the semi-independent feudal domains and the related establishment of a system of regional prefectures subordinate to central government.
3 The effective practical abolition of the class and caste of warrior-bureaucrats, and the related establishment of a rational bureaucratic system with positions filled by merit rather than birth.
4 The establishment of a central rational state apparatus (cabinet, parliament, civil service ministries).
5 The promulgation of a constitution.

In brief, an authoritarian modernizing state had been created. Thereafter, in society, the reforms included:

(a) the abolition of the class/caste system;
(b) the reform of the continuing family such that it was reoriented to the needs of a national developmental state rather than the local loyalties of domain;
(c) educational reform such that all children received a basic practical education;
(d) military reform to establish a modern style navy and army;
(e) infrastructural reform, such as roads, railways and telegraphs;
(f) a spread of economic reforms to encourage the upgrading of old industries (such as silk) and the development of new heavy industries.

In brief, a modern economy and society had been constructed. Finally, in the cultural sphere, the reforms included:

(a) the promulgation of ideals of nation in place of the particularisms of domain-loyalites;
(b) the establishment of state-shinto as a further mechanism to affirm a national identity.

In brief, a modern national identity had been constructed. What all this does is to rework the legacies of Tokugawa in order to establish an industrial-capitalist developmental state, which in turn provides the legacy for present-day Japan.

Conclusion

The shift of Japan to the modern world can be analysed, in terms of the intellectual resources of the classical European tradition of social theorizing, as a series of phases where each represents the way in which the ruling groups read and reacted to patterns of internal change and external pressures. The Tokugawa shogunate had become moribund and could deal neither with internal problems occasioned by growing populations and modest economic prosperity, nor with the demands of the European and American colonial traders. The Meiji Restoration saw the seizure of power by a group determined to reconstruct the country so as to resist the encroachment of the colonial powers. The Meiji Restoration secured its objectives with great success. If we look at the way in which this past is present within contemporary Japanese life, then the legacies, residues and continuities are many. Japan has a developmental state, a weak and underdeveloped polity, an hierarchical society and a culture which mixes tradition, local accomplishment and foreign borrowing.

The initial objectives of the Meiji Restoration were achieved in a relatively short period of time. The pursuit of development at home, security within the region and the search for recognition/status within the existing international system found summary expression and achievement in the Sino-Japanese war of 1894–5. The Japanese nationstate was acknowledged by the Western powers as a member of that exclusive club of modern industrial nations. Thereafter, the country continued its slow expansion within the region, defeating Czarist Russia in the Russo-Japanese War of 1904–5, annexing Korea in 1911, advancing into China, taking over German possessions in World War I and participating in the establishment of the League of Nations. However, by the early 1920s, as the original Meiji oligarchs died, the system slowly began to drift into confusion and was unable to cope either with the internal pressures of success and political conflict occasioned by global depression, or with external pressures occasioned by diplomatic responses to its wars in East Asia. The system was drawn into the ambit of the military who eventually launched a quixotic war against the USA.

Note

1 Henshall (1999) offers a series of 'lists' whereby the legacy of one period of Japan's history for subsequent generations is noted (see pp. 19, 47, 69, 102, 135, 179).

3

LOCATING JAPAN WITHIN THE MODERN WORLD

Success, Instability and Competing Political-Cultural Projects

The period of late Meiji, Taisho and early Showa extends from 1894, when Japan waged a successful war against China for influence on the Korean peninsular, through to the 1945 experience of defeat at the hands of the USA and its allies, and encompasses the second great phase of Japan's ongoing shift to the modern world. The success of the project of national development undertaken by the Meiji reformers had given rise to a series of domestic debates about how, precisely, to locate Japan within the extant modern world.

It is possible to trace a complex pattern of domestic advance, tension and debate in respect of the appropriate future for Japan. The experience of Japan within the modern world in the early years of the twentieth century can be grasped, in outline, in terms of three broad intermingled patterns of response to the modern world: the successes of late Meiji when Japan became one of the great powers within the international system; the more problematical period of Taisho, which combined economic and social advance with early tensions in respect of ordering the region with the West in general and the USA more particularly; and the final period of depression, domestic political instability and a slide into militarism which was to provide the context for a military option to deal with US pressures.

Late Meiji, 1894–1912

The late Meiji era, 1894–1912, can be characterized in terms of two government preoccupations: domestic development and regional security. The first related to industrial development and the associated social, cultural and political changes. The second was the vehicle for a series of anxieties and aspirations:

1 For security within a region whose historical centre, China, was undergoing a process of collapse as its ruling elites failed to deal with the demands of the business of effecting a shift to the modern world.
2 For security in respect of an economic area which could provide both raw materials and markets for the growing Japanese industrial economy.
3 Finally, for the status of 'great power' within the Western international system which at that time was characterized by the pursuit of empire.

Late Meiji: domestic developments

The domestic development concerns of the late Meiji era related to further industrial development and the associated social, cultural and political adjustments to the Japanese form of life.

THE PURSUIT OF INDUSTRIAL DEVELOPMENT The pursuit of industrial development was central to government policy in Meiji. In the early years much was achieved, in particular the broad shift away from rural feudalism into the modern world, but in 1881 there was a change of direction. A new Minister of Finance, Matsukata Masayashi, reordered the nation's financial system and a national budget and state bank were established. The Bank of Japan was established to order the nation's finances and by the turn of the century there was a network of specialist banks able to serve industrial activity as it subsequently developed. At the same time, as the economy began to advance Japan looked to integrate itself into the contemporary global trading system. The broad structural changes within the economy began in areas linked to international trade. In all this the role of the government was crucial. It was deeply involved in moving Japanese economic activity forwards, from agrarian feudal to industrial-capitalist. Sheridan (1993: 46) says: 'The case of Japan may be seen as one in which the government translated the greater portion of its national aims directly into economic terms, and consequently pursued economic development to the maximum extent.' In other words, this is a matter of broad mobilization, the pursuit of a political-cultural project, formulated by the elite and disseminated through the population.

SOCIAL, CULTURAL AND POLITICAL REFORMS The drive for industrial development entailed widespread social, cultural and political reforms. Yet the reform programme was essentially conservative in that it sought to retain elements of Tokugawa social ideas so as to manage and order this rapid shift to the modern world. An invented past, a 'traditional Japan', was contrived which presented the ideal of an harmonious hierarchical national community. The patriarchal continuing family was the key social organization. The civil code of 1898 enshrined the role of the continuing family in law. The model was copied to other social organizations such as firms and the state. The relationship of individual and collectivity was quite distinctive and centred upon membership of social groups such that an individual lived within a network of duties and obligations to others.

The process of rapid industrialization occasioned extensive change in the form of life of ordinary Japanese but the core ethos of individual membership of overlapping sets of groups was retained. In this sense, the social structure and social ethic of the life of the Japanese rural agrarian village was retained. The state made the ethos of membership into a key part of the official ideology, the idea of the 'family state', such that all the Japanese were enjoined to understand themselves as members of one national family, with a wise benevolent head in the person of the emperor (Hunter, 1989; Large, 1997).

ECONOMIC DEVELOPMENT AND ROLE OF GOVERNMENT The role of the government in economic development was extensive. Sheridan (1993: 57) notes that between 1939 and 1990 the population rose from 44 million to 71 million. Real national income rose by a factor of 2.8. The early industrial expansion was in light industry but from the 1920s it shifted into heavy industry. Overall, by the 1930s the industrial sector was producing more than one-third of the national product. Thereafter, Sheridan (1993: 58) is concerned with the question of how much the government contributed to these developments and reviews three related lines of argument: the nature of capital formation; the changing composition of the capital stock; and the history of government regulation of the financial sector.

In respect of capital formation, during the early Meiji period the government built on the resources of the feudal economy and change and development were slow. Yet by 1900, as economic, social and cultural changes were made and the country began to advance, there were resources available for more extensive programmes of capital investment. The government was strongly committed to building the capital stock and the country's economic growth was fuelled by capital investment rather than consumer demand. It is clear that other countries have acted similarly in the early phases of industrialization. However, in Japan this pattern has persisted through the twentieth century, as has the state's concern for development. Sheridan (1993: 61–2) notes that a significant share of this capital investment went to military expenditure, either directly, in the form of plant and equipment, or indirectly, via the provision of necessary infrastructure, such as roads, railways, ports and so on. It might be noted that Japan was actively at war for roughly twenty years in the period 1895–1945. The experience of modern war, which has an intimate relationship with advanced industry, reinforced state involvement in the pursuit and ordering of economic growth. At the same time, of course, the preoccupation with capital investment and the demands of military production also reduced the welfare effect of economic growth for the population at large. Overall, Sheridan (1993: 64) takes the view that early Meiji investment did not contribute very much to production growth. The trends of growth from the Edo period continued through the final years of the century, but thereafter growth did improve after 1900.

On the composition of the capital stock, Sheridan (1993: 72) points out that until 1885 public capital formation was greater than private. There was investment in infrastructure – road, railways and government offices. In contrast, private investment was slow to show itself. The state continued, therefore, with model industrial plants. These were not economically successful because they were capital intensive and the money could have been spent more broadly within the extant economy to greater short-term effect. However, these patterns of investment were part of a long-term government political-cultural project to effect the shift to the modern world. Sheridan (1993: 73) notes that from 1886 to 1900 there was a rapid increase in modern industry. Eventually, after 1900, available private money was invested in industrial development. Sheridan (1993: 73) reports that from 1901 to 1916 there was optimistic private investment alongside continuing government investment so that problems of underinvestment in social infrastructure became apparent in the guise of slums, pollution and degradation of natural resources. Overall, Sheridan makes the point that the government was not merely investing to assist an extant market, but was pursuing a project which aimed to alter peoples lives:

> In fact, this was the essence of the public capital formation in the period. The government aimed to modernize the lifestyle of the population along with their values and thinking habits by effective and swift industrialization. The modernization of private industry and production techniques was expected to follow from the *social* effects of public investment in these areas. (Sheridan, 1993: 74)

As regards the financial sector, the Meiji financial system of banks worked well until the demands of economic growth, empire and competition with the West, following World War I, began to strain the system. In the early years of development the banks extended credit more readily than Western banks would have done, so there was over-borrowing by firms that were closely tied to banks. A characteristic relationship was thus established and behind all these relationships was the national bank. In the financial system, as with production, everything was oriented to growth. In general, summarizing the review, Sheridan (1993: 86) notes that the state has been central to the pursuit of the project of development and that it has pursued this over-riding goal in close conjunction with the private sphere. It is clear that by the end of the nineteenth century the Japanese government had fostered the development of a successful industrial-capitalist economy.

GROWTH, WELFARE AND ECONOMIC POLICY   As the twentieth century opened the Japanese economy was growing strongly. In broad terms, the economy grew much as the Western economies had at similar stages of development. Yet the costs of progress were high as rapid industrialization entailed population movement, urbanization and the familiar spread of associated poor living conditions. The issues of growth, welfare and economic policy came to be important.

A series of familiar views of Japanese welfare are noted by Sheridan (1993: 93):

1   The idea of growth at the cost of equity, which suggests growth was key and welfare ignored.
2   The idea of growth without welfare, which suggests growth based on subsistence level toil for masses.
3   The idea of growth with increasing disposable income, which suggests that the Japanese story is pretty much like the Western one.
4   The idea of the need for a better welfare index, thereby suggesting that Western idea of 'welfare as transfer' needs to be adjusted to see the welfare effects of Japanese economic activity.
5   The idea of Japan as welfare superpower, thereby suggesting that misanalysis by Westerners blinds them to extensive welfare provision.

Against these diverse lines of analysis, Sheridan (1993: 94) insists that what is crucial in the Japanese case is that policy for economic growth includes welfare; the two are not opposed as they are in Western thinking.

Sheridan (1993: 95) suggests that in early debates, between 1901 and 1916, the successful wars against China and Russia reinforced the 1881 shift towards national development and older Tokugawa traditions of growth together with welfare (keisei-saimin) were rather neglected. However, the movement of the population to the towns, plus rapid economic development and generally poor conditions, led to labour unrest (which was suppressed using the Public Order and Police Law of 1900) and the matter of welfare was thereby represented within political discourse.

There was some government thinking about welfare but Sheridan (1993: 97) points out that bureaucrats tended to think in terms of borrowed Western models, where a distinction was drawn between the needs and demands of economic activity on the one hand and problems of welfare provision on the other. On the basis of the distinction, the role of the state was characterized in terms of a responsibility to organize general welfare provisions paid for from general tax revenues. The Japanese industrialists opposed these sorts of measures, so in the event little was done. It was only later, as the economy made further advances and as 'rice riots' occurred, that a distinctively Japanese welfare pattern began to emerge. The developing welfare system tended to be centred on the efforts of private firms to make provision for their own employees, rather than any broad prescriptive general initiatives from the state.

Overall, the period can be characterized in terms of the shifting adjustments of the Meiji state to the structural circumstances within which perforce it operated. At the outset the Meiji state avoided either the formal colonization which was the fate of large parts of Pacific Asia or the informal quasi-colonialism forced upon China. The Meiji state was thereafter determined to secure the twin interlinked objectives of national economic development and regional security. The achievement of a measure of autonomy of national action was a necessary condition of any longer-term development objectives. In the later years of the twentieth century the Meiji state steered the country to the status of a great power.

Late Meiji: Japan and Northeast Asia

The concerns of the governments of the late Meiji period for national development and regional security found domestic expression, as noted, in the pursuit of economic growth. The related concern for regional security focused on Northeast Asia. The region, whose historical centre, China, was undergoing a process of collapse, was seen as a source of raw materials and markets for the growing Japanese industrial economy. It was also thought that Japanese advance was necessary to forestall European and American ambitions (Iriye, 1997). It came to be thought that Japanese control could secure regional stability, domestic and regional economic growth and firmly establish the status of great power within the Western international system for Japan.

The Meiji oligarchy was determined to avoid the fate of China by competing with the West on its own terms (Beasley, 1990). The Japanese elite responded to the West by initiating a drive for national development (Moore, 1966). The Japanese drive for industrial equality with the West was the central consequence, but related policies were developed in respect of the other countries of East Asia (Tanaka, 1993; Iriye, 1997). The Japanese elite reasoned that the old tributary relationships with China which had ordered East Asia for centuries were no longer appropriate to the new global system. The Japanese elite therefore assumed responsibility for the countries of East Asia and began a process of establishing a sphere of influence which was to issue in the construction of a formal colonial sphere, and, rather later, in the drive to establish an Asian co-prosperity sphere in the years of the Pacific War (Iriye, 1987).

CONTENT AND RATIONALE OF EXPANSION   The indigenous pattern of international relations in East Asia had centred upon China – the key economic, political and cultural power. The region was ordered as a series of politico-cultural concentric circles with the Chinese empire lying at the centre. The broad territory of East Asia was acknowledged as a sphere of civilized peoples. Thereafter, the distant territories lying beyond were consigned to the status of barbarian regions. Overall, the system was organized in terms of 'tribute', whereby rulers of the countries bordering China acknowledged the pre-eminence of the Chinese empire and thereby secured favourable economic and political relations. As the modern period began this tribute system remained in place. However, by the nineteenth century the key East Asian powers – China, Korea and Tokugawa Japan – were weak and unable to resist the encroaching demands of the expansionary Western industrial-capitalist system. Hunter (1989: 41) notes that 'by the mid-late nineteenth century . . . the East Asian cultural area no longer possessed the might of earlier years'. It is within the context of an historically weakened East Asian sphere that Japan enters the modern world.

The experience shaped the posture of the Japanese government towards its neighbours. The Japanese elite had to confront both the strong powerful modern Western world and the weakened debilitated traditional East Asian sphere. The Meiji elite had to pursue domestic economic development and regional security at the same time. This involved not merely the mechanics of economic growth, but also the political-ideological reordering of East Asia such that Japan could both assume responsibility for inherited cultural traditions and open a route to the modern future (Tanaka, 1993). In simple terms, Hunter (1989: 42) notes that as the strength of Japanese economy grew 'so did her ambitions on the Asian mainland'. What followed was the construction of a colonial sphere. The precise political rationale is difficult to pin down, just as it is in the case of the development of the Western empires, but domestic discontent, strategic position vis-à-vis the West, the problem of economic resources and markets, population pressures and the ideology of pan-Asianism all made their contributions.

The rapid development of the later years of the century generated social tensions and new popular understandings of Japan's position within the modern world. The two wars within East Asia generated popular nationalist support and there was resentment at Western reactions. A particular contribution, as noted by Tanaka (1993), was the new scholarly based discussions of the historical cultural dynamic of the country within East Asia. It was argued that the Japanese were the inheritors of the clearest expression of the essential culture of the East and had, therefore, a responsibility towards the region in the face of the demands of the rapidly changing global system. It was an ideology which was available to serve efforts to emulate the West and achieve great power status.

In the event, Japanese expansion took on the shape of formal colonialism. The country had acquired Taiwan in 1895 and the next phase of expansion began in 1910 with the annexation of Korea. This expansion was justified in terms familiar from the Western expansion. Hunter notes:

While Japanese expansion in Asia was still influenced by a preoccupation with defence and strategy, Japan's need for security in terms of raw materials, trading opportunities and an outlet for her expanding population became of increasing importance . . . Japan justified her expansion by a public relations rhetoric aimed at making it appear as altruism. Japan, it was said, sought the benefit of Asia as a whole and had a national mission to lead and coordinate the nations of Asia in resistance to the West. A Japanese-led block of Asian nations would be militarily and economically secure, and able to stand up to the threat posed by the nations of Europe and by the United States. (Hunter, 1989: 51)

PROCESS OF EXPANSION IN EAST ASIA: KOREA, TAIWAN AND CHINA   The first area of concern was Korea which was nominally independent but lodged within the Chinese sphere of influence. However, with the unstable situation in China the Japanese government feared a Western encroachment into the area to their eventual detriment. Japan imposed 'unequal treaties' on Korea in 1876 and proceeded to struggle with the Chinese for dominance in the area. Both governments stationed troops in the country from 1882 onwards. The Sino-Japanese war of 1894–5 saw the Japanese defeat the Chinese on the basis of their superior Western military technology. The peace accord was made with the Treaty of Shimonoseki and Japan received an indemnity and acquired Taiwan and areas of influence in Korea and Manchuria.

However, Russia, Germany and France then intervened diplomatically and the Japanese government was obliged to relinquish its gains in Manchuria. This caused public dismay in Japan where the view was that the great powers had deprived Japan of gains legitimately secured. The reaction of the government, having acquiesced, was to reaffirm the ideas of 'rich country, strong army' and to increase armaments spending in order to be able to resist more effectively any future impositions. The Anglo-Japanese Treaty was signed in 1902, as both countries had anxieties in respect of Russian expansion, and Japan's place within the network of powers was acknowledged. Over the next few years the Japanese government became involved in the great power manoeuvring in East Asia and slowly drifted into conflict with Russia over Manchuria and Korea.

The Russo-Japanese war of 1904–5 was an early experience for the Japanese of the mechanized warfare of industrialized countries. The costs to both combatants were high, although militarily the Japanese had the greater success. A mediation effort by the USA achieved a peace with the Treaty of Portsmouth and the Japanese consolidated their influence in Korea and Manchuria and received half of Sakhalin island. These were modest gains when set against public expectations and on their announcement there was rioting in Tokyo. However, in 1905 Korea was made a protectorate and in 1910 was annexed outright. In Manchuria the South Manchurian Railway Company was to become a key agent of

Japanese colonialism. In these years there was further manoeuvring against China but it met with little success.

It was also the case that these later imperialist moves met with displeasure from the Western powers, which in turn provoked a negative reaction among the Japanese political elite whose view of the West became yet more sceptical. At this time it is possible to identify the beginnings of a new expression of Japanese nationalism, hostile to the Europeans and Americans.

LEGACIES OF THE PERIOD   The shift to the modern world inaugurated by the Meiji Restoration continued in the years of the late nineteenth century and by the early twentieth century Japan was accepted by the Europeans and Americans as a new great power. The Japanese had also established an empire in East Asia. The legacy of this period we can note as twofold: first, it marked an early expansionist exchange with the countries of Pacific Asia; second, as Dale (1986: 205) notes, it fixed in place a reactionary and latent anti-Western nationalist view of Japan as both unique and misunderstood.

The Taisho era, 1912–26: success, confusion and doubt

The patterns of advance established over the Meiji period were continued during the Taisho era, 1912–1926. The period encompasses further domestic economic advance, social reforms and significant political reforms. Externally there was a significant extension of Japanese involvement in Korea and Manchuria. In addition, the alliance of Japan with the British and French during World War I allowed Japan to take over German interests in the region, including island territories in the Pacific and trading interests in China. It is in respect of China, where Japan made diplomatic demands to be treated at least as favourably as other great powers, that we find the first elements of discord with the Western powers.

Taisho Japan: domestic advance

In the 1920s and 1930s there are new developments. A crucial political change occurs as the Meiji oligarchs and their immediate successors slowly leave the political scene. This has the effect of removing one important source of ideas in respect of the appropriate trajectory of development for Japan. There is a measure of democratization in the Taisho period and the beginnings of more extensive party political activity. It should also be noted that an element of unclarity within the Meiji Constitution becomes evident, namely, the lack of political control over the armed forces. The Great Depression of the 1930s has severe consequences for Japan and there is widespread unemployment. There is also significant rural poverty and the proponents of ultranationalism find support in these areas and within the military. The Japanese elite become ever more influenced by the military and the country both turns inwards and looks to the resources of East Asia.

ECONOMIC, SOCIAL AND POLITICAL CHANGE   World War I had triggered an economic boom which in turn had shifted population to the urban areas and thereafter fuelled demands for greater democracy in Japan (in line with the optimistic liberalism of President Wilson and the League of Nations). In Japan it was the period of Taisho democracy.

Overall the period saw a mix of economic boom and bust (with the power of the zaibatsu rapidly increasing). As the economy grew it began to assume a now familiar dualistic structure with government-sponsored modern heavy industry and small traditional firms working in light manufacture. Sheridan (1993: 99) reports that from 1917 the mood was optimistic. However, after the post-war boom there was a depression in Japan from 1920 to 1927, with a severe financial crisis and state-sponsored reorganization of the banking system. The period was punctuated by the 1923 disaster of the great Tokyo earthquake.

There was rapid social change, in particular the growth of the progressive towns at the expense of the more traditional and conservative rural areas. The period between 1917 and 1923 sees the start of the search for a Japanese approach to welfare in the context of the new industrial economy. Yet Sheridan (1993: 75) argues that the late Meiji pattern of development entailed a lack of social infrastructure and that from 1917 to 1932 the relative shortage of social infrastructure continued.

Henshall (1999: 103–7) notes that the period was confused politically. On the one hand, there is liberal Taisho – thus in 1925 the government introduced universal manhood suffrage. On the other, there is the growth of a strong nationalism. During this period the, although illegal, unions, developed and there were strikes and social unrest in the form of 'rice riots'. A further problem was that the Taisho emperor developed debilitating health problems (Large, 1997). There was further confusion as the original Meiji oligarchy slowly left the scene. The state system which they had made slowly came apart as factions within the state machinery vied for control.

The global depression of the late 1920s and early 1930s effectively destroyed the Taisho democracy. There were two areas of problems: first, inside the country the polity did not see the establishment of a democratic form of politics and instead the nationalistic military gained in strength; second, externally the country's relationships with the outside world became increasingly problematic. Thus, the collapse in world trade effectively removed the Japanese from the international system within which they had operated and propelled them into a self-contained East Asian yen bloc. At the same time the economic slump created a mass of unemployed in Japan, with strikes in urban areas and widespread poverty in rural areas. In this environment of political confusion the nationalist and militarist right wing came to the fore.

Taisho period: external problems

World War I provided the Japanese government with a further opportunity for expansion in East Asia when, citing obligations under the Anglo-Japanese Alliance of 1902, it moved to take over German interests in China and to seize German Pacific Island territories. The various Japanese concerns with China were summarized in the guise of the 1915 'Twenty One Demands' in respect of privileging Japanese interests in China. Later the Versailles Treaty left the Japanese with their gains, although not with full Western approval. The Treaty also saw the establishment of the League of Nations, in which Japan participated, notwithstanding a Western rejection of their suggestion that the founding articles include a declaration on equality between the races. Thereafter in the 1920s the Japanese participated in the discussions of the great powers and were party to decisions designed to stabilize the situation in East Asia.

Early Showa era, 1926–45: nationalism, empire and the military

The early Showa period, 1926–45, sees dramatic domestic problems: the Kanto earthquake; the Great Depression; political upheaval. Japan is a militarized society by the mid-1930s. The early Showa period sees equally dramatic external changes. The crucial issue is China. The Japanese military continue a haphazard advance into China and this earns Japan the enmity of the USA. The exchanges between the two countries lead to the outbreak of the Pacific War.

Showa: depression and the rise of the military

In the early period encompassing late Meiji, Taisho and early Showa the economy, broadly speaking, made significant progress. However, in the early 1930s the government faced widespread problems as the global Great Depression developed. At first the response of the government was orthodox, as elsewhere, which exacerbated the problems. But from 1931 Finance Minister Takahashi expanded government spending to counteract the depression. The government encouraged light and heavy industry, made credit easily available, abandoned the gold standard and ran a large budget deficit. This was a Keynesian style policy stance and it was successful. However, Takahashi resisted social and military spending as wasteful. He was assassinated in '2–6 incident' in 1936 and the military came to have greater influence and military spending increased.

The depression was confronted by a government determined to solve the problem. The banks fell under tighter government control and the dual economic structure became more pronounced. The economy became more unequal. Yet Sheridan (1993: 104) argues that the period sees a long recession because the response of the government was largely ad hoc. Sheridan (1993: 105) points out that the assistance which the government did offer was skewed towards the zaibatsu – who thus increased their importance at the expense of the more traditional network of medium and small firms in light manufactures. All this, as politics developed, assisted the drift into the fascism of the inter-war years.

On the issue of welfare, Sheridan (1993: 99) notes that the years from 1924 to 1932 are known as the Showa recession. The public mood was pessimistic, with the government unable to formulate a coherent strategy of action. It was in the new heavy modern industries that management began to work out a fresh approach to social welfare in the form of paternalistic management and associated welfare benefits. Sheridan (1993: 101) takes this to be the new Japanese policy relevant to industrial society. The role of the government was not clear but it favoured contributing to welfare via public works programmes. The trend in both areas is to subsume welfare concerns within economic concerns. In sum, Sheridan (1993: 107) argues that from early in the Taisho period through to eve of war, as the economy moved ahead the firms began to sketch out a novel form of welfare in the context of industrial employment while the state lagged behind, preferring to attend to capital investment projects, and rather left the traditional approach to welfare, keisei-saimin, neglected.

Showa: the decision for war

The upheavals of the late 1920s and early 1930s began the slide into war. In 1931 Manchuria was occupied and in March 1932 the state of Manchukuo was established. Japan left the League of Nations in 1933 as a direct result and in 1936 signed the Anti-Commintern Pact with Germany. Of course the pattern of events in Europe acted to encourage the militarists in Japan.

PACIFIC WAR   By 1937, following the incident at the Marco Polo bridge when Chinese and Japanese soldiers clashed, a general war against China was in progress. This developed and extended in stages until it enveloped a large part of Northeastern and coastal China. It would seem that the Japanese never had a coherent strategy in China and the war simply drifted on. Its prosecution increasingly led to sharp conflict between the Japanese and American governments and to tension with the governments of the European colonial empires in Asia.

The final breakdown in relations with the USA and the European colonial powers was precipitated by the Japanese movement into Indo-China and led to the wider war against the West from 1941 to 1945. The whole of Southeast Asia and large areas of the Pacific were drawn into the conflict when Japanese armed forces launched a series of daring attacks across the northern Pacific area. In the space of six months they drove the Americans out of the Philippines, the Dutch out of the Dutch East Indies and the British out of Hong Kong, Malaya and Burma. They neutralized the French in Indo-China and found allies in Thailand. All European and American holdings in China were seized. However, the high water mark of the Japanese advance was quickly reached and the outcome of this war was the complete military defeat of Japan, which was then occupied by the Americans (Ienaga, 1978; Iriye, 1987).

READING THE HISTORICAL RECORD   The decline of the Japanese polity into a variant of fascism has been subject to post-World War II analysis by American scholars. However, in retrospect these scholars can be seen to have been anxious to run with the contemporary political-cultural grain and establish good relations with the Japanese. The upshot of this concern was to push scholarship towards the view that Japanese fascism was an aberration in an otherwise smooth movement towards the estab-lishment of a liberal-democratic polity. The role of the US occupation forces is thus one of assisting in the re-establishment of extant trends. Against these optimistic apologias two other lines of analysis are routinely presented:

1 The cultural stereotyping which suggests that the Japanese are fundamentally different from the West in the ways in which they regard the social world – a line of argument that has on occasion found final expression in racist characterizations (Thorne, 1980).
2 The line of argument favoured in this text which follows Moore (1966) and suggests that the Japanese shift to the modern world was such that it was susceptible to authoritarian collapse.

LEGACIES OF THE PERIOD   The legacies of this period are complex and to an extent overshadowed by war:

1 The Japanese military expansion through Pacific Asia caused exten-sive destruction and has left a widespread residual hostility (although this is shaded to some slight extent both by memories of wartime Japanese encouragement of those nationalists who subsequently won independence from European colonial powers and rather more strongly by post-war Japanese economic success and ODA transfers).
2 At the same time the wartime economic and social mobilization left many organizational forms available for subsequent post-war use (in particular via MITI).

3   A linkage with the USA was made which is central to contemporary Japanese international relations and politics.
4   The determination to repair Japan's position in the world found expression in the post-war drive for economic success.

Conclusion

Over the late Meiji, Taisho and early Showa periods the transformation of Japan was dramatic. On the basis of 'late industrialization' the Meiji rulers went on to add 'late imperialism' within Northeast Asia. The patterns of advance established at this time were continued during the Taisho era, with further domestic economic advance, social and political reforms, coupled to a significant extension of Japanese involvement in Northeast Asia. Thereafter the early Showa period, 1926–45, sees dramatic domestic political upheaval and Japan is a militarized society by the mid-1930s. Overseas, the crucial issue is China where the Japanese military continue a haphazard advance which earns Japan the enmity of the USA.

It might be noted that the involvement which contemporary Japan has with Pacific Asia can be seen to date from the very earliest years of the modern period of Japan's history. It is to the matter of 'late imperialism' that we now turn.

4

IMPERIAL JAPAN

Expansion and the Project of Empire in Asia

The Meiji period established two key preoccupations for the Japanese elite: economic development and national security. In the late nineteenth century development and security were pursued in parallel and a Japanese sphere of influence was established in East Asia. During World War I Japan was allied to the British, French and Americans and afterwards became a major power within the global system. The subsequent Japanese pursuit of further influence within East Asia generated tensions with the Western powers. The impact of the worldwide depression led to the rise in influence of the military. A combination of trade tensions, diplomatic problems in regard to the wars in China and aspirations to lead an Asian bloc precipitated a rupture in relations with the West and led to the Pacific War. Overall, the pursuit of empire can be taken to have three phases:

1 The early expansion from 1868–1905 in Northeast Asia which had the tacit approval of the Western powers.
2 The subsequent further expansion as a recognized 'power' from 1905 through to the Versailles Treaty and the foundation of the League of Nations.
3 The later inter-war period which sees the growth of the influence of the military and the clash with the USA.

The context of empire: Western expansion and Japanese response

The construction of the Japanese empire in Northeast Asia was undertaken in the late nineteenth and early twentieth centuries as part of the wider drive to join the modern world. At the time, the Western powers were establishing patterns of colonial holdings which were to reach their imperial apogee in the early years of the twentieth century before World War I. In this context, Japan's success is all the more remarkable. It is also clear that the early pattern of Japanese imperial expansion was accepted by the established Western powers.

European expansion, the Meiji Restoration and the political-cultural project of modernity

The early modern expansion of industrial capitalism reached a key stage in the mid-nineteenth century when the Europeans and Americans forced the Chinese government to open up a series of trading ports. A mixture of technological superiority, commercial vigour and military force drew China into the Western economic system. All this was watched by the Japanese government with anxiety. The traders began to look to Japan. In the mid-nineteenth century the American and European powers all secured treaties which allowed trade, controlled tariffs and extra-territorial rights for foreign nationals. The Japanese called them unequal treaties and regarded them as a national disgrace.

The Meiji Restoration of 1868 was occasioned by the inability of the declining Tokugawa shogunate to formulate a satisfactory response to the demands of the European and American powers for open trading links with the Japanese islands. The shogunate was confronted with a dilemma: on the one hand, they had no wish to remake a system that had prospered over some 200 years in seclusion from the wider world; on the other, with the Europeans and Americans insistent on trade links, they had no desire to find themselves subjected to the same process of quasi-colonization that had occurred in China. The result was confused inaction on the part of the shogunate.

The Meiji Restoration saw a group of regional lords seize power. The Meiji government deployed the power of the machineries of state in order to remake Japan as a modern industrial-capitalist society which would be able to resist the demands of the foreigners, and thus the fate of China, and thereafter to join as an equal within the new global community of great powers. The Meiji government proceeded to borrow from the model of the developed countries in Europe and America and in a relatively short period restructured the Japanese political-economic, social-institutional and cultural structures. However, changes in received political-cultural ideas and patterns of authority were held to a minimum and the first modern constitution of 1889 was presented as a gift of the emperor. Moore (1966) characterizes the episode as an authoritarian modernization from above.

In the late nineteenth and early twentieth centuries the economic development of Japan was very rapid and the country quickly associated itself with the contemporary modern international state system.

Meiji Japan, security in East Asia and the political-cultural project of empire

In the late nineteenth century the European powers and the USA were extensively involved in China. The Europeans and Americans had established a series of trading ports which served to link China to the global industrial-capitalist system. The system was ordered as a series of empires and associated spheres of influence. In the nineteenth century nationstates had routine recourse to war in order to settle disputes. At the outset the Japanese had responded to the West by initiating an elite-ordered drive for development. The Meiji oligarchy was determined to avoid the fate of China by competing with the West on its own terms. As the Japanese drive for equality with the West was initiated a similar set of concerns were developed in respect to the other countries of East Asia. The Japanese elite reasoned that the old tributary relationships with China which had ordered East Asia for centuries were no longer appropriate to the new global system. In the late nineteenth and early twentieth centuries the Japanese government moved to secure a sphere of influence for itself in East Asia.

The indigenous pattern of international relations in East Asia had centred upon China as the key economic, political and cultural power. The region was ordered as a series of concentric circles: China, East Asia and the distant barbarian territories. Hunter (1989: 41) notes that as the modern period began 'the tribute system and the superior-inferior relationship upon which it was premised remained the basic concept behind the conduct of formal relations between the countries'. However, by the nineteenth century the East Asian powers, China, Korea and Tokugawa Japan, were weak. Hunter (1989: 41) notes that 'By the mid-late nineteenth century these three East Asian kingdoms were weak and divided, and the East Asian cultural area no longer possessed the might of earlier years.' It is within the context of an historically weakened East Asian sphere that Japan enters the modern world. The experience shaped the posture of the Japanese government towards its neighbours. As Hunter (1989: 41) remarks, 'as Japan re-entered the wider world and embarked on a programme of change to deal with it, in dealing with her neighbours Japan faced a mirror image of her relations with the West'. The substantive relationship found an intellectual counterpart in what Tanaka (1993) refers to as the construction of 'Japan's orient', an elaborate intellectual and ideological construct whereby Japan was both geo-culturally located within East Asia and allocated the role of cultural leadership as the inheritor of the historically undamaged line of Eastern culture which had flowed from China. What followed was the construction of a colonial sphere.

Morris-Suzuki (1995: 190) locates the germ of modern Japanese national sentiment in the response to the West made by elite and popular groups in the period of late Tokugawa and Meiji and notes that 'nationalism was . . . associated with efforts to overcome the economic and military gap between Japan and the West. These efforts came to be inextricably connected to the issue of overseas expansion and the creation of Japan's own empire in Asia'.

As Japanese power increased, so too did the country's ambitions. As with the Western powers, the precise rationale was difficult to pin down.

Hunter (1989: 42) notes: 'The motivations – both many and complex – behind Japan's desire to exert her influence in Asia have received considerable attention from historians.' A series of lines of analysis have been proposed:

(a) the desire of the government to distract the attention of domestic critics;
(b) the evaluation of the East Asian mainland as strategically important to Japanese security;
(c) the need for raw materials;
(d) space within which Japan's expanding population might be accommodated;
(e) the ideological estimation of Japanese superiority in respect of the peoples of East Asia;
(f) a desire to emulate Western nations and secure the status of a great power.

In regard to construction of the empire, there was early Japanese activity in the area of the Russian Far East, in the Korean peninsular and in Manchuria and China. All these areas were geographically contiguous with Japan and the obvious places for the expansion of Japanese interests. The Japanese empire in Pacific Asia involved the early seizure of Taiwan and Korea, the creation of a new state in northern China, Manchukuo, and the quasi-colonization of large areas of China. In later years in the period of the Pacific War the empire expanded in Indo-China, Southeast Asia and the Pacific islands. At its height in early 1942 the imperial Japanese empire covered a vast area ranging from the Kurile Islands in the north to the Solomon Islands in the south and from Java in the west to the Marshall Islands in the east. Hunter notes:

> While Japanese expansion in Asia was still influenced by a preoccupation with defence and strategy, Japan's need for security in terms of raw materials, trading opportunities and an outlet for her expanding population became of increasing importance . . . Japan justified her expansion by a public relations rhetoric aimed at making it appear as altruism. Japan, it was said, sought the benefit of Asia as a whole and had a national mission to lead and co-ordinate the nations of Asia in resistance to the West. A Japanese-led block of Asian nations would be militarily and economically secure, and able to stand up to the threat posed by the nations of Europe and by the United States. (Hunter, 1989: 51)

Overall, the shift to the modern world inaugurated by the Meiji Restoration continued in the years of the late nineteenth century and by the early years of the twentieth century Japan was accepted by the Europeans and Americans as a new power. The Japanese had also established an empire in East Asia. The subsequent actions of Japan as a great power were met with some European and American resistance and the stress made by some on traditional Japan was reinforced. In the 1930s there was a further turning away from the model of the West and a preference for traditional roots and cultural resources. In general, the legacy of this period we can note as twofold: first, it marked an early expansionist exchange with Pacific Asia; second, it fixed in place a reactionary and latently anti-Western nationalist view of Japan as unique and misunderstood.

Phase one: early activity within Northeast Asia, 1868–1905

The movement into Korea began in the late nineteenth century as the Japanese attempted to prize the territory away from the influence of China, while at the same time blocking the advance of Russian influence. These concerns issued in war against China in 1894–5. The colonial style expansion pursued by Japan involved conflict with Russia in respect of spheres of influence in Manchuria and Korea. The war of 1904–5 saw military success for the Japanese. Korea was made a protectorate in 1905 and formally annexed in 1910. The Japanese also enhanced their position in Manchuria. In general all this seems to have attracted the passive sympathy of the Europeans and, particularly in regard to the naval victory over the Russian navy, a measure of approval from Asians (Barraclough, 1964).

The first area of concern was Korea which was nominally independent but lodged within the Chinese sphere of influence. However, with the situation in China unstable, the Japanese government feared a Western encroachment into the area to their eventual detriment. Japan imposed 'unequal treaties' on Korea in 1876 and proceeded to struggle with the Chinese for dominance in the area. Both governments stationed troops there from 1882 onwards and the country saw extensive political manoeuvring among the parties contending for influence as Korea slowly began its move into the modern world (Cummings, 1997). The tensions between the Chinese and Japanese eventually led to war.

The Sino-Japanese war of 1894–5 lasted nine months, in which time the Japanese armed forces expelled the Chinese from Korea and captured Port Arthur and the Liaotung peninsular. The Japanese defeated the Chinese on the basis of their superior Western military technology. Beasley (1990: 146) notes that in the negotiations leading to the Treaty of Shimonoseki Japanese aims included 'demands for an indemnity; for the handing over to Japan of Taiwan (which she had not even occupied) and Liaotung; and for a commercial treaty which would put Japanese privileges in China on a par with those of the Western powers'. The Chinese government conceded all these points. However, the Triple Intervention by Russia, France and Germany obliged the Japanese to withdraw from Liaotung and Port Arthur. As the Europeans and Americans had at that time very extensive colonial holdings, this generated disapproval among Japanese ruling circles. The view was that the great powers had deprived Japan of gains legitimately secured. There was public dismay which fed popular complaint and thereafter nationalist sentiment. The reaction of the government, having acquiesced, was to reaffirm the ideas of 'rich country, strong army' and to increase armaments spending to resist any future impositions. The Anglo-Japanese Treaty was signed in 1902 and this signalled the Japanese government's preference for involvement with the British and US notions of the Open Door in respect of China trade such that all were to have access. Over the next few years the Japanese government became involved in the great power manoeuvring in East Asia and slowly drifted into conflict with Russia over Manchuria and Korea.

The Russo-Japanese war of 1904–5 was an early experience for the Japanese of the mechanized warfare of industrialized countries. The costs to both combatants were high, although militarily the Japanese had the greater success. A mediation effort by the USA achieved a peace with the Treaty of Portsmouth and the Japanese consolidated their influence in Korea and Manchuria and received half of Sakhalin island. These were modest gains when set against public expectations and on their announcement there was rioting in Tokyo. However, in 1905 Korea was made a protectorate and in 1910 was annexed outright. In these years there was further manoeuvring against China but it met with little success. It was also the case that these later imperialist moves met with some displeasure from the Western powers. This in turn provoked a negative reaction among the Japanese political elite whose view of the West became more sceptical. It is at this point that we find the beginnings of the nationalist literature of Japanese uniqueness – nihonjinron (Dale, 1986; Yoshino, 1992).

Thereafter, there was intermittent war in China from the late nineteenth century when the Japanese borrowed Western ideas of colonial expansion and intervened in China through to the military invasions of the 1930s which sparked warfare that ran on until 1945. The Japanese motivation for these exchanges combined geo-strategy, as they searched for security within the unstable area of Northeast Asia, and geo-economics as they looked to secure supplies of raw materials and access to markets in order to sell their manufactured goods. It was in pursuit of these objectives that the Japanese looked to secure from China the same sorts of trading rights as those enjoyed by the Western powers. The Chinese resisted these demands and only granted concessions slowly as a result of pressure.

Overall, the European and American powers looked on early Japanese advance with tolerance. However, a few years later in 1915 when Japan began to make further demands on China, Western sympathy rather tended to fade away and Japan came to be categorized as aggressive. It is argued that this early rebuff by the Europeans and Americans to

Japanese borrowings of the notion of empire had the effect of encouraging an aggressive Japanese nationalism which subsequently found expression in the fascism of the inter-war period.

Japanese nationalism from Meiji to military rule

In the period of late Tokugawa there were a series of new political and intellectual currents which moved beyond the rather conservative Confucian-inspired official ideology. One source of new ideas was the West which had slowly percolated into Japanese cultural life in the form of the 'Dutch learning' associated with the long-established trade through Nagasaki. Another source of new ideas was to be found in the renewed interest and codification of Japanese folk religion, Shinto. In the mid-eighteenth century these debates grew more urgent as Japanese elites became concerned about European and American expansion in China and anxious in respect of their intentions towards Japan.

The Meiji Restoration established a modernizing oligarchic government in power and a broad series of reforms were put in place as the feudal system was remade as a modern, law-governed nationstate. Morris-Suzuki (1995: 194) comments: 'Throughout the Meiji period the question of how best to combine the necessary Western knowledge with Japanese culture and traditions was a topic of intense debate. Newly established newspapers and journals . . . carried articles discussing issues such as Western education, the role of elected parliaments, the rights of women and the possibility of writing Japanese in the Roman alphabet.' The extent and breadth of the cultural exchanges between the Japanese and the West over this period were extensive. Wilkinson (1991) argues that within the context of this exchange the Japanese learned rather more than the West.

The intellectual debates in Japan were complex. One line of argument associated with Fukuzawa Yukichi, a leading educationalist, looked to repeat within Japan the European enlightenment, in particular in its British liberal form, while a softer line, associated with the late-Tokugawa philosopher Sakuma Shozan, looked to blend Eastern ethics with Western science. The debates were important in establishing how national sentiment and the country were to develop. One crucial shift was from liberal economic thought to the German Historical School of economics which focused on the needs of a national economy. At the same time the Meiji oligarchy borrowed extensively from the Prussian model of constitutional law. Morris-Suzuki (1995: 194) notes that the tension between liberal and conservative viewpoints ran through much of the debate at this time.

One issue concerned the business of colonial expansion. It was argued in the Meiji period that imperial expansion was necessary to secure an economic and military zone around Japan and to gain the respect of the

Western powers. The Japanese government then pursued military and economic advantage in Northeast Asia. The expansion received popular domestic support and the results of treaty negotiations that were popularly judged to be less than satisfactory provoked a strong nationalist reaction which was to some extent anti-Western – sentiments which were to be reinforced at the time of the Versailles Treaty and the founding of the League of Nations (where a Japanese proposal to enshrine a commitment to racial equality was blocked by Australia).

The reforms of the Taisho period, 1912–26, saw new political activity in the form of parties and reform groups. However, all this was swept away in the late 1920s by the growth of radical nationalism and military influence. The cultural priority of the Japanese within East Asia was asserted and responsibility for the peoples of Asia assumed and the rhetoric of the projected new order in Asia developed.

The nature of early Japanese colonial rule

Beasley (1991: 142) points out that the Japanese colonial empire in East Asia was acquired very quickly. The dual preoccupation of the Meiji oligarchy with economic development and security found expression both in domestic advance and overseas expansion. The island of Taiwan was acquired in 1895, Karafuto (the southern part of Sakhalin) in 1905 and Korea was annexed in 1910. A lease was obtained in 1905 for Liaotung in southern Manchuria, which was subsequently known as Kwantung. In addition a number of minor German possessions were reassigned to Japan at the end of World War I. As Beasley (1991: 142) remarks, these territories were relatively compact but together with the Kurile, Ryukyo and Bonin islands constituted a coherent security zone for Japan.

The pattern of colonial rule varied somewhat but in essence the government in Tokyo appointed governors-general and thereafter left them to rule their territories. The broad expectation of colonial rule was that these territories would eventually be integrated with Japan having first been economically modernized. The relationship between the colonial peoples and the metropolitan power thereby reproduced a familiar model: the key decisions were made by the functionaries of the colonial power and the local people had only minor roles and thereafter serviced the needs of the colonial economy.

The colonial administrations in Taiwan and Korea pursued the two goals of modernization in the expectation of eventual integration. The economies were developed, primarily agriculture, and the population was encouraged to look to Japan as the relevant political and cultural centre. The programme had some success in Taiwan but met with extensive resistance in Korea. In the other territories there was also some advance. It can be noted that Kwantung became the base for the advance into Manchuria, which territory saw development via the efforts of the South Manchurian Railway Company. Karafuto saw some timber and fishing developments.

In Korea, after the Sino-Japanese war, the Japanese promoted a pro-reform Korean government. Borthwick (1992: 151) reports that the Japanese tried to draw a local reform movement into government in order to pursue a modernization programme on the model of the Meiji Restoration. The Kabo reform movement lasted from July 1894 to February 1896 before strong opposition from conservative forces within Korea caused it to be abandoned. After a further period of confusion and conflict with the Czarist Russian empire the Japanese formally annexed Korea in 1910.

The subsequent development of Korea can be analysed in terms of shifting patterns of class-based production as economic modernization was pursued in the context of a largely agricultural society. Hamilton comments:

> In Korea the Japanese took much greater direct control of agricultural production by acquiring large tracts of land . . . The traditional Korean landed aristocracy was seriously weakened . . . The twin executions of pre-colonial feudalism and Japanese colonialism caused widespread agricultural pauperisation . . . While the Japanese were diligent in pursuing improved agricultural productivity, they were equally diligent in siphoning off the rural surplus, and more, through high rents and taxes. (Hamilton, 1983: 38–41)

Yet there was some industrialization, particularly in the north, to support this colonial economic pattern, but it was not until the 1930s that the production demands of rearmament generated significant industrial development. Borthwick (1992: 197) comments: 'The Japanese colonial policy vastly strengthened Korea's transportation and communication infrastructure, but Koreans were pressed into labour gangs to build the roads and telegraph lines that spread rapidly across their country. Borthwick (1992: 197) notes that at 'the end of the colonial period Korea could boast one of the most advanced transportation and communications systems in Pacific Asia'. However, the occupation also acted to undermine established Korean culture as Japanese models of education, language and family names were imposed.

The colonial regime drew protests. In Korea in 1919 the March First Movement began with a group of patriots meeting in a restaurant and reading a declaration of independence, only to be promptly arrested by the Japanese police, and thereafter a series of demonstrations were begun in cities across Korea. Borthwick (1992: 194) comments: 'Stunned by the massiveness and boldness of the protests, the Japanese responded with brutal violence . . . Schools, churches and houses were burned . . . From this nation-wide slaughter there emerged a more organized Korean resistance movement directed mainly by those who fled the country after the March First Movement.' A government in exile was formed in Shanghai, with Syngman Rhee as president, who subsequently relocated to the USA where he successfully gathered support. Nonetheless, after the March First Movement was suppressed the Japanese colonial authorities tightened their grip on the country. The economy of the territory grew quickly. However, as the military gained power in Japan the pressure of foreign rule in Korea increased. The outbreak of the Pacific War led to Korea being used as part of the Japanese war economy and the exploitation of the population attained heightened levels. In subsequent years the situation in Korea was not made easy by the manner of the ending of the Pacific War, which saw the country divided within the context of an intense Cold War competition that found expression in open warfare between 1950 and 1953 (Cummings, 1997).

In Taiwan the nature of colonial rule was somewhat different. The territory was underdeveloped and had a small immigrant Han Chinese population in addition to a small local population. Hamilton (1983: 39) reports that the slogan governing the colonial relationship was 'agricultural Taiwan, industrial Japan'. The territory was developed as an agricultural economy with the rural social structure left largely intact. Beasley (1991) reports that educational opportunities for the local population were improved, with some opting for higher education in Japan. At the same time there were signs of nascent national sentiment. However, these were not encouraged by the colonial authorities. The country developed as an agricultural supplier to the metropolitan core. It was only as the Japanese economy prepared for war in the 1930s that some industrialization took place. Hamilton (1983: 39) reports that: 'In Taiwan a boom occurred in 1936–42 and in addition to the earlier-developed food-processing factories . . . some industry emerged (machine and ship building, petroleum refining).'

On the impact of colonial rule generally Hamilton comments:

> All in all, colonial domination in the two countries had a fundamental impact on domestic class structures . . . It severely weakened the traditional governing class and landed aristocracy, robbing them of much of their political power, appropriating large portions of their material base and causing them, particularly in Korea, to be tarred with the collaborationist brush. During the period of intense colonial rule there was no potential, indigenous leadership stratum to speak of, except for scattered cabals of intimidated nationalists. No strong merchant class could develop, nor was indigenous industry allowed to flourish. Enclave industrialization did breed significant numbers of industrial proletarians, especially in Korea . . . but skilled workers were encouraged to emigrate to Japan or Manchuria. (Hamilton, 1983: 40)

In a similar vein, Beasley (1991: 155) remarks that the colonial regime was harsh and there was little in the experience which 'led naturally to Asian partnership, or co-prosperity, or the coordination of industrial growth'.

Phase two: the achievement of great power status

Iriye (1997: 8–10) locates the germ of modern Japanese diplomacy in the pragmatic concern of the Meiji government to catch up with the West and join in the system of states. Japanese government anxieties about Western trade intentions in the region led to concerns for security, first in Korea and then China. The movement into East Asia was motivated initially, suggests Iriye (1997), not by pan-Asianist ideology but by a pragmatic desire for security in the face of Western expansion. In the early twentieth century a series of upheavals provided the Japanese government with new problems and opportunities.

The Chinese revolution of 1911 fostered a new nationalism inimical to Japanese interests. Yet World War I in Europe provided the Japanese government with further opportunity for expansion in East Asia when, citing obligations under the Anglo-Japanese Alliance of 1902, it moved to take over German interests in China and to seize German Pacific Island territories. The various Japanese concerns with China were summarized in the guise of the 1915 'Twenty One Demands' in respect of privileging Japanese interests in China. However, the instability within China did provoke wider debates in Japan, not merely about its relationship with China, but also about the identity of modern Japan and its position within the wider world (Tanaka, 1993; Iriye, 1997).

The Versailles Treaty, which ended the war in Europe, provided new challenges to the Japanese. The energetic promotion of Wilsonian liberalism by the USA pointed to a new system of rule-based international relations which would order the interactions of states (Stern, 1998: 199), but which would again inhibit Japanese activity in the East Asia region. Iriye (1997: 40–5) reports that the Japanese government offered no clear response to these challenges and pan-Asianist sentiment grew. Nonetheless, in the 1920s the Japanese participated in the discussions of the great powers and agreed to measures designed to stabilize the situation in East Asia.

However, Iriye (1997: 40–5) notes that the Chinese revolution and the rise of Wilsonian liberalism cut against Japanese ideas about the development of East Asia and while there was no change in Japanese policy, pan-Asianism grew. Iriye (1997: 66–71) presents this set of circumstances as the context within which the military came to exercise increasing influence.

Phase three: the inter-war period and rise of the military

The period of optimism helped to shape Taisho democracy. In 1925 the government introduced universal manhood suffrage and there was more extensive party political activity. Overall the period saw a mix of economic boom and bust (with the power of the zaibatsu increased), rapid social change (in particular the growth of the progressive towns at the expense of the more traditional and conservative rural areas) and political confusion as the original Meiji oligarchy finally left the scene and the state system which they had made slowly came apart as factions within its state machinery vied for control. As matters unfolded it became clear that there were two areas of problems:

1   Formulating a clear political-cultural project whereby the country could move forward on the basis of the legacy of Meiji; in retrospect it can be seen that inside the country the polity did not become a democracy and instead the nationalistic military gained in strength.
2   Formulating a clear strategy in respect of managing relations with the countries within the region and the wider international system; where, in retrospect, it is clear that the country's relationships with the outside world began to decline.

The domestic situation

The domestic situation can be characterized in terms of the unhappy interaction of an unstable political system with the radical economic disturbance of the Great Depression.

As the Meiji oligarchs and their immediate successors left the political scene, an important source of ideas in respect of the appropriate trajectory of development for Japan was lost. The politics of the Taisho and early Showa periods were confused, with party conflict, social unrest and political violence (Stockwin, 1999: 20). An element of unclarity within the Meiji Constitution became evident, namely, the lack of political control over the armed forces who had direct access to the emperor and could therefore bypass the civilian politicians.

The Great Depression of the 1930s had severe consequences for Japan. The collapse in world trade effectively extracted the Japanese from the international system within which they had operated and propelled them into a self-contained East Asian yen bloc. At the same time the economic slump created a mass of unemployed in Japan, with strikes in urban areas and widespread poverty in rural areas. The global depression of the late 1920s and early 1930s effectively destroyed the Taisho democracy. It is in this environment of economic dislocation and political confusion that the nationalist and militarist right wing came to the fore.

The military came to exercise great influence on the country in the 1930s and in some practical respects they became the government. Initially they worked within the 'gaps' in the Meiji constitution which did not precisely specify lines of responsibility and left the military able to claim they were acting on behalf of the emperor, the theoretical core of the system. A series of assassinations took place and from 1932 onwards party politics gave way to rule by non-party cabinets which attempted to

reconcile the various interests of the major state machine players –
inevitably the military came to dominate matters. A military dictatorship
might have been established if the army had not been riven by factions.
There were two key factions: the Imperial Way Faction (a conservative
group stressing martial values, national unity and the centrality of the
emperor) and the Control Faction (looking to military modernization
within the context of a modernizing economy and society). A failed
Imperial Way coup in 1936 led to the dominance of the Control Faction
over the whole of Japanese politics. An authoritarian regime then
established a 'national defence state' with a controlled polity, and a
controlled economy and society (Beasley, 1990: 184–92). This pattern was
reinforced as the decade wore on and the imbroglio in China became
ever more demanding.

The international situation

The colonial holdings of the Japanese were developed over the latter
years of the nineteenth and the early years of the twentieth century
without significant Western opposition. In this period the European and
American powers had significant colonial holdings of their own. At the
time, of course, all the powers had interests in China.

    The Japanese had an increasing role in China as their industrialists
became more involved and as Japanese troops were deployed to offer
them security. At the same time the Japanese asserted control over
Manchuria and made effective use of the South Manchurian Railway
Company as the vehicle for army sponsored industrial development. In
this context it is important to note that the role of the military in China
and Manchuria slowly came to escape the control of the politicians in
Tokyo. It was locally sponsored military adventurism in China and
Manchuria that drew the Japanese into war with China. In the 1930s the
Japanese invaded China. Japan left the League of Nations in 1933 and in
1936 signed the Anti-Comintern Pact with Germany. Of course the
pattern of events in Europe acted to encourage the militarists in Japan.
The Imperial Japanese Army was a key actor in this drama. They had by
the 1930s become the dominant force in Japanese politics. The Kwantung
army staged an incident at Mukden on 18 September 1931 and began
the seizure of Manchuria. In March 1932 Tokyo officially recognized
Manchukuo, with Henry Pu-yi as emperor in 1934.

    Thereafter, an incident in 1937 at the Marco Polo bridge outside Peking
proved to be the spark which ignited a general war in China. This war
developed and extended in stages until it enveloped a large part of
northeastern and coastal China. It would seem that the Japanese never
had a coherent strategy in China and the war simply drifted on. The
various elements of the Japanese military could never make up their
minds just what their war aims were and with whom they might deal at
the local level. The prosecution of the war increasingly led to sharp

conflict between the Japanese and American governments and to tension with the governments of the European colonial empires in Asia.

The war in China turned out to be fatal to Japanese military expansion as the involvement in China drew the criticism of the USA and Europeans. The exchanges of the Western powers and the Japanese slowly degenerated. Iriye (1987) identifies a series of interweaving streams of action which precipitated war:

1   In the wake of World War I an international system was established, the Versailles–Washington system, whose universalist liberal aspirations proved awkward for the Japanese empire and relations with the Americans, in particular, gradually cooled.
2   As the Meiji oligarchs left the scene the military slowly gained the space for action independent of civilian political control.
3   The military launched a war in China which both ran out of control and further encouraged the idea of pan-Asianism as an escape route from the Versailles–Washington system.
4   The USA did not handle negotiations well and in effect pushed the Japanese government into a corner.
5   The military made the rational calculation that their best option was to try to solve basic dilemmas of policy through a war to secure a sphere of Japanese control in Asia.

The Pacific War

Japan was allied with Britain, France and the USA during World War I. However, in the 1920s this relationship came under strain and as the Japanese military became more deeply involved in wars against China it broke down completely. In late 1941 Japanese armed forces swept through the Asian and Pacific territories of the Western imperial powers. A general war ensued. Ienaga (1978) records that this war was a disaster for the Asians whom the Japanese attacked and also ended in disaster for Japan, with an extensive reconfiguration of the entire Pacific-Asian region.

The military campaign

The Japanese had been at war in China since 1937 and had battle-hardened armies and airforces, together with a large modern navy. In December 1941 the Japanese navy attacked the US Pacific fleet at Pearl Harbor. The operation was successful and followed by a spread of further attacks throughout the region – in the Philippines, Hong Kong, Indo-China, Malaya and the Dutch East Indies. In a brief six months' campaign the Japanese armed forces swept all before them in an unbroken series of victories.

However, a subsequent series of Japanese advances in mid-1942 proved unsuccessful. The Japanese navy suffered a strategically crucial defeat at the Battle of Midway Island when the military initiative passed to the Americans. A double line of naval advance from island to island was pursued: in the Southwest Pacific it moved towards the Philippines; and in the Central Pacific the line moved towards Okinawa and the Japanese home islands.

In the Southwest Pacific in late 1942 the battle for Guadalcanal in the Solomon Islands represented a turning point. The allies thereafter advanced island by island until in mid-1944 they were able to invade the Philippine islands at Leyte Gulf, thereby precipitating the last major naval action of the war which saw the remnants of the Japanese navy largely destroyed. In the Central Pacific the American's launched a series of attacks supported by aircraft carrier task forces on islands held by the Japanese which enabled the long-range bombing of the home islands until finally the island of Okinawa was seized, thereby cutting the links to Southeast Asia and providing the base for the direct invasion of Japan.

The Japanese naval and airforces were virtually destroyed by late 1944 and the overall Japanese position was militarily untenable. However, the Japanese army continued to be heavily involved in China and waged a series of campaigns. In 1944 the Japanese army launched a major new offensive in Burma which proved unsuccessful. The British army then began an advance through Burma.

By early 1945 it was clear that the military position of the Japanese was untenable. However, the war cabinet in Tokyo was most reluctant to acknowledge defeat. The war was only brought to a close after the August 1945 atomic bombing of the cities of Hiroshima and Nagasaki.

Altering established balances through the wartime exchanges of Japanese, European, American and Asian peoples

Thorne (1978) argues that in the pre-war period two time scales were coming into phase: first, the decline of the European colonial empires as latent nationalism, the growing concern for development and the slow acceptance of the case for reform all advanced; second, the process of the overthrow of white political, economic and social supremacy in Asia. In a rather more mundanely practical sense there were specific areas of tensions between the USA, UK (the largest colonial power) and the Japanese. In terms of the general positions of the relevant governments, the Japanese understood these matters in terms of survival, the Americans saw opportunity and the Europeans were anxious to defend the status quo. In the event, the episode of the Pacific War sees the European colonies dissolved (with the Japanese interregnum playing an ambiguous role), the Japanese defeated and occupied and the USA emerging as the key power in the region.

During the period of war there were a series of shifts in the relationship of the Western allies. The USA quickly came to be the key partner as it recovered from the opening military reverses of 1942 and began to order a reply. The USA was the dominant Western power in the military conflict with Japan as the UK and its empire were largely unable to contribute until late in the war. As regards the fighting in China, Thorne (1978) reports that the USA had illusions about the value of the KMT, whom it actively sought to support, which were only slowly dissipated. In the large swathe of territory within Southeast Asia and Indo-China, which had been the colonial holdings of the Europeans, the USA took the position that it was not fighting to re-establish colonies (which is precisely what it did in respect of the Philippines). In other words, the early war years saw a shift of power from the UK (and the other European powers) towards the USA which continued as the Americans fought their island-hopping war across the Pacific. The final phase of wartime cooperation saw the Americans laying exclusive claim to Japan and leaving their European allies to reoccupy their colonial holdings in Southeast Asia and Indo-China. A variant of the status quo ante was precariously and provisionally re-established only to be submerged in the twin processes of decolonization and Cold War bipolarity.

In all this the Japanese had a quite particular perspective. There were economic conflicts between the Japanese, European and US empires in the Pacific. In particular the war in China was a considerable burden and source of tension with the West. Thorne (1986) also records that there were racist sentiments overlaying these problems. The Japanese military government came to see war as an opportunity to settle all three matters in favour of Asians. It is clear that this line of argument did command some sympathy from Asian nationalist leaders and that the region was in flux.

Thorne (1980) argues that the Pacific War had its occasion in strategic economic interests and sets of internal politics, but nonetheless a belief did persist that the whole business was a revolt of Asia against the West. It is true that nationalist sentiment in Asia did have an anti-Western side. Barraclough (1964) notes that the defeat by Japan of the Czarist Russian empire in 1904–6 was widely read as an Asian defeat of Westerners. In post-Meiji Japan a nationalist stream of thought spoke of Japan leading Asian emancipation from the West and in the period of military fascism these lines of argument found more emphatic expression. It is true that Europeans and Americans responded with a taken-for-granted assumption of the priority of their concerns which were to be quickly destroyed by the success of the Japanese in 1941–2. Once the war had begun, the East–West, coloured–white, European–Asian distinctions were available to be used by all the combatants, and the terms were used by both sides in racist propaganda (Downer, 1996). Yet the conflict did have significant cultural implications. Thorne (1980: 343) notes that the Japanese victories of the early war years 'greatly increased the readiness of large numbers of Asians to discard any remaining loyalty to their European rulers'. Thorne (1980: 343) adds that the sense of shock in the West was acute. The Japanese sought to inculcate an idea of 'Asianess'. The key vehicle was the proposal for a Greater East Asia Co-prosperity Sphere. They found nationalist sympathizers in Burma, Indonesia, and the Philippines and among Indian communities in Southeast Asia. These nationalists voiced similar ideas and linked the pursuit of independence to the rise of Japan, as in the cases of, for example, the Indian nationalist leader Subbash Chandra Bose, the Burmese independence leader Aung San and the Indonesian independence leaders Sukarno and Hatta.

Consequences of the war

In August 1945 the Japanese government surrendered unconditionally and the country was occupied by the USA. The Japanese empire was dismantled and the country was subject to enforced reform. The war also saw the pattern of development of the region radically remade as the pre-war influence of European and US governments and commercial interests were fatally disturbed. As the confusions of wartime dislocation found a measure of resolution and stability the region came to be divided into an American-dominated sphere and an autarchic socialist bloc centred upon China.

The Japanese invasion of China overlay an indigenous civil war. The nationalist Kuomintang had been supported by the Americans before the outbreak of the Pacific War and they continued to offer some material support via Burma during the war years. After the war with Japan came to an end there was a nominal ceasefire in China, during which the USA made extensive assistance available to the nationalists. However, the conflict resumed and was to resolve itself in 1949 in favour of the Communist Party led by Mao. At this time China withdrew into an autarchic socialist path of development while the island of Formosa provided the base for a US-backed Kuomintang regime. Relatedly, the situation in Korea during the war years saw an indigenous resistance movement develop which seized control of the country in the wake of the Japanese surrender only to find the Americans imposing an anti-Communist nationalist upon the southern part of the country, thereby precipitating the division of the country (Cummings, 1997). A similar situation was to obtain in Vietnam (Duiker, 1995).

In the former holdings of the colonial powers the disturbance of war had opened a space for nationalist movements. In 1941–2 the Japanese army moved into Vietnam, displacing the colonial French, and thereafter extended its influence throughout Indo-China, including drawing Thailand into the war against the West. The holdings of the Japanese were extended by military conquest in the period 1941–2 when the European and US empires in Southeast Asia were seized. These territories included Malaya, the Dutch East Indies, the Philippines,

Burma and many Pacific Island territories. The wartime interregnum had encouraged nationalist sentiment within these territories and as the war came to an end these sentiments were asserted. The Americans were sympathetic to these nationalists and unsympathetic to the European colonialists (notwithstanding the militarily unnecessary invasion and recovery of its former territory of the Philippines). The colonial spheres of Indo-China and Southeast Asia quickly became independent nation-states.

In general, the Pacific War had far-reaching effects:

1   Most immediately it broke the power of the European empires.
2   Thereafter it undermined the legitimacy of the American colonization of the Philippines.
3   It had the effect of destroying the military dominated pre-war Japanese polity.
4   It provided an occasion for the advance of communist influence in China and thereafter the Chinese revolution.
5   It led to a period of US hegemony and Cold War competition in Asia.

Legacy of the Japanese political-cultural project of empire

After the arguments of Grimal (1978) it can be suggested that the manner of withdrawal from colonial holdings had an impact on the subsequent relationship of ex-colony and ex-colonial power. In the case of the dissolution of the Japanese empire in Pacific Asia we have an abrupt ejection occasioned by war. The political status of the occupied territories changed with independence and the status of the Japanese occupiers similarly changed through their occupation by the USA. Moreover, the entire region was reconfigured and quickly took on a bipolar form with a socialist grouping centred on China and a Western-oriented group looking to the USA, whose key regional ally was Japan.

The manner of the ejection of the Japanese from their colonial holdings was quite particular. At the end of military hostilities, following the use of atomic bombs, the Japanese were left in control of all their territories until the Allied forces arrived. At that point the military withdrawal took place over a relatively brief period. The relatively ordered nature of the withdrawal of the Japanese can be noted in contrast to the general debacle which befell Germany in 1945 (Buruma, 1994). The German economy, society and state all collapsed. In contrast, the Japanese military defeat did not entail total collapse. Thus, the Europeans and Americans used Japanese soldiers as police in parts of East Asia, Southeast Asia and Indo-China for the temporarily recolonized territories in the interval between the collapse of the Japanese empire and either the return of the civilian and military powers of the various pre-war colonial powers or the establishment of post-Japanese, post-colonial era regimes.

In Japan itself the occupation was relatively benign with an administration which was initially distinctly idealistic, subsequently rightwing, and arguably broadly inept (Buckley, 1990).

The diplomatic rehabilitation and economic reconstruction of Japan began with the outbreak of the Korean War, itself a product of the US drive against 'world communism', which saw the Americans looking to Japan as an ally and base for their Cold War in Asia. Thereafter, the general business of reordering the global system around its new US centre – with processes of decolonization, the establishment of the Bretton Woods economic settlement, the related founding of the UN system and the pervasively deployed US conservative ideology of anti-Communism – gave the Japanese rulers an umbrella under which to shelter as they rebuilt their economy and their links to Pacific Asia. It seems fairly clear, as van Wolferen (1989) argues, that this episode of rebuilding involved a great measure of continuity with pre-war patterns of economy and society.

In brief, notwithstanding that in the wake of World War II the Japanese had to re-establish links with Pacific Asia, it turned out that they had a relatively smooth path to such a re-establishment of linkages. One first contact was via the forerunner of aid links, that is, war reparations (Rix, 1993b). Overall, the historical legacy of Japanese colonialism is complex. We find a mixture of long-established colonialism, wartime violence and some political and economic reforms which took a different character in the various territories. The official ideological rationale of Japanese expansion was the establishment of a co-prosperity sphere which would allow both the Japanese and the peoples of Pacific Asia to flourish in a cooperative fashion.

The inner periphery

In the late nineteenth century Korea lay within the ambit of the Chinese. In the process of Japan's shift to the modern world the Korean peninsular was seen as strategically important. The Japanese established a protectorate in 1905 and annexed the territory in 1910. In Korea the colonial episode saw harsh treatment of the indigenous population and it would seem that there is a legacy of bitterness at the present. Again, while it is initially difficult to see any positive legacy, it was the case that the colonial period brought a measure of industrialization and the post-war economic rise of South Korea, in particular under the leadership of Park Chung Hee, was to a significant extent modelled on Japan (Cummings, 1997). Again, at the present time pragmatism and geographical proximity underpin economic linkages.

In Taiwan the colonial episode was inaugurated when Formosa, as was, was handed to Japan at the peace treaty in 1895 which settled the Sino-Japanese war. Japan pursued the development of the territory with significant success. The situation was made more confused by the end of the Pacific War and the Chinese Revolution which saw the defeated Chinese nationalists retreating to the island and being supported by the USA. Among some older residents of Taiwan memories of the Japanese are positive.

The outer periphery

In the Dutch East Indies the early period of war and exertion of Japanese control gave way to a measure of cooperation. An army of indigenous people was formed, as was a political representation organization led by Sukarno. In this sense the Japanese had a role to play in fostering an eventually successful nationalist movement. Relatedly, in Burma a similar situation held with Aung San's army and political organization, which in a rather different way modulated into the independence movement that in due course secured this goal.

In Malaysia the Japanese encouraged Malay nationalism while harshly treating the Chinese. The Japanese interregnum has had a lasting impact on Malaysia in the form of communalist politics, whose occasion may in part be traced to the wartime period. In Singapore the wartime episode was harsh and is remembered as such by the largely Chinese population. However, as with other areas of Pacific Asia there is a pragmatic focus on economic cooperation.

In the Philippines a similar pattern is visible. The Filippino elite cooperated with the Japanese and ideas of independence were floated. However, the return of the USA saw the re-establishment of the status quo ante – leading directly to the Huk rebellion (Kerkvliet, 1977) and instituting a pattern of American-dependent crony capitalism that culminated in the era of Marcos. It is difficult to identify a positive legacy of Japanese colonialism. Again, the current determinants of the relationship are the pragmatics of economic growth coupled to geographical proximity.

If the above notes the political impact of the period of Japanese colonial rule for the outer periphery, it must be said that the economic impact at this time was severe, but of short duration. These territories were absorbed as materials supplying elements of a war economy that quickly collapsed. Rix (1993a: 23), in regard to ASEAN, points to a prewar Japanese concern for resource security, noting that the 'economic rationale for military domination of the region from 1941 to 1945 was paramount'. It is also quite clear that this continues to be the key interest – trade, investment, resources, and security in general for the Japanese. Rix (1993a: 22) characterizes official development aid for ASEAN as an 'expensive insurance policy'.

In China and Indo-China

In mainland China including Manchukuo one might suppose that the record was one of simple violence, remembered with hostility by

the victims today and unacknowledged to date by the Japanese government save for rather ritualistic apologies. In such a case it would be
difficult to see a positive legacy in this episode. However, notwithstanding
the disruption of war there was considerable Japanese investment in
Manchukuo and China, and that the wartime legacy included a significant
measure of industrialization. At the present time contemporary economic
links are well established. It would seem that a mix of historical and
cultural similarities plus delicacy over World War II provide the base for
pragmatic links. The Chinese secure a source of capital and the Japanese
markets plus stability.

The French authorities of the Vichy regime in colonial Indo-China
were obliged to submit to the Japanese. Indo-China was a wartime base
for the Japanese. An attempt to recreate the status quo ante by the French
failed, as did the subsequent US attempt. In Indo-China the eventually
successful nationalist resistance movement was the Vietminh. It is difficult to identify a positive legacy of the brief period of Japanese colonialism and once again we note the overriding influence of present economic
power – with the end of the US boycott announced in February 1994 by
President Clinton, Japanese firms are investing in Vietnam.

Contemporary popular recollections

In regard to the recent historical episode of war, it seems safe to say, at a
very general level, that these years are either ignored or taken as essentially unproblematical, in the sense that states are taken to have wars and
the Japanese state had one which it happened to lose. The idea that Japan
was the aggressor and wrought unparalleled destruction across the area
is not widely entertained.

In this instance the position of the Japanese political classes, and
thereafter population generally, is in stark contrast to the response of
the German governments and people where the episode of national-
socialism has been subject to extensive public debate. It has been pointed
out that the removal of Hitler and the Nazis left the German people able
to acknowledge their responsibility and reach back to a rich cultural
history separate from the Nazi era, whereas the SCAP decision to leave
the emperor in place, and thus the symbolic heart of the polity in significant measure unchanged, blocked the Japanese people from making
this sort of move (Buruma, 1994). They could not reach back beyond a
discredited group of wartime leaders because the key symbol (and much
practice) of that group stayed in place with US support. The subsequent
reluctance of the Japanese political elite to acknowledge the country's
history is often cited as one of the reasons why the Japanese elite are not
trusted either in the West or Asia.

More broadly, because the history of Japanese involvement with
Pacific Asia is longer and deeper than the wars of the twentieth century,
an available theme characterizing the relationship generates the view

that the unique and gifted Japanese are able to lead the rest of Pacific Asia in development.

Conclusion

Tokugawa Japan evidenced a mixture of economic success and political immobility. In the later years of the Tokugawa shogunate there was inter-han conflict, structural political-economic change (as some groups prospered and others did not) and growing dissatisfaction with the shogunal government. The Meiji Restoration grew out of the mixture of economic advance and political conservatism which characterized late Tokugawa Japan and was precipitated by the fears of elements of the Japanese feudal elite in respect of the demands of Western powers for trading opportunities. It is this mixture of internal and external factors which propels Japan's 'shift to the modern world'.

The Meiji oligarchy had two interrelated preoccupations: the first was to pursue economic development; the second was to secure their position within East Asia and thereafter the wider international system. A period of revolution from above secured 'late industrialization' and this in turn provided the military and organizational basis for 'late imperialism'. Over the period from 1868 to the eve of World War I the Japanese carved out an empire in East Asia. These developments were watched with equanimity by the European and US colonial powers. However, the depression years encouraged the rise of a nationalistic military that pursued wars in China which, in turn, drew imperial Japan into conflict with the West in general and the USA in particular.

5

JAPAN IN THE CONTEMPORARY WORLD

The Political-Cultural Project of Economic Nationalism

The American occupation lodged Japan within the Western sphere and partially reordered Japan domestically. The occupation authorities, SCAP, showed an initial enthusiasm for reform which quickly gave way to the desire to secure an ally against mainland Asian communism within the context of the developing Cold War. An extensive reordering of the Japanese economy, society and polity was accomplished under American direction and produced a mixture of change and continuity with pre-war Japan. Thereafter, the role of the Ministry of International Trade and Industry (MITI), achievement of social solidarity and the dominance of the Liberal Democratic Party are crucial to the success of the Japanese 'developmental state'. The economy continued to advance and by the early 1980s trade friction with the USA had begun. In 1985 the Plaza Accord revalued the yen against the dollar and a new phase of development was inaugurated as Japanese companies moved production offshore and accelerated structural processes of regional integration.

Occupation, 1945–52: an American political-cultural project for Japan

The American occupation undertook a restricted reordering of the Japanese economy, society and polity. The result was a business-dominated conservative Japanese system which showed a mixture of change and continuity with pre-war Japan.

End of the Pacific War

The Pacific War came to an end in August 1945 and the occupation forces arrived in September (Beasley, 1990: 208–12). The occupation was nominally an allied matter but was in practice almost entirely an American affair.

The wartime allies were intensely suspicious of each other and manoeuvred for advantage as best they could with the USA, which through the war years became the dominant economic and military power, attempting to advance its position throughout Asia. The USA opposed the re-establishment of the European colonial empires, sought to buttress the nationalist side in the Chinese civil war and took the central role in the war and occupation of Japan. Thorne (1978, 1986) locates American wartime policy within the context of the shifting patterns of structural economic power among the major industrial-capitalist countries and characterizes US actions in Asia as opportunistic. Thorne (1986: 295–9) notes that while the socio-political impact of the Pacific War, and World War II more broadly, encouraged progressive change, and the growth of democracy, the great exception was the USA where there was a sharp lurch to the right. The vigorous pursuit of national advantage was represented in universalistic terms. As Kolko (1968) makes clear, the US government spoke about freedom and democracy, but in practice sought to construct a global liberal-market trading order centred upon Washington.

The make-up of SCAP

The American General Douglas MacArthur was made Supreme Commander for the Allied Powers (SCAP) and under his direction the SCAP authorities endeavoured to remake Japan after the model of the USA. The broad objective was to construct an open market, liberal society. The goal unpacked into a series of areas of reform:

1   The economy of pre-war Japan with its large firms linked closely to the government would have to be radically reconstructed so as to generate a pattern of firms competing within a regulated liberal-market place.
2   The society of pre-war Japan with its hierarchical form, restricted roles and routine denial of American-style individualism would have to be radically reconstructed so as to generate an open society where individuals came to the fore in pursuit of their own particular wants.
3   The polity of pre-war Japan, with its oligarchic, militaristic and nationalist state, absence of autonomous political institutions and acquiescent population, would have to be radically remade in order to secure a liberal-democratic form of political life.
4   The culture of pre-war Japan, with its conservative celebration of the particularity of the Japanese, would have to be radically remade in order to permit the broad secular progressive ethos of the modern world to be affirmed.

It is clear that the initial SCAP objectives constituted an ambitious programme of radical social engineering. Yet the SCAP authorities had relatively few personnel and all American sponsored reforms had to be put into practice through the agency of the Japanese bureaucracy. The Japanese resisted quietly. The political, rural and education reforms were all taken to have had significant effect. However, other than displacing the military, the depth of the changes to Japanese political economy, society and polity accomplished by SCAP has been the subject of extensive subsequent debate. It is clear, for example, that the immediate post-war situation in Japan was radically different from that of Germany and while the latter was extensively remade, Japan was not similarly treated.

The SCAP authorities comprised a mixture of New Deal supporters and nascent anti-Communist conservatives. This divergence of opinion mirrored the divisions of political opinion in Washington. The pattern was not stable and in the early post-war years the Truman administration slowly began to give ground to the political right (Kolko, 1968). These shifts of opinion were repeated within the SCAP authorities. Thus, in the early period of SCAP administration the reformers had the most influence in framing policy. A little later, as the Cold War in Asia began, the anti-Communist conservatives came to have the greater influence. The conservative faction became dominant as the Cold War was slowly established. The reform programmes of SCAP, which were designed to remake Japan after the style of the optimistic New Deal model of the USA, were scaled back in favour of the US right's preference for a business-dominated Cold War ally. When Mao became leader of China in 1949, followed shortly afterwards by the outbreak of the Korean War in 1950, the Cold War became a fixed part of Western political thinking. Buckley (1990) comments that the issue of reforming Japan was finally abandoned in favour of a preference for Japan as an ally in the containment of Communism.

The familiar criticism of SCAP is that it did too little (Buckley, 1990). The perceived failure is taken to have flowed from an initial naivety in the matter of making reforms and the subsequent desire to have Japan as an ally in the US anti-Communist crusade. A series of elements came together:

(a) the limited nature of the SCAP reforms;
(b) the use of Japanese bureaucracy to effect reforms specified by SCAP;
(c) the start of the Cold War;
(d) the US–Japan defence agreement;
(e) the active US sympathy for the Japanese political right;
(f) a conservative-dominated and US-oriented Japanese political-bureaucratic ruling group.

At the time many of the reforms were viewed unfavourably by the Japanese political elite (Beasley, 1990: 228) and aspects of SCAP rule such as war crimes trials were resented even at popular level (Tsurumi, 1987). Yet, in total, the reforms undertaken by SCAP were rather modest and the outcome of the process was a business-dominated Japanese system firmly lodged within the US sphere of influence.

The reform programme, 1945–52

The ambitions of the optimistic SCAP reformers implied an interrelated series of reforms to the Japanese economy, society, polity and culture.

THE MILITARY, POLITICS AND SOCIETY   The most pressing task facing the occupation authorities was dismantling the still extensive Japanese military machine. Installations and equipment were destroyed all over Japan and the armed forces were demobilized and sent home. Many civilians from overseas were repatriated as all Japan's territorial gains since Meiji were removed. A war crimes tribunal was held in Tokyo.

In politics the Japanese aristocracy was abolished. There was an extensive purge of the machineries of state to remove potentially anti-democratic personnel. The emperor was left in place, having first renounced his divinity and thus embraced a Western-style notion of constitutional monarchy. This was a matter of some debate at the time: Why leave in place the figure on whose behalf the Japanese had waged their wars, and in any case did he not carry responsibility? The US authorities elected to keep the emperor as a figure of authority who would make their occupation of the country easier than it might other-wise have been. It was a contentious decision and remains a matter of debate. In the early occupation period the existing political system was used. There was therefore continuity of government (although, of course, power rested with SCAP). A new constitution was promulgated by SCAP in October 1946 and brought into force in May 1947. In general a US-style system was put in place with extensive devolution of powers to regional prefectural governments. The central government machine was modelled after the British system of a cabinet reporting to parliament (originally the Japanese had borrowed this form). The suffrage was broadened to include women. In 1952 a peace treaty was signed, a part of which was a 'defence agreement' which made Japan in effect a military protectorate of the USA.

In society the 'continuing family' was abolished in 1947, women were given the vote and an extensive educational reform was undertaken.

THE ECONOMY   Sheridan (1993: 121–3) points out that the war years caused considerable destruction in Japan. The empire was dissolved and there was no international trade. In the aftermath of the Pacific War Japan was isolated and poor. In reviewing the economics of the immedi-ate postwar period, the necessary starting point for any renewal, Tsuru (1993: 9–10) reports that the war and defeat had severe consequences:

1 Territorially, Japan was reduced to four main islands and all post-
   Meiji gains were stripped away.
2 Materially, approximately 25 per cent of available material wealth
   was gone and there were 2.5 million casualties.
3 Organizationally, business, government and society were extensively
   damaged and disrupted.

The initial US Presidential Policy Statement of 22 September made it
clear that economic reconstruction was a Japanese responsibility. The
Basic Initial Post Surrender Directive to SCAP made the same point.
The Pauley Reparation Mission in November 1945 reiterated this stance.
Yet the Japanese had few ideas about reconstruction. In the run-up to
defeat there had been some thought given by the government to the
postwar period, but Tsuru (1993: 15) reports that in the early days of
peace the ideas for reform presented by the Japanese side were meagre.
Indeed, the population was exhausted. Nonetheless, Sheridan (1993:
126–7) records that in August 1946 the Economic Stabilization Board
(ESB) was established to formulate a national strategy for the economic
reconstruction of Japan.

In time, SCAP shifted its position in respect of responsibility for
economic reconstruction and came to the view that it was necessary to
become more directly involved. In March 1947 SCAP demanded action
from the Japanese government. The ESB was strenghthened by new
powers for economic planning. In 1947 the socialist Katayama government came to power and asked the ESB to produce an overview of
Japanese economic requirements. In June 1947 a comprehensive national
plan was announced, the Emergency Economic Policy. It was followed a
month later by the First Economic White Paper, known after its chief
editor as the Tsuru White Paper, which analysed problems and
explained to the population what had to be done. The stress was on
economic recovery and advance. Interestingly, Sheridan (1993: 129) notes
that the White Paper raised the status of economists and planners at the
expense of the previous key group with legal backgrounds. Tsuru (1993:
16) suggests that in retrospect these actions were a start in stabilizing the
economy. However, Tsuru (1993: 18) reports that when the Katayama
government fell in February 1948 and the conservative Ashida came to
power, the ESB lost most of its staff and its reforming elan. Nonetheless,
as Sheridan (1993: 128) notes, the 'Tsuru White Paper set the pattern
from which Japan's unique style of indicative planning developed
through the following four decades'.

It is clear that SCAP had begun its work in Japan with extensive plans
for economic reform. The early concerns involved the process of dis-
solving the zaibatsu, legalizing the trade unions, elimination of cartels
and, overall, the drive to establish a weakly developed competitive liberal-
market capitalism lodged within a Western-style liberal-democratic
polity. A key area was the dissolution of the zaibatsu in order to foster a

more US-style competitive market capitalism; a tall order, remarks Tsuru (1993: 19). The key policy document was Directive 230 made by US government to Far Eastern Commission in Washington and thence to SCAP. The Diet passed a relevant law in December 1947 and the Holding Company Liquidation Commission (HCLC) came into being, which in February 1948 designated 325 companies for deconcentration. However, the plan drew opposition from Japanese and US business and the proposals were slowly watered down.

Tsuru (1993: 20–2) records that another key initiative was land reform and a law was passed by the Diet in October 1946. This shifted absentee landlord holdings to small farmers and rents from kind into cash and was supported by Japanese bureaucracy who translated it into practice.

A reform was also made to labour law. In pre-war Japan the 1925 Peace Preservation Law suppressed unions and similar activity in order to protect the notion of kokutai, the national polity. SCAP introduced US-style law and procedures, passed by Diet in December 1945 as Trade Union Law. Tsuru (1993: 24) notes that after such long suppression and in the context of the confusion of defeat, union activity expanded very rapidly. There was much labour activism and SCAP obliged the Diet to pass a further law in September 1946, the Labour Relations Adjustment Law, that provided for conciliation and banned strikes in key industries, which included large swathes of public sector. In January 1947 SCAP banned a projected general strike and in July 1948 prohibited a projected strike in the public sector. Tsuru (1993: 26) notes that the unions were thus significantly weakened and the US-style reform experiment was over.

It is clear that international circumstances contributed significantly to the recovery of Japan. In particular, a strengthening Cold War psychology, from the Truman Doctrine of 1947, to Mao's victory in 1949, all led to US policy toward Japan being changed; an episode known as the 'reverse course'. Sheridan (1993: 126) reports that the 'reorientation of American policy came suddenly in April 1947 . . . The USA now helped Japan to regain her prewar economic position as the workshop of East Asia. Obsessed with Russia and communism, the USA desired a strong and prosperous Japan. American loans and credits poured into Japan and Japanese leaders were quick to exploit the situation.' Overall, the US occupation, which lasted six years and eight months, had two distinct phases: the first was typified by the Pauley Report, Japan was responsible for remaking its economy; and the second saw the USA determined to protect Japan against Communist infection and turn it into an economically successful bulwark of the West.

The reverse course had two rapid effects: the reparations issue was quickly settled; and the reforms of zaibatsu were halted with little achieved. Tsuru (1993: 13) notes that the reparations issue was dealt with in the context of a peace treaty with the Western allies which, in effect, demanded very little from the Japanese. Yet in the early months of the

occupation the general view, especially among the Japanese, was pessimistic because of the reparations issue which could have been made into
an intolerable burden. In the event, after originally high US demands
expressed in the Pauley Report, relatively little was achieved. The USA
realized that it would have to subsidize both removals and aid for a
weakened Japan, and per cent GNP outflow was much less than per cent
GNP US aid inflow. Relatedly, the arguments to drop zaibatsu reform
were effective in part because there was no social support within Japan
for their reform, and they had played a role not merely in war but over a
longer time from Meiji in contributing to Japan's shift to the modern
world (Tsuru, 1993: 42–3).

The pursuit of economic recovery was handicapped by the upheavals
associated with defeat and occupation. In the immediate post-war years
there was serious inflation as money chased few goods; in addition the
costs of the occupation had to be met. SCAP became concerned after the
reverse course as money stability was a condition of economic revival. A
related concern was an exchange rate for the yen so that Japan could
effectively re-enter trade relations. The Young Mission came to Japan in
June 1948 and recommended a rate of 300 yen to the dollar coupled to a
cut in spending to stabilize the economy. SCAP realized this would have
cut real wages at a time when they were trying to raise them and resisted
the plan. But Washington was unhappy and the National Security
Council issued the 'nine-point programme' in December 1948 and
despatched Joseph Dodge in February 1949 as the personal representative of President Truman. The nine-point programme looked to establish
stable state finances, wage and price stability, to increase domestic
production and to enhance exports. Tsuru (1993: 47) comments that this
recalled the SCAP Economic Stabilization Programme of 1947, so the
nine-point programme was not oriented to policy per se but to performance of that policy.

The Dodge Mission concentrated on stable state finances and also
settled the exchange rate issue. In the former there was a wide-ranging
budget rationalization and in the latter the rate was set at 360 yen to the
dollar. The impact of the Dodge reforms was immediate. The state
finances were put in a conservative order and the price of these deflationary measures was a severe economic slowdown, which hit small and
medium firms the hardest and favoured zaibatsu-related activities. A key
post-war linkage between state and big business was fostered thereby.
As Tsuru (1993: 48) points out, the undervalued yen had the effect, over
time, of aiding exports. However, in the short term, the economic
distress found expression in a polarization between classes which, in
turn, found expression in politics.

Tsuru (1993: 57) reports that the situation was changed by the outbreak
of the Korean War. In a matter of days the USA turned Japan into its key
base. SCAP ordered the formation of a 75,000 Police Reserve Corps and a
spread of orders for materials were placed with Japanese firms. The

psychology of Japanese firms changed and they pursued expansion vigorously. Thereafter, the Cold War provided the context for a uni-lateral peace treaty between Japan and the Western allies which was signed in San Francisco in September 1951 and came into effect in April 1952. An important security treaty linking Japan and the USA was signed at the same time. This was not well received in Japan and although it was amended in 1960 the one-sided peace treaty situation remains. Overall, by 1952 Japan had regained its sovereignty, was undergoing economic recovery and was firmly lodged within the Western sphere.

Recovery and advance, 1952–85

In the immediate post-war period the recovery of Japan was rapid. The shift in US policy towards Japan was significant, as was the Korean War. However, the subsequent rapid economic development owed more to domestic agendas. Waswo (1996: 107) comments that 'the first and argu-ably most crucial step the Japanese took was to toss aside the model of their economic future bequeathed to them by the Occupation'. The SCAP economists had looked at Japan through liberal-market eyes and seen cheap labour as the primary Japanese comparative advantage. They plotted a route to a low technology economic future with other industrial nations taking the technological lead. However, the bureaucracy, politicians and industrialists strongly supported the goal of running a first-class economy at the very highest levels of available technology; a policy goal which had been in place since Meiji.

In broad terms, the Japanese miracle was a product of state-regime commitment, the fortuitous circumstances of the post-World War II 'long boom' and the tolerance of export success within the US market because of Cold War alliances. In addition, it is important to note the deter-mination of ordinary Japanese people to redeem themselves and their country after the debacle of the war. Waswo (1996: 110) recalls that this has been referred to as 'GNP nationalism'. The early period of post-war growth came to be dominated by heavy industries (steel, ships, chemi-cals, coal). It is true that by the early 1960s Japan was beginning to emerge as a significant economic power. In the early 1970s their economy was to experience some shocks – the oil price rises and Nixon's decision to float the dollar – but these were made the occasions for further success. The first oil shock caused a sharp economic downturn and triggered inflation (Henshall, 1999: 163–4). Nonetheless, after internal reconstruction and export-orientated growth the economy began to run a trading surplus. It was clear by the middle 1970s that the post-war recovery was a significant success. The restructuring of the 1970s moved the economy to higher value added goods (cars, consumer appliances, machinery), and the second oil shock of 1979 was weathered fairly easily.

Recovery, 1952–71: the miracle economy

The early advice of SCAP was that the Japanese economy should be reconstructed as a relatively low wage, low technology economy operating in a subordinate position within a global liberal-market economy effectively dominated by the USA. Yet the Japanese planners had the objective of establishing a first-class economy (Waswo, 1993: 107).

The economy had recovered its pre-war levels by 1951 and subsequently advanced rapidly. In 1955 the economy was still semi-industrialized with 40 per cent of the workforce in the agriculture and primary product sectors, yet from 1955 to 1965 growth was pursued singlemindedly. Sheridan (1993: 136) reports that the 1956 Economic White Paper announced that it was no longer 'post-war', and that with basic reconstruction accomplished further economic growth would have to flow from upgrading the economy. The White Paper discarded a pessimistic view of Japan as a small vulnerable island. The following years saw further economic growth. Thereafter, from 1965 to 1972, the concern for growth was intermingled with a desire to solve particular problems of full employment and the dual economy. An increased concern for external economic trade was established.

At first, through much of the 1950s, growth was pursued using capital that had survived the war plus abundant labour. The period was plagued by balance of payments crises and was politically unstable, with a turnover in political leaders and labour unrest. Then in 1960 Ikeda became Prime Minister and inaugurated the National Income Doubling Plan which ran until 1965. The aim of the plan, which had its origins in 1958 discussions among academics and politicians, was to draw the unrest into a programme of economic activity.

Ikeda seized the moment. The plan had two elements: the pursuit of high-speed growth and freer trade. In regard to the first element, the state undertook to upgrade social capital – social security, infrastructure, education and training and the elimination of the dual economy. In regard to the second element, the freer trade aspects were occasioned by US complaints about trade restrictions as Japan's balance with the USA moved into positive. The plan called for trade liberalization and more Japanese exports in order to finance greater development. Industry objected. However, the state went ahead and MITI had the role of assisting those infant industries identified as good or potential exporters. However, it is not clear whether MITI helped, as the evidence is ambiguous (Sheridan, 1993: 151). More generally, the National Income Doubling Plan succeeded, but it is not easy to be clear about the role of the government. Indeed, Japan's success in these years may be quite particular to that country as the restrictions of post-war years and the doubts of a confused political period were left behind and optimistic business moved forward supported overall by the plan (Sheridan, 1993: 156–7). Nonetheless, as the miracle ran on through the 1970s into the

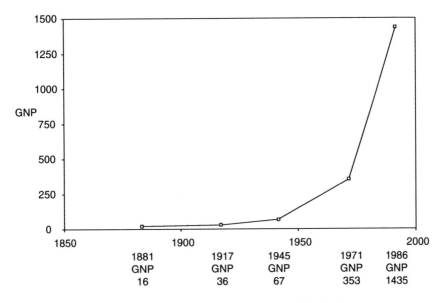

Figure 5.1 *Long-term Japanese growth (after Sheridan, 1993: 9–17)*

early 1980s, Sheridan (1993: 139) reports that Japan 'could claim to have transformed itself into one of the most advanced industrial and welfare societies in the world, equal if not better than the USA, West Germany, France or the Scandinavian countries'.

RAPID GROWTH   Tsuru (1993: 66) notes the period of high growth rate is quite remarkable. A series of domestic factors was involved, including state direction, the reassembly of the zaibatsu and a drive for export markets (Figure 5.1).

   Tsuru (1993: 67) recalls that Keynes remarked that long-run growth rates rarely exceeded 1 per cent and adds that in West Germany post-war rates were over 6 per cent, earning the tag 'miracle economy', and in Japan they were for several years above 10 per cent. These figures raise the question of how this growth is to be explained. One suggestion is offered by commentators who have spoken of 'creative defeat' – a strong national response to catastrophe. Tsuru (1993: 67) suggests that there could be a 'transcendental explanation' for Japan which points to long-term growth rate and process of post-war recovery of trend line growth. However, he adds that this is implausible because, while the familiar growth equations can tell us something (about labour availability, new technology and savings rates), this is not enough. A series of wider issues must be addressed, including sources of effective demand, the role of government, relevant industrial restructuring and exchange rate policy.

   The Korean War and the separate peace helped Japanese recovery but the changed atmosphere which followed the subsequent reversal of many of the occupation reforms was most important. The government and people put the war behind them as the war crimes trials ended in 1948. The SCAP reforms were being set aside, as noted, even prior to the peace and more were reversed thereafter. At the same time the conservative political forces within Japan established their domestic dominance. All in all, Japanese capitalism was rejuvenated.

The zaibatsu were reassembled. The old networks, the old banks and the old names quickly reappeared. There were differences: thus the networks each had 'one set' of key economic activities and competed against each other across the range of activities. Another key difference was the power of the banks. In pre-war days much capital was internally generated, but post-war the banks played a much bigger role in providing capital,which gave them, and the state behind them, strong influence.

The effective demand for these goods came from Korean War procurement at first and then, with the aid of an undervalued yen, exports. Tsuru (1993: 78–81) details the case of sewing machines and the role of state and industry groups in developing the industry and opening up markets. After sewing machines came cameras and watches, followed by steel, cars and ships where the same story holds true. Tsuru (1993: 85–6) notes that the precise relationship of exports to Japanese economic growth is disputed by economists but their important role cannot be denied. Overall, what makes Japan different is the role of the state, in particular MITI, and the one-set zaibatsu behaviour which had companies competing in all industrial sectors as soon as technology would let them.

ROLE OF THE STATE AT THIS TIME   A significant role was played by the government in the high growth period. The state employed a series of strategies. It tried central planning briefly but thereafter used indicative planning and a range of administrative devices.

In the early reform period of SCAP there was an attempt to utilize development planning in the construction of a liberal-market system to replace the state monopoly capitalism of pre-war days (Tsuru, 1993: 91). Following the socialist victory in April 1947, Premier Katayama set up a planning secretariat which produced plans for almost ten years, but after the first two, the fall of socialist government and the US reverse course, little weight was put on such plans per se (Tsuru, 1993: 90–1).

The Draft Plan for Economic Rehabilitation of May 1948 was followed by the Economic Rehabilitation Plan of May 1949. However, the conservative premier Yoshida, who came to power in January 1949, did not stress planning. Yoshida remained in power until December 1954 and only then did the state look again explicitly at planning. In January 1956 the Five-Year Plan for Economic Self-Support was published, followed in December 1957 by the New Long-Range Economic Plan, which identified a high growth rate as the target. In 1960 the Plan for Doubling National

Income was produced with a target of 7.2 per cent growth, but Tsuru (1993: 96) takes the view that this was simply political rhetoric, adding that any idea of effective planning was now gone.

Tsuru (1993: 97) notes that administrative guidance was widely practised and was effective, in particular, in coordinating investment programmes in major industries. An early example is the steel industry. The state has also provided industrial development land and undertook reclamation work.

It is also clear, Tsuru (1993: 104–10) reports, that the state has provided important financial mechanisms. There has been a light tax regime for firms and individuals. Relatively light expenditure has been made on armaments and welfare. The system has also allowed firms to carry a high external debt as interest payments are tax deductible. There have been many special incentives for different sorts of development. Credit rationing and direction via 'window guidance' issued by the Bank of Japan to big commercial banks specifying how much to lend to which sectors have worked to favour the zaibatsu. The system has had a large volume of savings available from the public via banks and the post office savings system, which allows the state to direct investment moneys. Tsuru (1993: 112–15) also comments that over the years the state has carefully ordered the relationship between the domestic economy with the external economy and has agreed to liberalization (GATT, IMF, OECD) only when Japanese companies could deal with the consequences, of which few have been untoward.

In a similar vein, Sheridan (1993: 180) reports 'the role of government in Japan's economic development has been unusual by Western standards . . . it gives Japan an unusual capacity to think strategically, and at times to make deliberate changes of direction as a national society'. Japan has had a strong effective public sector throughout the post-Meiji period. Sheridan (1993: 181–2) argues that the state has used a series of strategies to achieve its goals and has changed its overall character as the tasks confronting it have changed. There have been a series of policy cycles with policies for growth and policies for efficiency. Many of these cycles occur as bureaucrats shift from one policy disposition to another (Table 5.1).[1]

The continuing thread is the concern of the state with national development, which has been central to its activities and has forged a consensus among the population. In all this, reports Sheridan (1993: 202–8), a key group is the economic bureaucrats, and it might be said that Japan has a 'planned capitalism'. Against this, Sheridan (1993: 213–17) notes that it has been argued that a mature economy does not need the state, because the market can do the coordinating job. But Sheridan insists that this is not true as the mix of state and market is always a political decision. To shift from the established Japanese model to a more liberal-market centred model, as advocated for example by Kenichi Ohmae, would be a political decision in favour of Americanization.

Table 5.1 *Policy cycles, 1868–1999*

Date	Policy
1868–1880	The effort to industrialize
1881–1900	Reworking the effort along national(istic) lines
1901–1916	Expansion overseas and a concern for welfare at home
1917–1937	Taisho democracy, depression and militarization
1937–1945	The war economy and economic collapse
1946–1955	Occupation reforms and the basics of subsequent success
1956–1970	The years of rapid growth
1971–1985	Responses to crises, upgrading and decelerated success
1986–1991	Bubble economy
1991–present	Domestic recession and concern for global position

Sheridan (1993: 215–17) is confident that this would be a mistake because the Japanese system is strong and should attend to the many outstanding qualities of life tasks.

It is clear that the pattern of development over the post-World War II period was successful in raising the economic level of the country. Waswo (1996: 108) notes that 'with the publication of its New Long-Range Economic Plan in December of 1957, the Japanese government made it clear that the static and somewhat self-serving model devised by the Occupation had been replaced by a dynamic development plan that would, if successful, bridge the economic gap between Japan and the leading nations of the world'. Thereafter, the early years of growth were successful, but it was clear that the government had not addressed social welfare issues and in the late 1950s there was social unrest. In 1960 Prime Minister Ikeda inaugurated the National Income Doubling Plan, which aimed to deploy government resources to provide social capital, raise the level of living of the population and liberalize trade relations to allow the benefits of trade. The government undertook to foster economic growth and MITI moved to plan key sectors in chemicals, heavy industry and other modern technology sectors. The business community reacted negatively, but the plan went ahead. The strategy was pursued explicitly until 1965 when a change of government resulted in policy revisions which nonetheless continued along familiar lines. Sheridan (1993: 139) records that by 1970 'the demand for workers by the heavy industrial and chemical sectors had led to an exodus of younger workers from villages to factories, thus transforming the economy into a fully industrialized one'. Nonetheless, Sheridan (1993: 153–7) argues that government policy failed to address questions of success (such as high levels of employment, growth and accumulating social problems) and genuinely new thinking had to await the shock of the 1973 oil price hike.

As the high growth rates continued during the 1960s structural inflation emerged and there were concerns about environmental problems (the costs of high growth). The first oil shock of 1973 brought the whole high growth period to an abrupt end and opened up new agendas. Tsuru (1993: 120) argues that the high growth could not have continued as most of the factors aiding it, such as a favourable exchange rate, catching up with latest technologies, slow acceptance of liberalization and subsidized land, had disappeared. Yet the optimism in ruling circles prevailed. Following the 1972 Income Doubling Plan, Prime Minister Tanaka inaugurated the Plan for Remodelling the Japanese Archipelago which grandiosely looked to upgrade the national infrastructure on a massive scale, spreading industrial centres throughout the islands and linking them with rail and roads. Tanaka came to power in July 1972 and the oil crisis hit in October 1973.

The 1970s and 1980s: shocks, upgrading and further success

In the early 1970s the Japanese economy began a process of transition from the drive for recovery and advance, typical of the economic nationalism of the post-war years, to the first realization of the achievement of the role of a regional core economy which came in 1985 as the Plaza Accord revalued the yen. As the Japanese economy advanced, the position of the USA weakened. However, the route to regional core status was not smooth.

DECELERATED ECONOMY OF THE 1970S   Sheridan (1993: 158) records that there was a series of economic booms in the post-war period. Then came the 1970 slowdown and a number of long-term problems were revealed, in particular the environmental and social costs of rapid economic growth. The year 1971 marked a new phase in economic development and policymaking.

Sheridan (1993: 160) recalls that the policy of successive governments had been to grow the Japanese economy through trade pursued by state-supported large industrial sectors. This was a success for many years, but, as the economy became large and joined the rich economies in the global system, the positive linkage between the state and large firms within Japan began to look like a cosy arrangement. When new problems arose the policymakers found it difficult at first to respond. Sheridan (1993: 161) comments that while MITI had promoted networks of producers over the years in order to advance national growth, these links now looked like cosy collusion; where they had worked to advance growth, now they looked like lobby mechanisms for special interests.

However, in the early 1970s the Japanese government was obliged by popular opinion to introduce controls on industry to combat pollution. This was the first curb to an otherwise wildly successful policy of rapid growth. Then in 1973 there was a further curb in the form of the first oil shock. Tsuru (1993: 121) points out that the oil shock had a sharp impact as Japan was dependent on imported fuels and raw materials.

The initial public response was anxious and there was some business profiteering. The result was that private consumer expenditure and company investment dropped. The problem of structural inflation was aggravated and stagflation appeared. The economy was obliged to adapt to high oil prices and the impact was severe, with negative growth rates which did not recover until 1978. Over time the demands of the economy for energy were reduced, environmental standards were raised and new product lines established. Sheridan (1993: 162) reports that the second oil crisis in 1979 was not nearly so problematical.

The response of Japanese policymakers to these events was to argue that the economy had to shift into a lower growth pattern which could be accomplished by refocusing expectations on creating a knowledge intensive economy with a higher level of social capital. MITI discussed these issues and pointed to a future of lower growth with more focus on the quality of life in Japan, based on more knowledge intensive industries and less government direction of large industries in the economy. Sheridan (1993: 164–6) notes that MITI reorganized itself and began publishing 'visions' which sketched out the future for Japan. The MITI visions provided an overall blueprint and the economy was restructured as anticipated. In addition, there was movement on the quality of life front, with better welfare, but the key remained a commitment to economic advance, itself taken as the key to social advance. The new strategy was successful and the broad growth of the Japanese economy continued. Over the period of the two crises the economy was restructured both to be less dependent on oil and to centre on higher value added activities. Sheridan (1993: 163) argues that the period saw the economy shifting to a new lower growth path, a 'decelerated economy'.

However, one issue did cause concern. The economy ran with a persistent trade surplus and friction developed with the USA. In 1985 the Plaza Accords revalued the yen in the expectation that this would curb the economy and thus shrink the trade surplus. This did decline for a short period, but the response of the Japanese government and industry was further to upgrade the domestic economy and to relocate other activities within the Pacific-Asian region.

COSTS OF SUCCESS IN THE 1970S AND 1980S   The oil shock had a sharp impact on Japan The problem of structural inflation was aggravated as the economy was obliged to adapt to high oil prices. At the same time a related concern was the environmental costs of high growth. The recognition of environmental concerns by industry and government was very slow and reluctant, but eventually the issue was acknowledged. Over time the demands of the economy for energy were reduced, environmental standards were raised and new product lines were established which allowed the economy to resume its upward growth path. Nonetheless, there were further problems emerging in the late 1980s. Tsuru (1993: 147) speaks of a 'double price revolution'. The price revolutions impacted upon energy and land, two key resources in an industrial-capitalist economy. The oil shock was external, but the rise in land values was internal and resulted in a frenzy of speculation.

The bubble economy developed over the 1980s. The oil shocks of the 1970s produced one price rise and domestic land price inflation produced a second. These led, in turn, to the expansionary enthusiasms which followed the revaluation of the yen. It is at this point, in the phase of what Tsuru (1993: 160–9) characterizes as the 'third high tide', from 1986 through to 1990, that commentators speak of the 'bubble economy'.

Tsuru (1993: 149) recalls that the term price revolution relates to European countries in the late sixteenth and early seventeenth centuries when silver from Spanish America led to price inflation. The inflation saw profits from trade and landowning rise quickly whereas wage rates rose more slowly. The increased wealth and power of the traders and landowners contributed to the rise of the capitalist system in Europe. The situation in Japan was different under the oil shock as the price rise was not general but restricted to one sector, which then impacted upon the rest, leading to a 'new price revolution' (Tsuru, 1993: 149). The oil price shock caused a sharp change in the general pattern of prices. The Japanese economy adjusted by making minor reductions in domestic expenditure on energy and significant reductions in industry expenditure (Tsuru, 1993: 150–8). The land price rise was internally generated, accompanied by a series of contributory factors: available easy credit; commercial speculation; tax regimes having the effect of favouring land holding; and government policies of development. The rise in land values generated capital gains and skewed the pattern of economic power within society.

Tsuru (1993: 158–69) notes that a myth of ever-rising land values was generated which fuelled the speculative bubble. The rise in land values had socio-economic consequences: men on average salaries could not afford to buy a house; firms began to offer ever-improved subsidized housing to attract the best employees, who then used their disposable income for consumption; the overall pattern of economic wealth was skewed in favour of a few; the effect on public works has been unfortunate as these rely on land, so provision is held down; and slowly the old neighbourhoods have changed character as land ownership has become a matter of firms rather than individuals.

CORPORATE CAPITALISM IN THE 1980S Tsuru (1993: 184) is confident that the post-war growth record of Japan is unquestionably remarkable. It seems that a new form of capitalism has emerged, a 'corporate capitalism' which lodges great power within large companies. In retrospect it is clear that the occupation authorities, SCAP, tried to rebuild the Japanese economy, but partly failed and partly changed their minds. The zaibatsu were reconstructed in a somewhat less predatory form and have become sprawling conglomerates which have expanded overseas – an aspect of globalization. Tsuru (1993: 205–11) suggests that the high tide of corporate optimism was achieved in the privatization programmes of the 1980s.

Yet a key element of this pattern of development has been the quite particular role of the state. Sheridan (1993: 180) reports that 'the role of government in Japan's economic development has been unusual by Western standards . . . it gives Japan an unusual capacity to think strategically . . . to make deliberate changes of direction as a national society'. Japan has had a strong effective public sector throughout the post-Meiji period and has used a series of strategies to achieve its goals. It has changed its overall character as the tasks confronting it have changed and throughout has run the continuing thread of concern of the state with national development.

In general, the Japanese economy has grown throughout the post-World War II period, and between 1971 and 1985 became the economic core of the region. The key Japanese trading partner is the USA, but there are extensive linkages with other regional economies. The development of these links has been a deliberate Japanese policy. At the present time the relationship of Japan and Pacific Asia is bound up with trade, investment and aid networks.

A regional core economy

The global system is sustained and ordered through a number of institutions and patterns of activity including: first, the inter-state system of treaties which underpins the exchanges of states; second, the formal intra-governmental organizations such as the IMF, World Bank and GATT/WTO which together provide a regulative framework for economic activity; third, the presence and activities of global economic organizations (multinational corporations, MNCs) and practices (the financial markets) which integrate economies at regional and global levels; fourth, the surprising capacities of new technologies (communications, via many channels, some outside the control of state-governments, thus satellite TV, and relatedly human movement on the basis of long-haul airlines) which underpin new patterns of social activity. At the same time the givens of geography, history and culture, coupled to present economic and political imperatives, are pushing the global system towards a set of regional groupings. In brief, there has been both a measure of globalization in production and exchange (although consumption is still skewed towards the developed countries) and a drift towards regionalization.

The Japanese elite has been concerned with relations with its Asian neighbours since the period of the Meiji Restoration. Government policy has looked to the creation of a stable regional environment within which the Japanese economy could prosper and advance. In the early phase of the Japanese shift to the modern world this concern came to be exercised in colonial terms within the context of the disintegration of the traditional Sino-centric system in East Asia. However, after the debacle of 1945 this strategy could not be used and in its place over the post-World War II period the Japanese government has looked to foster economic linkages.

The earliest expression of this new orientation was the provision of war reparations to countries in the Asian region. These took the form of credits for Japanese manufactures rather than simple money transfers. In this way an economic linkage was established between Japan and a series of Asian countries. These links have been developed over the succeeding years and presently involve trade, investment and development aid. Rix (1993a: 23) comments that 'Asian development was more a means of achieving Japanese objectives than a goal in its own right'. Yasutomo (1986: 26) notes the emergence of the concept of 'comprehensive national security', which suggests that national security depends upon regional security, which in turn is helped by economic growth in the area. Yasutomo (1986: 112–14) argues that the Japanese government pursues five interrelated goals with its aid programmes:

(a) economic well-being;
(b) national prestige;
(c) domestic support;
(d) peace diplomacy;
(e) national security.

It might be noted that the pattern of Japanese direct investment within the region tends to parallel the pattern of aid. There was an early post-World War II concentration on primary product production which has been broadened significantly in recent years to include manufacturing plant. Overall, Yasutomo (1986) argues that what is crucial in the Japanese aid programme is not the absolute sums of money, but rather 'the manner of giving' – it is creating an integrated industrial-capitalist region.

INTRA-REGIONAL LINKS AND INTER-REGIONAL LINKS The pattern of relationships which Japan developed over the period of its recovery and growth can be analysed in terms of their regional and inter-regional global aspects. The two aspects are intertwined and have at their core the extraordinary productive economic power secured by Japan in the years following the Pacific War.

The regional expression of Japanese productive economic power is found in its increasing role as a regional core economy. The role of Japan within the regional economy has been developed through aid, trade and foreign direct investment. The involvement has been seen by some as problematical in view of the history of Japanese colonialism within the region. The involvement has been subject to extensive theoretical analysis revolving around the nature of regional integration (Bernard, 1996; Zysman, 1996).

The inter-regional global expression of Japanese productive economic power is to be found in its trade and investment relationships with the USA and the EU. The relationship with the EU is, in principle, straight-forwardly economic, with patterns of trade and investment at the core of the relationship. The relationship with the USA is more problematical and includes, in addition to trade and investment, a military security relationship (whereby the USA guarantees the defence of Japan) and a financial relationship (which sees Japanese money funding US deficits).

The patterns of intra-regional and inter-regional development had a particular contingent intersection in the 1985 attempt by the developed countries of the West, in particular the USA, to address the problem of trade imbalances between Japan and the USA. The result of the meetings held at the Plaza Hotel in New York was an agreement to revalue the yen against the dollar. The expectation had been that the resultant shift in relative prices of goods would reduce Japanese exports to the USA while making American goods more competitive in Japan, with the overall result that the trade deficit would be reduced. In the event this did not happen. The reaction of Japanese policymakers and industrialists to the pressures of an upwardly revalued yen was to relocate manufacturing activity to offshore production platforms within the Pacific-Asian region. The Japanese trade imbalance with the USA continued and the relocated activity had the effect of generating a further round of regional integra-tion within Pacific Asia. At the same time, it should be noted that the revaluation of yen holdings against the dollar represented windfall gains for holders of yen and a spiral of domestic inflation was initiated. In Japan, as noted earlier, this developed into the bubble economy of the late 1980s and, after a heady period of capital investment and consump-tion, the inevitable collapse led to a lengthy period of domestic recession in the 1990s.

REVALUATION OF THE YEN AND DEVELOPMENT OF REGIONAL PRODUCTION PLATFORMS   The revaluation of the yen in 1985 had the effect of forcing Japanese industrialists and policymakers to formulate a rapid response to the sharply changed financial structural circumstances within which they operated. The strategy adopted was to engage in foreign direct investment throughout the Pacific Asia region. The pattern of new foreign direct investment was shaped by established trade links and supported by official development assistance. Aid, trade and foreign direct investment comprised the trio of vehicles for the expansion of Japanese economic engagement with the countries of Pacific Asia.

The particular response to the negative implications of the Plaza Accord revaluation for Japanese business – in brief, a sharp contraction of trading opportunities in the USA – was to relocate industrial production to sites within the Pacific Asia region. A series of objectives were secured by this strategy:

1 Lower tech production was removed from Japan, creating the domestic space within which higher tech production could be developed.
2 The costs of production moved offshore, typically to lower wage environments, could be reduced, thus aiding the recovery of price advantages lost in the yen revaluation.
3 Goods sourced in Pacific-Asian production platforms could access the USA with less political opposition from the country offering the final market.
4 As the countries of the region were active participants in this relocation, new alliances could be developed (Phongpaichit, 1990; Dobson, 1993; Katzenstein and Shiraishi, 1997).

REFLECTIONS ON THE FUTURE OF JAPAN   The contemporary situation of Japan has been the subject of intense debate. There is a market-liberal line of criticism popular among American commentators which suggests that the current problems of the Japanese economy revolve around the reluctance of bureaucrats to acknowledge that the economy has matured and that deregulation and liberalization are now necessary. A sophisticated proponent of this position has been Kenichi Ohmae (1987). A wealth of journalistic commentary is also available (*Economist*, 1994) and critics content to draw on market liberalism can be found in Japan (Gibney, 1998). Indeed Sheridan (1998b) notes that 'deregulation' has come to be seen as something of a cure-all in popular debates in Japan. However, against these easy borrowings an alternative line of commentary draws on indigenous Japanese resources to propose, variously, a Japanese route to a Japanese future.

Tsuru (1993: 213–19) recalls that in pre-war days both liberal-market and Marxist theorists agreed that there would be a form of convergence, around the logic of technological advance. In the post-war period the ideological conflict between the USA and USSR repeated this debate until the dissolution of the latter tempted some to argue for the victory of capitalism. But this is an error. The demands of modern technology in respect of elaborate mechanisms of social order and planning continue to work against any simple liberal market model. Indeed, the real world seems to be organized in three fashions in the trio of economic blocs, the USA, Europe and Pacific Asia. Tsuru (1993: 224–35) concludes that in the case of Japan the presently powerful corporate capitalism needs to be criticized in the light of two principles: the prioritization of people; and the affirmation of the peace constitution. The criticisms imply a series of policy proposals which would serve to make Japan an exemplar of a peaceful, sophisticated, industrial society. In a similar way Sheridan (1993, 1998b) argues that a rational route to the future would deploy

Japan's ability to make policy decisions to advance long-established concerns for national development by upgrading the quality of life concerns of the mass of the people, the neglected producers. In summary, we can note that the post-war experience of Japan has been both celebrated and subject to sharp criticism.

Conclusion

The US occupation initiated a programme of reform which was designed to remodel Japan economically, socially and politically along the lines of the USA. The work was begun optimistically (and arguably naively). However, the 'reverse course' saw the abandonment of this project in favour of the policy of economically and militarily strengthening an ally against mainland Asian Communism.

It is this early post-war period which sees Japan drawn into the Western sphere. A quite particular balance of interests was achieved as the American elite secured an ally and the Japanese elite secured the space within which they could engineer their national recovery. After the reverse course, the role of MITI, the achievement of social solidarity and the dominance of the Liberal Democratic Party are crucial to the success of the Japanese 'developmental state'. The upshot has been a conservative, business-dominated country whose political-cultural project has been justly tagged as a thoroughgoing 'economic nationalism'.

Thereafter, the economy continued to advance and the process of post-war Japanese recovery became the subject of considerable debate. At first the debate concerned academic specialists on Japan and the somewhat wider issue of 'Third World' development. However, in time the success of the Japanese economy was such that trade friction with the USA began to develop. In this context, the debate about the fundamental occasion of Japanese success attained a new quality as policy advisors and political actors became energetically involved.

Note

1 The bulk of this is taken from Sheridan (1993: 190–5) with my additions to embrace the confusions of the 1990s. These are also pursued by Sheridan (1998b) who re-states her preference for 'Japanese solutions to Japanese problems'. The role of the state and the mix of policy concerns is also pursued by Penelope Franks, *Japanese Economic Development: Theory and Practice* (1992).

6

THE JAPANESE MODEL

Success Debated, Celebrated and Disputed

The fundamental occasion, detailed nature and dynamic trajectory of modern Japan are intellectually problematical issues which have generated sharp debate. The logics of the political economy, social institutions and culture of Japan have been vigorously discussed by political agents, policy analysts and social scientists. The debate has a recent occasion in the context of the Pacific War (Benedict, 1946) and a more particular expression within discussions of development, where the Japan of the late 1950s and 1960s was taken to be an interesting model. The debate has had a subsequent centre in the often sharp and somewhat racist reactions of American commentators concerned with the phoenix-like quality of Japanese recovery following the Pacific War and the apparent dissemination of the development strategy around the region of Pacific Asia.

A series of objects of debate have been specified: Japan, the Western sphere of Cold War Asia and, most recently, the region of Pacific Asia. The discussion of Japan per se often becomes tangled up in related debates (and given that Japan is the economic core of the region this is perhaps unsurprising). In very general terms then, on the one hand there are those like Krugman (1994b) who argue that nothing special has happened in Pacific Asia save for a process of catching up with the West, combined with heavy protection for domestic economic activity, now no longer justifiable and, in the light of the financial crisis of the late 1990s, unsustainable. On the other hand there are those like Wade and Veneroso (1998) who argue that the Pacific-Asian pattern is distinctive, successful and perfectly well able to continue into the future. The argument unpacks in a series of areas – economic, social and cultural/political – and a related aspect of the debate touches upon the status of Western social science (in particular, mainstream market-liberal economics with its claims to universal positive scientific status). The heady brew of intellectual, policy analytical and political issues has generated an often heated debate.

This study is grounded in the classical European tradition of social theorizing. It is focused upon Japan (while granting that the country is indeed the core economy of a region). If we analyse the historical development experience of Japan in the light of the intellectual resources of the European tradition we can identify the sequence of phases whereby Japan has ordered its ongoing shift to the modern world: Tokugawa, Meiji, and Taisho/Showa. The subsequent phase, following the Pacific War, has seen the development of a sophisticated industrial-capitalist system which is the core of the region of Pacific Asia. Recalling the development history of Japan opens up a wide spread of areas of debate. The material presented here both follows from the discussions of the opening chapter and will be the subject of further reflection in the final chapter. In this chapter we will look at the following: the political-economic system of Japan; the social-institutional structure of Japan; the polity of Japan; and finally the culture of contemporary Japan.

Contemporary Japanese political-economic arrangements

In the period from the Meiji Restoration to the turn of the century the Japanese economy made rapid advances which continued through the years of war in Asia. However, the Pacific War left the Japanese economy in ruins. The post-war recovery has been a remarkable achievement and the success has been a mixture of planning mechanisms and the marketplace. The iron triangle of bureaucracy, business and politicians has been overwhelmingly committed to the pursuit of economic growth. The role of the bureaucracy has been crucial in guiding the development of the economy. By the mid-1980s the economy began to run a persistent trading surplus. An attempt to correct these surpluses by revaluing the yen led to production being relocated in Pacific Asia and Japan now seems to be the core economy of an increasingly powerful economic grouping.

The nature of the Japanese economy has been the subject of much debate. The sphere of the economic is often addressed in orthodox market-liberal terms which speak of the spontaneous, human wants grounded, givenness of markets. Against this view, those working within the classical European tradition would prefer to speak of the social and cultural construction of patterns of economic life, which thereafter might be elucidated in critical social scientific reflection. In Japan the shift to the modern world was first conceived in market-liberal terms, but after only a few years the Meiji economic policymakers shifted their attention to the German Historical School. It is this tradition of thought, coupled to local intellectual and ethical resources, which has shaped Japanese policymaking. Against market-liberal analyses cast in terms of modernization, the result has been described as an essentially corporatist system pursuing mercantile trading strategies, a modern-day version of medieval Venice (Johnson, 1995).

Standard characterizations and familiar debates

In discussions of the Japanese economy a series of factors are routinely adduced to explain the success:

1   External factors in the global system including rapid general economic growth and US tolerance of trade deficits (as part of Cold War alliances).
2   State direction of development with an extensive system of 'administrative guidance' at the level of the firm and protection at the level of the economy.
3   A structure which privileged large keiretsu firms with extensive links to bureaucracy and politicians, who in turn worked sympathetically with small-scale suppliers.
4   Compliant labour relations with house unions and life-time employment for those in the core firms of the economy.
5   A large service sector which soaked up unemployment and provided the equivalent of a welfare network.

However, if we retreat from description a little and consider the matter analytically, it is possible to identify a series of ways in which the sphere of the economic is construed by Western social science, and each sets up the whole business in a different way – concepts, descriptions, problems and prescriptions. We may speak of three lines of analysis and a fourth more radical position.

In the first case, the conventional wisdom centres on the neo-classical economics of rational-calculative behaviour in a liberal market and the language used will be of scarcity, markets, competition, efficiency and price. In the second case, the institutional line of analysis, economic behaviour is taken to be embedded within social life and thereafter the line has recourse to the language of the social and cultural construction of patterns of livelihood and the institutional ordering of markets. Third, the line of political economy looks to analyse patterns of economic activity within society itself lodged in phases within history, and the language of structures and agents is used. Finally, there is a position available which suggests that the entire language of markets is tainted by Western ideology and that it would be better to leave the discourse and attend instead to the great diversity of available real world social processes. The claim here is that there are no universal models, but only local models (Gudeman, 1986; Dilley, 1992).

The debate in respect of the nature of the economy of Japan can be grasped in terms of three broad approaches: orthodox market-liberal theorists; institutionalists; and those working with reference to the classical European tradition (including the materials of critical and structural international political economy).

THE MARKET-LIBERAL THEORISTS   The analysis of the nature of the Japanese economy is a deeply problematical issue for those Western analysts who affirm the orthodox economics of the marketplace. This is because it is both difficult to deny the success of the Japanese economy and even more difficult to claim that it is a liberal-market system. In the USA this difficulty of response adds to the real problems which are apparent in trade deficits and the dependence of the USA on Japanese investment money to finance this deficit.

On the arguments of the social scientific economic orthodoxy, those who work with a model of liberal markets, the Japanese system is riddled with unacceptable practices: a state which routinely intervenes in the economy; companies which eschew the capital markets in favour of cosy relationships with banks (and thereafter ignore their equity holders); employees who enjoy life-time contracts; and consumers who pay high prices and do not complain. In orthodox market-liberal terms the system should not work. However, clearly it does. Thereafter the debate revolves around how to characterize the Japanese economy. Is it successful despite its great handicaps, or is it to be judged according to institutional and political-economic terms, in which case it is an interesting and wholly intelligible tale of a national developmental success plan rationally achieved (Appelbaum and Henderson, 1992: 21).

Of course these debates are made the more fraught as economic theorizing (and social theorizing more generally) overlap with government policymaking, and here we meet ideological commitments head on. In the policy communities of the Anglo-Saxon world the attempt is automatically made to read Japan in terms of market-liberal ideas – and there is a good case for saying that this is only productive of error and unhappiness. Sheridan (1993: 1) notes that there has been extensive discussion of Japan's successful industrialization and that many explanations have been offered by outsiders, including, pointing to a submissive culture enabling mobilization, the role of government and a neglect of welfare in favour of development. Some in Japan rehearse these arguments and look for a shift from state to marketplace as the economy matures. Sheridan does not agree, arguing that unaided market forces did not determine Japan's development in the past and need not in the future, unless there is a political decision that they should. Sheridan (1993: 3) argues four points:

(a) that Japan's government does not intervene in the economy from the outside but is an integral part of it;
(b) that it is possible to identify deliberate changes in economic and national direction in the past;
(c) the capacity for making such choices still exists;
(d) it offers a programmatic new direction.

Sheridan (1993: 47–8) notes that this integral role for the state in national economic development has proved awkward for market-liberal economics. The problem lies in the preference for the notion of a self-regulating system, with government intervention as a contingent external influence, whereas in Japan such intervention has a routine, necessary and integral directing role within the political-cultural project of national development. Sheridan (1993: 54) identifies four basic aspects of Japanese government intervention:

(a) the notion of the 'state economy', which asserts that the state must secure the general interests of the community;
(b) integrated policies for growth, equity and welfare;
(c) competent public authorities;
(d) a cooperative relationship between planners and market.

Sheridan (1993: 55) adds that a distinctive trait of the Japanse system is that national development goals are routinely translated into economic terms via this system of intervention.

INSTITUTIONALISTS The tradition of institutional economic analysis argues that all economic systems are necessarily lodged within social systems, in turn located within cultures, which are thereafter shaped and understood by agents with reference to distinct moral and intellectual traditions (Preston, 1996). The patterns of economic life of peoples are diverse and each has its own logic. The proponents of institutional economics regard the claims of market-liberal theorists to the universal relevance of their model of rational-calculative economic behaviour in juridically regulated market systems as ideological (in the pejorative sense; Gray, 1998). In Gudeman's (1986) terms their universal model is simply one more local model. The institutional line of economic analysis is itself diverse, but it is the concern for the detail of patterns of social life which is important. An influential contribution to the debates about the nature of the Japanese economy which does access the detail of social relationships has been made by Ronald Dore.

Dore (1986, 1987) has analysed the corporatist political economy of Japan and shown how it contrasts with the regulated competitive liberal market of the USA. Dore (1986: 20–5) describes the sectors of the economy and notes that the core manufacturing sector is both ordered (with cross-shareholdings, industry organizations, supportive banking and various networks of suppliers and customers) and has strong links to the politico-bureaucratic establishment. Dore (1986: 25) calls it a 'developmental' industrial-capitalist political economy. It is this character which allows the Japanese state-regime to respond to patterns of change within the global system effectively, creatively and prospectively (thus change is not mere reaction) and this subtlety of response is the key to its success. Dore pursues this argument in three main areas: enterprise, workers and government.

The enterprise works as a community. There is an internal commitment towards those who run the firm. The firm itself works within an ordered market environment. This allows both long termism and confidence builds among the various players (employees, managers, customers, suppliers, bankers, ministries). At the level of individual firms there is ferocious competition, but thereafter there is an acknowledgement of the collectivity of producers. The system manages to combine both competition and cooperation. Dore (1986) speaks of 'relational contracting' whereby links with customers and suppliers are read as broader than orthodox market-liberal theories allow.

The workers are employed within a firm understood as a family and which responds to trading conditions collectively. In adverse conditions the firm as family attempts to accommodate and sacking people is a rare and last resort (as recently in the extended recession of the 1990s). With this management commitment employees are able to be flexible about their work and wages.

The government offers a spread of encouragements and services to retrain, redeploy and reassure employees in the matter of change; plus, of course, the economy through much of the post-war period has been expanding and this makes things easier. As regards the enterprise, the government has a role via industry associations, MITI, available high savings and long-established links of administrative guidance: in sum, a way of intervening extensively, cooperatively and subtly.

Dore (1986, 1987) insists that Japan is to be regarded as a corporatist system and that orthodox market-liberal economics has no intellectual purchase or relevance. Looking to the future, Dore can see no reason why a successful corporatist economy should or will change. In a developmental political economy, productive efficiency is more important than allocative efficiency (the obsession of market-liberal economic theory), and it depends upon an idea of society being fair (that is having an ethical base). In turn this requires corporatist arrangements in regard to consensus building within society about collective social goals. These arguments have been influential. Nothwithstanding further reflection – which illuminates, for example, the contribution of political and managerial repression of militant trade unionism in the immediate post-war years and then decisively in the early 1950s (Henshall, 1999: 159–9) – the system is routinely characterized as 'corporatist' (Appelbaum and Henderson, 1992; Sheridan, 1993, 1998a; Tsuru, 1993). Clammer (1997) argues that the fundamental social relations constituting the system – concerns for harmony, hierarchy, tradition and emotion – reveal a profoundly ordered society.

THE CLASSICAL EUROPEAN TRADITION   The classical European tradition of social theorizing is concerned with the emancipatory elucidation of the dynamics of complex change in the ongoing shift to the modern world. A clutch of analytical strategies is deployed, in particular, the political-economic, social-institutional and culture-critical analysis of the structural dynamics which are the product and ground of the routine behaviour of agents. A spread of contemporary approaches deploys, one way or another, these strategies of argument and action. In the case of Japan it presents us with an analysis of a series of discrete political-cultural projects which act to express the fundamental elite concern with national development and regional security.

The Tokugawa period left a legacy of organization, small-scale manufacturing and relatively prosperous agriculture. On this basis Meiji pursued a planned catching up and the state provided modern infrastructure and strategically important heavy industries. In the period to 1945 the economy gradually became more centred on manufacturing and old pattern agricultural activities declined. A series of very large and powerful conglomerates grew up, the zaibatsu. As the 1930s wore on the economy gradually became focused on war production – including all the apparatus of state direction. After the war the zaibatsu were abolished, liberal competition was encouraged and labour unions were set up. However, after an initial period the reforms were modified and a conservative business alliance came to power. The Japanese economy benefited from the Korean War of 1950–53 and this was the start of the 'economic miracle'. The state took the lead in ordering economic reconstruction and growth. The large firms reappeared as networks of companies called keiretsu. The economy retained its dual structure – a mix of large firms and a mass of small suppliers.

The early period of post-war growth came to be dominated by heavy industries (steel, ships, chemicals, coal) and they suffered in the first oil shock of 1971–3. Restructuring moved the economy to higher value added goods (cars, consumer appliances, machinery). The second oil shock of 1979 was weathered fairly easily and the move into higher value added goods continued with the microelectronics revolution. After the yen revaluation of 1985 some firms moved production offshore to Pacific Asia and the overall economic growth of Japan and its offshore production platforms continued apace.

One feature of the Japanese economy is the role of banks and the national postal savings system in gathering savings and financing companies. This means a greater involvement in the activities of the company and a greater concern for the long term. The banks in turn raise money from the state bank (which gives the state a significant measure of control over the economy). The Japanese as a whole have a high saving rate (Reading, 1992). The relationship of banks to manufacturing is often cited as one of the less obvious reasons for the post-war 'economic miracle'.

In pre-modern times Japan was a self-contained economy, but with the shift to the modern world the linkages with the evolving global system became deeper. The exchanges with East and Southeast Asia and the Western powers and the USA in particular in the pre-1945 period played a significant role in Japanese government thinking. After the manner in which the modern world impinged on Japan there was a deep-seated

concern for security. Many commentators have suggested that this characterizes the general economic trading posture of post-war Japanese
governments. It is now familiarly referred to as an 'export-oriented
growth strategy'. However, the success of an export-oriented strategy
depends on there being markets which will take and pay for all the
exports. In the case of Japan the markets have been Europe and the USA.

The Japanese economy has run a surplus on its import-export account
for many years and has also become a major source of capital for the
global system. The imbalance in trade has led to great friction between
Japan and its developed trading partners. Such is the salience of this
issue in Japanese–American relationships that a vast literature has
grown up dealing with the problem. In its modest versions it looks to the
model of Japan and suggests that the USA will either have to move to
managed trade (Thurow, 1994), or radically upgrade the performance of
its own economy (Vogel, 1980). In its radical versions it speaks of a
veritable 'clash of civilizations' (Huntington, 1993). Either way, the
business of the place of Japan and Pacific Asia within the evolving global
system is now a live issue.

The recession of the 1990s and the global financial crisis

The Japanese economy has run into difficulties in recent years. A mixture
of domestic, regional and international problems can be identified. The
result has been a long drawn-out and seemingly intractable recession in
Japan over the decade of the 1990s.

THE JAPANESE BUBBLE AND SUBSEQUENT RECESSION   The roots of severe
inflation can be traced to the oil shocks of the 1970s which produced one
price rise, with domestic land price inflation producing a second. These
two led, in turn, to the expansionary enthusiasms which followed the
1985 revaluation of the yen. It is at this point, from 1986 through to 1990,
that commentators speak of the 'bubble economy'. The bubble collapsed
in the early 1990s. A period of very slow or negative economic growth
followed. The government confronted problems of indebted companies
and a financial system that was carrying a large amount of non-
performing debt (both domestic and, after the Asian financial crisis,
regional).

The problem of domestic bad debt and a related post-bubble falling
away of domestic consumer demand prompted the government to
attempt to reflate the economy via Keynesian style pump priming.
However, successive attempts were unsucessful and in the late 1990s the
domestic problem became entangled in regional and global problems.

THE ASIAN/GLOBAL FINANCIAL CRISIS   The current crisis in Pacific Asia
has been the subject of considerable debate, which can be provisionally
summarized in terms of a trio of approaches: market-liberal,

institutionalist, and classical tradition. In the first case, the advocates of a Western market-liberal system have blamed the political and business elites of the region and have spoken of 'crony capitalism'. A sharp reply has been made by regional advocates of the particularity of the development experience of Asia (often unhelpfully summed up in terms of an idea of 'Asian values') who have spoken of a Western politico-financial conspiracy to undermine Asia's success (Lim, 1998). Thereafter, a more plausible line of institutionalist analysis has looked at the dynamics of liberalized deregulated markets and diagnosed an irrational – and all to be expected – panic that has seen a flight of capital which no economic system could sustain without damage. However, finally, the classical European tradition of social theorizing can offer further insight into the crisis and reveal something of its occasion in post-Cold War intra-regional adjustment within the increasingly integrated global system (Preston, 1998b).

The advocates of the universal relevance of Western models, buttressed by the universalizable work of Western social science, look to a continuing process of globalization driven by the powerful industrial-capitalist countries and entailing a continuing process of modernization for weaker countries as they are drawn into the global market-based system. In this perspective the current crisis in Asia is symptomatic of a failure of adjustment to the inevitable demands of globalization.

The regional advocates of the particularity of the development experience of Pacific Asia deny the claims to universality of Western social science and look to the need to resist the demands of Western 'predatory liberalism' as a necessary condition of the pursuit of locally or regionally specified development goals. In this perspective the current crisis in Asia is symptomatic, first, of a disinclination on the part of the Western powers to acknowledge the legitimate goals of others and, second, of a readiness to deploy for selfish ends their present relative financial and economic power.

It seems clear that the proponents of a market-liberal future for the region are guilty of an intellectually illegitimate affirmation of the priority of the model of Western industrial capitalism. At the same time it would seem that the advocates of a radically different Pacific Asia, captured in terms of a summary notion of 'Asian values', are overstating their case.

The intellectual materials of the classical European tradition of social theorizing – with its concern to elucidate the dynamics of complex change – would grant the claims of the institutionalist analysts (the unregulated global financial system is irrational and dangerous and certainly does need re-regulating), but would go on to add that the global system as a whole manifests a shifting mix of internationalization and regionalization. The global system is both extensively interdependent and ordered on a regional basis. There are three key regions (the Americas, the European Union and Pacific Asia) and the business of establishing a contested compromise to order their relations is now in process. It is a matter of shifting patterns of structural power and agreed sets of formal rules.

In this context it is clear that the Asian/global financial crisis has severely weakened the position of key liberal-market international financial institutions. The machineries of the Bretton Woods system of regulated liberal-market trade were established in the later years of World War II by Western governments determined to avoid any repetition of those policy mistakes of the inter-war years which had led to economic depression, regional blocs and war. The institutions included the World Bank, whose objective was the provision of long-term development funding, the International Monetary Fund (IMF), whose objective was to manage short-term problems within the global financial system and, later, the GATT, whose objective was to encourage and regulate free trade. In the context of the Keynesian theorized post-World War II long boom, the system broadly worked. In such a context the pronouncements of the constituent institutions could carry considerable authority. However, the system has changed. The Bretton Woods system collapsed in 1971 and the World Bank and the IMF have subsequently been vehicles for an assertive, American-centred, neo-liberal, political-cultural project. In this context, it might be noted that the actions of the IMF during the crisis in Asia have come under intense critical scrutiny. It might also be noted that Japanese proposals for an 'Asian IMF' were resisted by the USA (Higgot, 1998). Critics have considered the actions of the IMF and argued that the organization has acted not merely to deal with the transient financial effects of a bursting investment bubble coupled to investor panic (and done so incompetently), but has gone on to demand reforms oriented to market liberalization and market opening. In doing so the IMF has radically misunderstood the nature of the East Asian 'developmental capitalism'. On this basis critics suggest that the economic and social costs of the demands of the IMF, which they lodge within the politico-institutional context of the 'Wall Street-Treasury-IMF complex' (Wade and Veneroso, 1998), are likely to fuel a political reaction within Asia (Higgot, 1998).

In the context of the broad development experience of the Pacific-Asian region it seems unlikely that the crisis will be other than transient. The alternative lines of speculation, to collapse, disintegration and regression to the Third Word or to radical reorganization along Western specified market-liberal lines, seem deeply implausible. The EU, North America and Pacific Asia are the three major regions within the global industrial-capitalist system (Thurow, 1994). In each region there is a large population, a sophisticated scientific base, a well-developed industrial structure and a distinctive culture (Bernard, 1996; Zysman, 1996). In particular, the standard agency data show that the Pacific Asia region now has an aggregate gross national product of a magnitude similar to that of the European Union or North America. Overall, it may be suggested that the crisis can be read, after the style of the classical European tradition of social theorizing, in terms of the post-Cold War patterns of adjustment between regionalized economic spaces within the increasingly integrated global system. The central intellectual task is the piecemeal, dialogic elucidation of contemporary patterns of complex change as diverse groups within the global system read and react to ongoing structural change in order to make their own lives.

The Japanese political economy

The Japanese economy has been the subject of heated debate in respect of its fundamental logic. The proponents of the Western market-liberal orthodoxy find difficulty in analysing an economy which has been enormously succesful while apparently disregarding the fundamental axioms of market-liberal economics. In the USA these intellectual problems have coincided with political and policy difficulties. At back of these there is an available American racism in respect of Asia. The upshot is an unhappy and unfruitful debate. Against these approaches, attention to the historical development experience of Japan reveals a quite particular economic system: in brief, the economy is subordinate to an overriding elite commitment, which enjoys broad public support, to the economic development and national security of Japan.

Contemporary Japanese social-institutional arrangements

In analysing the social world a distinction can be draw between the 'system' and the 'life world' (Habermas, 1971, 1989). The first designates the social system in its entirety and posits a level of analysis appropriate thereto, while the second points to the realm of mundane lived experience, the world of routine, of life taken for granted. A key issue in respect of the system will be the manner in which it reproduces itself and thereby exists over time. A key issue in respect of the life world will be the extent of human autonomy realized.

In the case of Japan the system reproduces in the sphere of the economic via a top-down economy which requires that the population cooperates in decisions taken by an elite. In the political sphere the system reproduces itself via an elite-ordered, top-down politics which coopts but does not engage the population as a whole. In the sphere of the social, institutions of social learning and control enable the system to reproduce itself via the fashioning of a participative, cooperative and obedient population.

Social-institutional structure of Japan

The social-institutional structure of contemporary Japan can be elucidated in terms of historically generated and presently sustained patterns of organization and belief. The shift to the modern world effected by Japan has had two key episodes, the Meiji Restoration and the American occupation. During each of these periods the social-institutional structure of Japan was self-consciously remade (albeit with extensive continuities in both cases).

In pre-modern Japan the family unit was known as the 'continuing family', which was a unit of residence, family and state administration initially established in the Tokugawa period (Bowring and Kornicki, 1993: 236–41). The continuing family had a status within the community which members were expected to uphold and their lives revolved around it: work, benefits, marriage and child rearing, old age and broad social status. The head of the household registered the continuing family, which was the property owner, with the authorities. In each generation one person would become the head – ideally the eldest son. The society was ordered hierarchically, as was the continuing family. However, the continuing family was abolished in 1947 although its cultural influence continues in a slowly declining fashion. Thus the expectations of reciprocity between generations continue (ancestors must be remembered, and the younger generation is taken to owe duty to the older). The Japanese take the view that children are basically good. Children learn early the distinction between home and the outside world (where different patterns of behaviour are required) and between the formal world and real feelings. The parent–child relationship tends to be repeated in various settings: in companies, in politics, in the arts and among gangsters. It is a relationship of loyalty and benevolence. The older person takes a certain responsibility for the younger who reciprocates with loyalty.

In Japan formal education in the guise of learning Confucian texts by heart dates from the early years of Tokugawa (Bowring and Kornicki, 1993: 236–41). In the pre-contact years of the early nineteenth century Japan had a better educated population than the USA or Europe. The Meiji state was quick to capitalize on this legacy in its drive to catch up with the West. A series of study visits was made to the West and a new system rapidly put into place. It was hierarchically ordered from mass primary schooling through to elite tertiary universities and was controlled from the centre. It was also directed to the pursuit of national development: practical skills necessary to an industrial society and the inculcation of a national identity. The Meiji system was abolished by SCAP and a US pattern introduced. The idea of education for work is still very strong and the system is centrally directed, hierarchical and ostensibly practical. Much of the teaching and learning consists of what a US or European observer would call rote learning geared to examinations. The system acts to place people in the job market and is thus both formally meritocratic (hence the stress on examinations) and fiercely competitive (hence the famous examination hell). It produces generalists whom companies can thereafter mould to their own requirements. In recent years many foreign observers have paid attention to the system and have expressed admiration – in particular with regard to its per-ceived role in development. However, many Japanese are critical of the system. Parents complain of the pressure of the examination hell, bullying at school and child suicide (where Japanese statistics are not out of line with other developed countries). Employers increasingly think that maybe a less conformist workforce would be an economic advan-tage. In sum there is concern for quality rather than simple quantity in education.

There are clear gender roles in Japan. In the urban areas it is mostly the men who go out to work (although the pattern will be rather different when the economic activity is in the small business or service sector which might involve the family more broadly (Sugimoto, 1997)). Buckley (1990) characterizes the role of the 'salaryman', those employed in large companies, in terms of the priority for men of the workplace. It is within the confines of the small work group that the salaryman finds his identity. He will expect to work late routinely and then he will socialize with his colleagues in a local restaurant or bar. At weekends he may well play golf – a routine business activity. All this has an impact on family life and Buckley (1990: 85) notes that many 'Japanese children rarely have dinner with their parents'. The key to the salaryman's life is the company. Yet, in contrast, argues Buckley (1990: 93), the role of the wife centres on the business of childrearing and homemaking. However, as the time burden of childrearing falls along with family size women increasingly have time to devote to other activities. In middle-class households the women may not work and will instead have a round of leisure activities. In less well-off households women will return to work when the children go to school. Grandparents will help with childrearing activities. Overall, this separation of gender roles is extensive: men and women tend to live rather different patterns of life. There is an appreci-ation of feminist arguments among some younger Japanese women, but activity is presently restricted to practical matters, for example, in respect of improving employment conditions and welfare such as child pro-visions. Nonetheless, in recent years the matter of gender relations has begun to shift. As the nuclear family becomes more usual and the last vestiges of the 'continuing family' which was abolished only in 1947 fade away, and as the Japanese family becomes more wealthy and new wives more assertive, the pattern of power within the household is changing. This is leading to tension between the wife and her mother or mother-in-law (who may well come to live with the couple upon reaching old age). Another area of change is with young 'office ladies' (OLs) who live at home, have jobs and a high disposable income. The spending power is the basis of a consumerist life style which is quite different from that of young women a generation ago.

The pattern of the economy determines in broad terms the nature of the patterns of working life adopted by Japanese people (Bowring and Kornicki, 1993: 250–3). The economy has a small rural agricultural sector, some fishing and other primary production and a large service sector. The manufacturing sector, which of course dominates the economy, has a dual character with a mix of very large firms surrounded by a mass of very small firms. It is in the companies of the manufacturing and service sectors that we find the stereotypical pattern of work of the salaryman. These companies present themselves as quasi-families. They offer life-time employment to their core workers who will have been recruited as young graduates, put through an induction process and thereafter be promoted on a seniority system. Basic salary may not be very good but a range of benefits will be provided (subsidized housing, canteens, travel, plus pensions and health benefits). There will be an enterprise union and company leisure provisions. The world of the company is largely male dominated. Women are employed but often in less responsible positions. Young women are expected to work for a while and then leave to have families. The process of choosing a company depends on educational record – the better the status of your university or college, the higher you can aim in respect of prestige of the company or government department.

Dore (1986) argues that the typical Japanese firm is ordered around a 'firm as community' ethos which stresses the bonds of mutual obligation of employers and employees. More broadly the firm will operate within a corporatist system which stresses the long-term view. Dore (1986) argues that this style of working is responsible for Japanese economic success and he identifies three crucial points: what he calls 'x-efficiency' which focuses on production efficiency rather than allocative market efficiency; which in turn demands a precondition in a sense that society is fair in its organization; where such fairness flows from corporatist arrangements for securing consensus on social goals rather than market arrangements. However, van Wolferen (1989) is rather more critical, although his sympathy for the 'ordinary Japanese' is not in doubt. In a discussion of the 'submissive middle class', van Wolferen (1989) argues they should be regarded as victims of the system which they serve. The culture of the salaryman sets the general tone even though they account for only 30 per cent of the working population. After recruitment to the company there are rites of passage (sometimes harsh). One becomes a member rather as one joins the military and the company expects loyalty from its recruits. The member must demonstrate this loyalty with, for example, long hours and few holidays. The whole is legitimated with reference to an ideology of firm-as-family and it is claimed that this is lodged deep within Japanese tradition – tracing back to Tokugawa and Meiji. However, van Wolferen locates the rise of familialist ideology in the 1930s when a mix of fear of labour activism and the demands of production to support the wars in China led to its widespread promulgation. The ideology resonated with earlier ideas of conformity to the group most clearly expressed in the Tokugawa political-economic use of the 'continuing family'. However, van Wolferen (1989) argues that just as the continuing family was shaped by elite concerns, so too is the present-day company family ideology. Inside the company there is little real sign of a family but instead a bullying hierarchy that demands the obedience of the salaryman who is locked into the system as there is no free labour market. With Japan's electoral system skewed to the rural areas, the urban salaryman is politically under-represented (and over-taxed). On van Wolferen's (1989) account the salaryman is caught by the system which he serves.

Individual and collectivity in Japan

It can be argued that the key concern of sociology, as one discipline within the spread of social scientific disciplines which can be taken to be lodged within or derived from the classical European tradition of social theorizing, is with elucidating the nature of the social, the notion of society. The familiar discipline of sociology has three key preoccupa-tions: social relationship (patterns of behaviour within the social realm); social structure (regular patterns of behaviour shaped by common expectations or law, that is, social institutions); social change (the ways in which patterns of behaviour change over time). One fundamental issue for sociology is the nature of the relationship of individual and collec-tivity; how it is ordered, understood and legitimated. In the process of the ongoing shift to the modern world the relationship of individual and collectivity alters in line with the changes within the economy. In the case of Japanese society, the 'corporate society', we can note that the whole system is buttressed by an ideology which stresses consensus, harmony and equality. Yet, the claims to harmony and equality do in fact disguise some significant conflict and inequality (Sugimoto, 1997).

The Tokugawa shogunate had a population which was 80 per cent peasant farmer. Worsley (1984) argues that in peasant farming the central resource is the land which is held in common, farmed by households within a village for subsistence within the household, and with surplus used for barter exchange. In Tokugawa Japan peasant farming was ordered via the system of class and caste, whereby slots within the division of labour were allocated by birth and the system of the con-tinuing family which acted as the key practical social institution of the period. An individual was born into a family and their identity and social role was determined by their membership of that family. The members of Tokugawa peasant society owed obedience to their feudal domaine lord and filial piety to their parents and family. These patterns of obedience are to the group and the lord. It has been called a vertical society (Nakane, 1970). The impact of economic change on the system was pervasive and subtle. As the economy grew in prosperity the class and caste system began to suffer tensions and to change. The artisans and merchants grew in influence and the division of labour similarly began to alter. The official system of caste began to soften. As elite groups took on debts to merchants the tensions became more severe and extensive change, precipitated by the arrival of Western traders, took place in the process of the Meiji Restoration.

The Meiji oligarchy pursued a programme of elite-sponsored economic, social and culural reform. A series of elements can be noted:

1   The abolition of class and caste so that people and families could pursue a range of livelihoods within the rapidly developing industrial economy.
2   The reworking of the continuing family as a unit within a developmental state such that the members of the family owed obedience to the general demands of the national developmental state rather than the particular requirements of a local lord.
3   The invention of a tradition of 'Japan' to replace the regional particularisms of feudal Japan: hence, obedience to authority, filial piety, the pragmatic pursuit of consensus and patriotism.
4   The construction/invention of the family state where the role of education and national military service are vehicles for the promulgation of an ideology of collective Japanese familyhood, with the emperor as the father figure.

Overall, the individual remains subsumed within a family group. However, the context of that family group has changed – from an agrarian, stable, regionally particular feudalism to an urban, industrial, national state. Thereafter, as the economic reforms of Meiji advanced, the position of the individual altered as the continuing family began to decline as the key practical social institution under the impact of economic change.

The continuing family was the key practical social institution linking persons and society in Tokugawa and Meiji and in the later phase was also the vehicle of a developmental ideology cast in terms of the family state. The practical role began to decline with the development of the industrial-capitalist system. As industrialization and the shift to the towns continued, the key role of the continuing family declined. Over the whole period from Meiji to the present day there is a shift from continuing families located in rural areas and lodged within an agrarian system to nuclear families in urban areas lodged within an industrial system. As Japan becomes ever more deeply enmeshed within the routines of the modern world, the continuing family declines. However, the shift is overlain by the peculiarities of Japanese popular ideology. First, there are the mobilizing practices of the developmental state which celebrate the continuing family as the key to social organization. This ideological celebration continues even after the practical decline of the institution and its formal legal abolition by SCAP in 1945. In other words the continuing family within the village remains as a folk memory and

official ideological image. Then there are the ideas of Japanese specialness which again invoke the rural communitarian past. All this generates
a tension cast in terms of 'Japan versus the West', but this tension is a
spurious confection. Japan has its own particular ongoing route to the
modern world and it is here that the pattern of life of contemporary
Japanese is shaped.

The pattern of life is distinctive. The matter of the relationship of
individual and collectivity has been pursued with reference to the social
institution of the family. However, we could also talk about 'personal
identity' and here the debate shifts slightly to take up the theme of the
individuality (or not) of Japanese people. The stereotypical Western view
of the Japanese stresses their personal subsumption within a spread of
groups. However, there are alternative lines of analysis:

1 Yamazaki (1994) takes issue with the claim that the Japanese are not
   individualistic and suggests that not all forms of individualism are
   coterminus with American 'rugged individualism'. He suggests that
   the Japanese affirm a 'gentle individualism' expressed within the
   context of shared aesthetic principles.
2 Clammer (1995) argues for the centrality of the ethical commitment to
   harmony within Japanese society, a commitment that colours all
   social relationships and leaves individuality to be secured and
   expressed within these parameters in the multiplicity of ongoing
   social relations.

In contemporary Japan the demands of the group in respect of the
individual are still significant. In general the shift to the modern world
has been associated with the sharp diminution of ascribed status and the
rise of achieved status. In Japan we can make the following points:

1 The continuing family was abolished by SCAP.
2 Women were given legal and political equality with men within the
   context of a modern constitutional state.
3 Thereafter, we note that the ethic of the continuing family continues,
   albeit with much more fluidity and a drift towards nuclear families,
   especially in urban areas.
4 The group remains crucial within Japanese social life and the Meiji
   ideal of firm-as-family remains widely affirmed.

Overall, the relationship of individual and collectivity within modern
Japan has run through a series of phases which have in common that
the ethic of the subordination of the individual to the needs of the
group is still affirmed. The practical expression of the affirmation of this
ethic shifts and changes as the practical circumstances within which it
must be expressed themselves change. It is all rather Durkheimian: as

the economy advances and as patterns of social solidarity change, the relationship of individual to group is reaffirmed.

Ideology of the 'corporate society' considered

Japan is a deeply ordered society. The analysis of Japanese society has generated often sharp debate. There are many unsympathetic Western commentators who argue that the social system reveals a loss of individuality in dull conformity, but we can set these complaints aside. A more familiar route into these matters is offered by sympathetic commentators who take the system to be harmonious (in both operation and result) and fair (in both operation and result).

The ideology of harmony and equality expresses a complex package which we can schematically undo. It is argued that Japan is an island nation (geographical determinism); the Japanese are an homogeneous people (ethnic determinism); and Japanese psychology favours groups (psychological determinism) – all of which adds up to a claim for a natural base for harmony. It is further argued that Japan is a meritocratic country where reward is a matter of effort and natural difference (eugenic determinism), and this offers a naturally given base for fairness in social arrangements. Finally it is argued that the Japanese language is both very special and intimately linked to Japanese culture (linguistic and cultural determinism), which offers a natural basis for separateness. The package thus claims that Japan is a uniquely harmonious society as a result of a series of natural factors and that it is an egalitarian society because as a meritocracy everyone has opportunity. Finally critics are blocked by an assertion of the ineffable language-carried specialness of Japanese culture (thus critics cannot really understand).

A series of comments can be offered in regard to this ideological package:

1 Social science typically does not accept treatments of social behaviour which offer non-social explanations of social behaviour – and consequently the appeals to various determinisms in respect of Japan are not persuasive.
2 Social science is typically in favour of open debate and looks suspiciously at ideological discourses (most especially when they are making a rhetorical move to present their value-based claims as natural and thus neutral and technical). Consequently the appeals to the given basis of Japanese culture are viewed sceptically from the outset.
3 Social science notes that in Japan the standard claim to naturally given harmony and fairness is false – and to show this we can consider the two issues of conflict (harmony) and inequality (fairness).

The issue of conflict and inequality can be pursued in three areas: the distribution of income and wealth; the status of minorities; and the status of women.

INCOME, WEALTH AND TAX REGIMES   Eccleston (1989) considers the nature of social division in Japan. A series of questions can be raised about income, wealth and tax regimes. It is difficult to measure the pattern of income as data are incomplete. In the case of salarymen it is good, less so for small business men, quite unclear for savings bank accounts except for global figures and thoroughly obscure for the informal economy. Yet on the basis of data available it seems to be rather like other developed countries, that is, fairly egalitarian. It is more difficult to measure wealth – assets must be valued in the form of stocks, objects and in particular land – yet available data suggest wide inequality, particularly around the issue of land ownership. These two factors are further shaped by the different nature of work in the core and peripheral areas of the economy. The tax system shapes the ways in which given income and wealth may be deployed.

Compared with the situation prior to the Pacific War the spread of income and wealth is more equal as a result of the expropriation of rural landlords and family-owned zaibatsu. However, there are still significant differences which affect life chances (including education and job chances which are central to the meritocracy claims). We can identify a series of 'economic locations': land owners and stock holders, large business managers, salary earners, small business people, wage earners, unskilled day labourers, and thereafter the misfits and petty criminals. All of this is of course further skewed by gender and treatment of minorities. In brief, it is quite clear that the core ideological claims to equality and harmony must be qualified as the system is unequal and this does occasion conflict (Eccleston, 1989; Sugimoto, 1997).

MINORITIES   A standard ideological claim in respect of the Japanese is that they are a homogeneous nation. But this is not true as there have been waves of immigration over the centuries from the mainland and at the present time there are clearly identified minorities (Bowring and Kornicki, 1993: 241–4). The minorities include burakumin, Koreans, the Ainu of Hokkaido and the inhabitants of the Ryukyu islands.

In the first case, the burakumin, these people originate as a Tokugawa period outcast group when they were involved in economic activities involving animals and waste which were regarded as ritually unclean. The status was formally abolished in 1870 but continued modified in practice down to the present day where their social role is still somewhat marginal In the post-World War II period barukumin tended to live separately in the poor parts of town. Only in the middle 1960s did the government take some steps to ameliorate their position. In the 1990s the situation is much improved, yet the discrimination still continues and burakumin tend to find their life chances restricted. The estimates for numbers are unreliable as people are reluctant to declare this status and figures range from 1.5 million to 3.0 million. Second, there is a post-colonial population of Koreans in Japan who were born and raised in the country. They number approximately 1.0 million, do not hold citizenship (in Japan this is based on descent rather than residence) and must register as foreigners. They have restricted welfare and job rights and tend to work in the lower reaches of the job market. In a similar way, the people of the Ryukyu islands to the south of Japan were colonized in the late nineteenth century and held by the USA until the late 1960s. They too are regarded as somewhat second-class Japanese. Finally, the Ainu are a small population of indigenes living in Hokkaido. They have had rights since the late nineteenth century but are treated as second-class citizens. They number approximately 25,000, have poor jobs and receive little sympathy for claims in respect of 'traditional culture'. In other words, overall, there is systematic discrimination against sections of the long-established resident population and so life chances are not equal (and this again includes education and jobs, the key of the ideology of meritocracy).

GENDER   In the European tradition of social science there is a commitment to an idea of progress which claims, among other things, that as civilization proceeds there will be a shift from ascribed to achieved status. In practical terms this means that the presence of extensive ascribed status must be counted as cutting against individual achievement and choice and meritocratic achievement – thus acting to diminish equality of life chances. In Japan the position of women is very much a matter of ascribed status. The standard data in resepct of the situation of women in Japan are reviewed by Eccleston (1989: 177–94) who notes a pattern of systematic discrimination.

The standard model of the development of gender relations in Europe involves the dynamics of family and work in the process of the shift to the modern industrial-capitalist world. In particular, the rise of industrial forms of life saw the separation of dwellingplace and workplace and the related development of a spread of familiar gender divisions.

In agrarian societies the dwellingplace and the workplace are one and the same. In pre-industrial societies the key social and economic institution was the household, which was a unit of production and consumption. It was the key social space within which individuals operated. In general, the task of child rearing would mark the gender role of women. Thereafter, the business of working a peasant farm did not involve any functionally distinct tasks which could imply different roles for men and women. In this sense gender divisions within the work sphere were made within an essentially undifferentiated work sphere – farming is farming is farming.

In industrial societies the dwellingplace and the workplace are separate. The activities carried out within the dwellingplace are distinct from those carried out within the workplace. The role of childbearing and childrearing remained with women. In addition a spread of tasks developed, often inspired by the leisured lives of elite-class women (themselves determined by the social dynamics of the elite classes), which together constituted the domestic realm. In the shift to the modern industrial world this domestic realm became the female realm. The new world of work within factories became restricted to men (and in the nineteenth century the access which women had to this sphere was denied them on social reform arguments). Thereafter, in the twentieth century, there has been a slow process of reform to this pattern and a shift towards more equality.

In Tokugawa Japan the inherited model of the social role of women stressed the two roles of procreation and serving men. A woman had three obediences: to father, husband and son. There was change in the Meiji period with an initial enthusiasm for Western ideals of equality. However, this did not last as the drive for modernization from above gathered pace. In this context a traditional model of the appropriate role of women was reaffirmed.

In Meiji the patriarchal family state made women legally second class. Prostitution was legal and widespread. However, in the late nineteenth century there were many small reform groups, inspired by the political reforms which had been put in place by the Meiji government, and in the early twentieth century the socialist movement was influential. However, these were both the province of women from the elite classes and from artists and intellectuals and had little general impact. Indeed, in the 1930s the patriotic societies' supportive of the status quo recruited millions of women – who were slowly drawn into supporting the military.

The SCAP administration made important reforms: the continuing family was abolished; the patriarchal civil code was overhauled and women were given legal equality; the constitution was rewritten and women were given political equality; and legalized prostitution was discouraged and in 1956 prohibited. Yet the immediate post-World War II period saw little practical change as the population was preoccupied with the reconstruction of war damage. A little later, in the 1970s, under the influence of the rise of feminism in the West, laws prohibiting discrimination against women in the economy were passed but are not rigorously applied.

Today, women look to the domestic sphere and their role is that of homemaker and mother. They have authority within the domestic sphere and men are content with this, as are most women. In the workplace there is systematic routine discrimination against women. The political consciousness of women seems to have been displaced and they are active in the PTA and in certain civic organizations such as consumerism and the environment. Commentators suggest that little will change without the political elite giving a lead on this matter. It is also added that there is no sign of such a lead being given.

Finally, an intriguing lexicographic and ethnographic route into the matter of gender relations is taken by Kittredge Cherry (1997) who makes a glossary of colloquial terms used to capture the relationships of men and women. We can note a sample.

1   A 'daughter-in-a-box' is how a young unmarried women will be characterized. It recalls the way in which Japanese are careful to place precious objects in boxes to protect them. This concern for welfare and morals leads to young women leading somewhat sheltered lives. However, as times change so too are the connotations of the expression, now it can mean over-protected and unworldly.
2   'Mrs Interior' is the term used to designate a married woman. It points to her status as homemaker and housekeeper and derives from pre-modern times when only the wives of the rich were able to stay indoors rather than working outside. Some Japanese feminists have tried to substitute the term life partner but this has not proved widely popular. Many husbands and wives will address each other as mother/father thus stressing the child-rearing focus of familyhood.
3   An 'office lady' is the term which covers women who work in offices. It was picked out in a national competition in a magazine to replace 'business girl' which had fallen out of favour. An office lady will do all the general clerical jobs around the office. A sub-species is the 'office flower' who will be young and pretty and whose duties are mostly making tea and looking decorative.
4   The marital relationship of salaryman and wife is noted in the expression 'food, bath and bed!' which are supposed to be the three words which the salaryman utters to his wife when he finally returns late in the evening.
5   A 'cockroach husband' expresses the view that the kitchen is the women's preserve, and that a man in the kitchen is as useful as a cockroach. When the salaryman finally retires to spend much more time in a home which he may not have seen a great deal of over his working life he will be called 'giant garbage', like an old washing machine or refrigerator, in the way and useless.
6   When widowhood comes around she will become a 'not yet dead person', implying that with husband and family gone she is now redundant and merely awaiting death.

Social control in overview

The classical European tradition of social theorizing is concerned with the analysis of complex change in the shift to the modern world. The substantive work is macro-structural and historical in style. The shift of

Japan to the modern world has been considered in terms of the exchange of the internal dynamics of the country and the impacts of the external developing global system. In this present section related micro-sociological material has been noted, in particular the question of the relationship of individual and collectivity. A closely related set of issues centre upon the processes of recruitment to the system, its routine ordering and the matter of securing formal social order, in brief: education, work and deviancy.

EDUCATION   We can take the role of education to encompass three related matters: social skills, practical skill and social control. In Tokugawa Japan there was significant educational provision and all three issues were addressed. In Meiji Japan the same holds broadly, although the educational system was overhauled and made into an adjunct of the developmental society – both in the provision of technical skills and in the promulgation of the new national ideology of the emperor system. In the post-war period SCAP reformed the system in line with the US model. The militarist and nationalist ideas within the system were removed. Overall, the realm of education is contentious and some critics suggest it is over-regimented, over-examined and oriented too closely to the demands of industry and commerce. Other critics suggest that the system remains a vehicle for nationalist sentiment. Yet the practical outcome is an educated and disciplined population.

WORK   The issue of work can be approached in two ways: in the context of discussions about the Japanese economic system; and in the context of discussion of the micro-sociological details of the patterns of peoples lives. The second concerns us here (the first will crop up later).

The workplace, along with its demands and routines, provides people with three main rewards: it is a source of access to the social world – we earn money and we can join in; it is a source of structure in the guise of the daily routine of life; and it is a major source of identity and self-esteem. There are some negative features. The demands of the system within which the workplace will be lodged can override the needs of the individual – alienation or anomie. The practical counterpart of the trio of ideas noted above is found in the experience of unemployment – loss of access, pattern and esteem.

The basic patterns of work are different in the USA, Europe and Japan. In the USA the workplace is an element of a liberal market system with an homogeneous economic space and individual mobility. In Europe the workplace is an element of a social market sytem with a broadly homogeneous economic space, individual mobility and extensive social welfare provision. In Japan the workplace is an element of a state-ordered market system with an heterogeneous economic space supporting a strong community ethos.

The Japanese economy has a series of sectors: farming; large firm; small firm; retail/service sector; and state. These sectors sustain typical forms of life:

1 Farming is the province of family firms and part-time farming.
2 The large firm sector is the province of the salaryman and office lady.
3 The small firm sector is the province of family firms.
4 The retail/service sector is the province of the family firm.
5 The state is the province of the competitive, exam-recruited, career bureaucrat.

In addition, there would be an informal sector of day labourers, gangsters and petty criminals. Overall, notwithstanding the lengthy recession of the 1990s, the economy has been very successful and runs at a very low unemployment rate. The people work long hours and the standard criticism revolves around the idea that Japan has made a rich country but has poor people.

CRIME The central mechanisms of social control are found within the routines of social life where a variety of sanctions act to secure adherence to social rules. The state thereafter additionally shapes social behaviour through extensive intentional regulation. The state further establishes the criminal justice system which acts to enforce both civil and criminal legal codes. It is in this last noted sphere that we find discussion of deviancy and crime. Japan has a very low recorded crime rate compared with other developed countries. The explanations offered for these results include:

(a) an efficient neighbourhood-based police force;
(b) an effcient prosecution service and judiciary;
(c) a culture of conformity;
(d) a society suffused with a soft authoritarianism (and there are debates about civil liberties and police powers).

The police have a presence in every sub-department of every city and town. The local police will visit each household once a year and there will be a neighbourhood police box. The police are apparently tolerant of minor misdemeanours which can be cleared up with an apology or expression of regret. With other more serious crime their powers of interrogation are quite generous. Most wrongdoers are eventually convicted on the basis of confessions and often they will surrender themselves and confess.

Finally, one curious feature of the Japanese system is the presence of semi-acknowledged gangster groups, the yakuza. It has been argued both that they act to keep order in their local territories in unofficial connivance with the police and that they have links to politicians and bureaucrats (Saga, 1987). The system has its critics, with van Wolferen (1989) speaking of a semi-police state.

The harmonious and equal corporate society

The social system is divided in many ways into strata and groups who thereafter have different life chances (Sugimoto, 1997). The harmony of the society depends upon routine pursuasion (school, work and media) and the equality also depends on routine persuasion (school, work and media) and selective blindness towards minorities. It may be argued that the ideology survives because there is no functioning critical public sphere. In the absence of a critical public discourse, existing patterns of conflict and inequality continue to be disregarded. However, there is one final thought which cuts against any confident Western-centred summary judgement: we should be careful not to replace geographical, ethnic and other determinisms with a cultural determinism. The ideology of harmony and fairness does not deterministically shape Japanese society, rather it offers people a way of reading their circumstances. The ideas thread their way through social activity – a mix of mystification and structuration – as people make and remake their own lives (Clammer, 1995, 1997).

Contemporary Japanese polity

After the debacle of the military defeat in 1945 Japan was occupied and the political system remade by SCAP. The extent to which the real as opposed to formal system was remade is a matter of some debate, with less orthodox critics pointing to a significant measure of continuity with pre-war days and outright radicals suggesting that the Americans virtually resurrected the pre-war elite in order to secure Japan as an ally in their confrontation with 'world communism'. Hunter (1989: 11) notes that the 'occupation policy had two stated objectives: demilitarization and democratization'. Now it is clear, remarks Hunter (1989: 12) that the occupation largely failed in its own terms as the reverse course was adopted and that present success in Japan owes much to long-established patterns of life.

The view of Japanese political life among US and other Western scholars has been mixed. E.H. Norman had writtten just before the war using Marxist analyses that the authoritarian fascism was inherent in the structures established by Meiji. Others came to see the Pacific War as an abberation, a notion popular in the context of Cold War. Hunter (1989: 13) comments that the debate on the nature of the Japanese situation has been coloured by events in the West:

In the frenzied atmosphere of the Cold War and its aftermath, historical research on Japan was strongly influenced by political imperatives. The Pacific

War was viewed less as a failure brought about by long-term institutional factors and class and other divisions within society. Instead Japan's modern development was seen in more positive terms. Japan was a country which had achieved 'modernization', which could offer a model to other industrializing nations; the militarism and aggression of the 1930s was an abberation, explicable largely in political terms, the ability of a small group to turn back the liberal trends of the twenties.

If we review the particular route to the modern political world taken by Japan we can consider how changing sets of material circumstances have generated ideological, institutional and actual patterns of power. First, in Meiji Japan the ideology was oriented to catching up with the West and the institutions were those of the family state and power flowed from the oligarchy. Second, in 1930s Japan the ideology was nationalist and the institutions were those of the militarized family state with power centred on the armed forces. Third, in post-war Japan the ideology was liberal-democrat, the institutions were those of a developmental state and power centred on the iron triangle of bureaucracy, business and politicians. Thereafter, in making an overall summary judgement of Japan, we should note, first, that culturalists suggest that Japan is fundamentally refractory to outside judgement and that, having rejected this position, it is the case that from the available spread of notions – democratic, liberal, liberal-democratic, etc. – that Japan looks to be corporatist and perhaps communitarian. In this section we will begin with the orthodox view, before taking note of some of the influential critics.

An orthodox view of the Japanese polity

The standard analytical machineries of Western political science – constitutions, institutions, parties and electoral behaviour, all read in terms of theories of pluralism – offer Japan as a liberal democracy.

The Meiji constitution was promulgated in 1889 in the name of the emperor (Bowring and Kornicki, 1993: 280–3). It borrowed from French law and Prussian state theory and was the vehicle of Japan's late modernization drive. In the Meiji constitution sovereignty resided with the emperor and power was exercised by a modern state apparatus in his name with the advice of an unofficial grouping of 'elder statesmen' called the Genro. The Meiji constitution was rather vague as to lines of authority and responsibility and when the generation of leaders who had made the revolution from above left the scene the system rather drifted apart as the various factions of the overall state machine manoeuvred against each other for position. The military slowly gained power and in time precipitated war with the USA. This led to a new constitution. The constitution of 1947 was imposed by SCAP and is a variant of the familiar liberal-democratic patterns of the West. The emperor is symbol of state and power resides in the people and is exercised via a popularly elected bi-cameral parliament, the highest body in the state, which is led by a cabinet under a prime minister. The spheres of state and church are separate (and state Shinto was abolished). The judiciary is independent. Article 9 renounces the right of the state to wage war. The constitution is popular according to opinion polls. There have been periodic attempts to revise it by disgruntled rightwingers but thus far none have succeeded (Stockwin, 1999: 162–79).

The bi-cameral parliament consists of a House of Representatives (the lower house) and a House of Councillors (the upper house). The lower house is the main house and the upper house is a revising house. The government is drawn from parliament and the constitution provides for cabinet government on the British model. A prime minister selects his ministers and all are acknowledged by the emperor and approved (or not) by parliament. They sit in the lower house and a version of the familiar tripartite system of executive, legislative and judiciary is in use. However, as Stockwin (1999) makes clear, a key institution is the bureaucracy. The civil service is an elite which may be accessed by merit via competitive examinations (Bowring and Kornicki (1993: 288–98). The present system was set up in 1894 and remains in essentials intact. Relatedly, the judiciary, which was radically reorganized after 1945 so as to ensure its independence from the executive, is responsible to a Supreme Court which has a constitutional status equivalent to that of the executive and parliament. The Supreme Court is the pinnacle of the whole apparatus of law.

In the period since the Meiji restoration there has been a rich stock of political parties (Stockwin, 1999). In general they have been parties of the right – and parties of the left have been variously controlled or repressed. In the post-World War II era, after an early period of political movement, the LDP was formed in 1955 and has remained the dominant party in Japanese politics ever since.

The system has had vote inequalities built in and tolerated. Thus rural constituencies have been much smaller than urban constituencies. One vote in a rural area could have had the same weight as five or six in an urban area – in other words the urban areas of Japan (a notably urban country) were under-represented in parliament. In 1994 a new system was brought in by the Hosokawa government. The electoral reforms have ameliorated this situation and the discrepancy is now such that a rural vote is worth only double that of an urban vote (Stockwin, 1999: 128), but Stockwin (1999: 131) suggests that it has had surprisingly little impact. In particular, it is extremely expensive to run an election campaign and thereafter maintain a local office in the constituency. This has contributed to an insatiable demand for money by politicians, an aspect of 'money politics'.

The emergence of interest groups on a large scale is a post-World War II phenomenon (Bowring and Kornicki, 1993: 288). The following might be noted: trades unions, farmers groups, large and small business, professional groups and other employment categories, and many other social and cultural groups. All these groups can lobby parliament and in turn many parliamentarians belong to special parliamentary groups which follow the concerns of specific sections of the population. All these groups can feed information and seek support among parliamentarians. They have diverse goals: patronage, subsidy, licences, price supports, finance and so on, which all tend to be pragmatic.

Relatedly, popular protest (Bowring and Kornicki, 1993: 269) is another way of trying to influence local or central government. Thus, there were peasant rebellions in the Tokugawa period. There was manoeuvring by lords in court politics and during the Meiji period there were protests against land tax reforms. There was popular movement for democratization and in the wake of the Russo-Japanese war there was protest against the terms of the treaty. Similarly, in the Taisho democracy period there was much political protest and a popular movement for universal male suffrage. During the post-World War II period in the early SCAP years there were many social protest movements. However, with the onset of Cold War these declined. Subsequently there have been various outbreaks of protest – against pollution, against the US–Japan security treaties, against the Vietnam War, against Narita airport, and so on. However, since the 1970s such public protests have rather faded away.

A favourable commentary

A conventional commentary on the Japanese political system would say that over the post-World War II period it has worked remarkably well. It would be suggested that attention to the general condition of the country reveals that the political system has ensured stability and extensive citizen involvement via local parliamentarians and has pursued a successful spread of economic, social and international policies. In brief, it would be argued that Japan is a successful polity possessed of an equally successful economy. An early and influential version of this line of argument was presented by Vogel (1980), who took the view that Japan was an interesting case study for sociologists interested in ordered change because it had twice been self-consciously reconstructed: in the Meiji and SCAP periods. Vogel notes the post-World War II economic track record of Japan and details the usual features of this process of modernization. The upshot is taken to be a knowledge-based, post-industrial society. On the basis of his analysis Vogel concludes by urging the USA to become a little less individualistic and a little more collectivistic.

Vogel (1980) reports that there is a routine concern for education in Japan: both formal, in school, where there is considerable commitment to achievement read as a collective rather than simply individual responsibility, and continuing in the form of study groups, seminars, study tours and the like, all of which are undertaken by companies, politicians and the bureaucracy. The role of knowledge finds its expected post-industrial deployment in the role of the bureaucracy. The bureaucracy has a directive role within Japanese political economy and society and Vogel notes that it is meritocratic and powerful. The bureaucrats network with senior politicians and businessmen. Within this elite consensus emerges in respect of the overall direction of state and economic policy and thereafter administrative guidance is pragmatic, knowledgeable and oriented to the agreed overarching goal of economic expansion. The goals of economic advance are pursued within the context of Japan's distinctive company system with its long termism in respect of employment, investment and market presence.

Vogel goes on to argue that Japan could be regarded as substantively democratic as interests are expressed via group membership: village; neighbourhood; school; work; and clubs and societies. All these groups feed ideas, views and requests into the formal political system at local, regional and national levels. Vogel adds that business groups operate in the same way. In general, it is suggested, the metaphor for politics is not a US notion of 'fair play' but instead 'fair shares'. This may be regarded as disposition to a social inclusiveness and in the field of welfare this finds expression in a decentralized system of local provision, charities, companies and families. Overall the system is driven by a corporatist rather than liberal ethic.

In later years the line of argument evidenced by Vogel has called forth a series of negative replies, all of which one way or another make vehement criticisms of the Japanese model as economically restrictive, socially limiting and politically repressive (Eccleston, 1989: 88–90). We will set such material aside. What is clear is that judgements about the Japanese political system get bound up with wider judgements about the relationship of polity and economy (and this turns out to be a par-ticular concern for Western orthodox economists). Yet the lines of commentary are not clear. In general what the theorists sympathetic to Japan's corporatism try to say is that while the system is fine in regard to production, it under-rewards those who man the system and that a necessary condition of an improved pattern of life is political reform so as to shift power away from the present iron triangle towards the general population. On the other hand, those unsympathetic to ideas of cor-poratism call for nothing less than the wholesale liberalization of the Japanese economy and thereafter the better satisfaction of Japanese consumers (*Economist*, 1994).

Standard criticisms and problems

There are a number of familiar lines of criticism of the Japanese political system. Stockwin (1999: 66) points to 'revisionist theorists', Karel van Wolferen, Clyde Prestowitz, Chalmers Johnson and James Fallows, who

offer a variety of critical analyses (which have in common a rejection of
the complacency of orthodox US work) that move away from the idea
that Japan is a liberal democracy. A series of issues are presented:

1   The political system (organization and electoral system) is taken to be
    defective.
2   The bureaucrats are taken to be too powerful.
3   The judiciary is taken to be lacking in independence.
4   The politicians too riddled with faction fighting.
5   The system has fostered a pragmatic politics of material gain whereby
    each parliamentary representative must look after his constituency in
    simple pork barrel fashion.
6   The business of politics has become dominated by access to resources,
    hence 'money politics'.
7   The system has delivered power to the LDP for most of the post-war
    period and they have become profoundly corrupt and now prefer to
    service their various networks rather than give a lead to the country.

In other words, the political system does not work to express the
common concerns of the population, rather it is the vehicle of sectional
interests competing pragmatically for a share of available resources.

A striking analysis has been made by van Wolferen (1989) who argues,
overall, that the nature of the shift to the modern world made by
the Japanese has issued in an informally ordered system wedded to the
pursuit of security via economic growth. The system is not a formal state
and nor is it under any guiding political control. Political power suffuses
the system, which disguises its character via propaganda in respect of
the uniqueness of Japan. But the key to grasping the nature of Japan is
power – it is diffused through the system and nowhere clearly account-
able. The system grew from the Meiji period, found chaotic expression in
the militarism of the 1930s and continues in all essentials today. In effect
there is no state, rather there are shifting patterns of alliances between a
multitude of players in the bureaucracy, business, politics and pressure
groups. It looks like a liberal democratic system, and all say that it is, but
it is not.

The Japanese ruling class comprises the top ranks of bureaucracy,
business and politicians. It is a ruling class of administrators and there is
fairly open recruitment. They are wedded to the continuity of the system.
If Japan has a political debate then it takes place inside this class, which
is results rather than rules focused – money, politics and pork-barrelling
predominate. The role of politicians in regard to the population is to act
as a channel to secure material gains. It has been this way ever since
Meiji. The effective absence of a formal state means that the system
absorbs everyone. There is no formally established sphere (a public
sphere, or other institutionally distinct sphere) from which the system
can be criticized. Hence people are absorbed and conformist, while

pressure groups are coopted. In rural Japan the agricultural cooperatives are the key agents of cooption and in urban Japan the company unions. The general relationship within the political sphere construed broadly is one of patron–client. The system works, but only if you opt into it – one cannot be both a critic and a client.

The routines of social control which act to maintain the boundaries of the system are thoroughly effective. In the family the stress is on obedience and achievement and this is repeated in school. In the world of work a similar requirement is evidenced, nothwithstanding official ideas of work as family. More general agents of social control such as police and media similarly contribute to a culture of conformity. The system is thereafter extensively buttressed by an ideology of 'Japanese uniqueness' which reports on present arrangements as evidencing acultural givens of Japanese character and mentality and thus blocks critical reflection, and the few who do rebel get nowhere. Once inside the system it all makes sense.

In the end van Wolferen concludes that the system is successful in its own terms, but that these terms are quite particular to the system. The Japanese people are as much its beneficiaries and victims at home as are their trading partners overseas. The system cannot grasp either the costs to ordinary Japanese or the tensions caused overseas by its trading practices. Any change would require extensive reworking of the economy, society and culture and is thus very unlikely. The first move in such a sequence of changes would have to be political reform in Japan.

Reforms of the 1990s

The Japanese trade surplus with the USA was addressed in the 1985 Plaza Accord which revalued the yen against the US dollar. In the event the problems of the trade imbalance and the diplomatic friction which attended it were not solved. But the revalued yen did contribute to rapid economic growth in Japan and the region. Henshall (1999: 170) reports that price inflation became severe from late 1989 and the Bank of Japan raised interests sharply. The Japanese bubble was ended and the economy went into a sustained recession in the early 1990s. The government has made repeated efforts to stimulate new growth but the economy has continued to record very low growth rates. Sheridan (1998b: 9) argues that the Japanese economy 'underwent a period of chaos following the collapse of the speculative boom in 1991'.

The popular reaction was highly critical. In 1993 the LDP failed to win a majority in the lower house elections and its period of rule, which had lasted 38 years, came to an end. There was a period of intense political activity and reforms to the electoral and party systems were made. These reforms seem to have generated little significant change. However, Sheridan (1998b: 9) reports that by 'mid-1996 the [economic] situation had been brought under control, but industries and households have been left with the task of trying to recover their financial losses. All this has fuelled the general public's anxiety about the economic management of the country and the future prospects of society.'

Sheridan (1998b: 10) comments that while these anxieties are familiar within advanced industrial-capitalist countries, 'what sets Japan's case apart is the sudden appearance of this fear about the future prospects of the economy in the population in general'. Sheridan adds (1998b: 11) that while it is true that the Japanese face the task of reordering their economy (as a consequence of the effects of the bubble and also because the economy has shifted from capital poor and labour rich to capital rich and labour poor), a rational debate is presently pre-empted by 'a simplistic nationwide cry for deregulation of the economy, as if the removal of public control and guidance will create market competition which will then act as a panacea for the country's economic ills'.

Contemporary Japanese culture

In this section we will consider the ways in which the people of Japan read and react to those structural patterns which enfold their lives. The notion of culture will come to the fore. We can approach the idea of culture in several ways (Bauman, 1976):

(a) culture as praxis – which stresses the importance of the ordinary pattern of life of people and suggests that it is here that one can find the living culture of the people;
(b) culture as form of life – which stresses the general sets of beliefs which are espoused or evidenced in behaviour;
(c) culture as acquired manners – which stresses the idea that culture is something one acquires in social learning;
(d) culture as art.

We can also note that there is a series of ways in which 'culture' can be located and characterized within the social realm, often via dichotomous constructs:

(a) great tradition/little tradition – which points to the realm of formal and informal religious ideas;
(b) sacred/profane – which points to the sources, status and uses of knowledges;
(c) high culture/low culture – which points to the difficulty of acquisition of an appreciation of art works (and makes a status claim);
(d) refined/popular (or commercial) – which points to acquisition and status;

(e) elite/folk – which points to the social base of patterns of art and recreation;
(f) official ideology/mass ideology – which points to the realm of political culture which repeats these distinctions with its own substantive concerns.

The material on culture fits into this discussion of Japan in the following very broad way: where we have been dealing with structural analyses of Japan via a notion of corporatism, we now need to deal with an agent-centred strategy. By looking at the notion of 'culture' we can get some idea of how people read and react to the structures which enfold them. The material we now treat focuses on how people construe their own local and domestic circumstances. In other words, system and persons are linked via sets of ideas and practices, or culture.

The standard material of great traditions and the arts

The notion of great tradition designates those sets of formally elaborated ideas (doctrines) and institutionally embodied ideas (shrines and temples) which have authorized spokespersons (priests) and which relate to either the world of the spirits and humankind's relation to the spirit world, or to the ethically proper patterns of behaviour of humankind. The related idea of little traditions points to the informal patterns of belief affirmed by ordinary people. These ideas can generate an overview of religion in Japan (Bowring and Kornicki, 1993: 152–80).
  Shinto is the original folk religion of Japan, predating Buddhism and Confucianism. The term covers a spread of ideas which were originally rather distinct. The religion is focused on 'this world', with the spirit world as a non-moral realm of spirits who are called upon for assistance in this world. The key deities are known as kami and can be taken to be understood as manifestations of impersonal power. The kami inhabit a realm of their own and can be invoked to assist in the practical problems of this world. They can also be called to particular places – thus the village shrine. The spirits of the dead are known as tama. This spirit lodges within a person when alive and withdraws when the person falls ill or dies. Upon death the spirit must be acknowledged for 33 years, after which it fuses with the common family ancestor. As with kami, the tama can be asked for practical assistance in this world. Later, with the arrival of Buddhism in Japan in about the sixth century, Shinto underwent changes as it often fused with Buddhist teachings, and the kami were taken to be manifestations of Buddha.
  In the Tokugawa period there was an alternative move to fuse Shinto and Confucianism in order better to discipline the population to the will of the ruling elite. This tendency was accentuated in the Meiji period when the state endeavoured to purge Shinto of Buddhist teachings in order to create a State Shinto which served elite-specified goals of

national development with the cult of the emperor made central. State Shinto was abolished in 1945 by SCAP, but Shinto continues as the folk religion of Japan.

Buddhism arrived from India in about the sixth century. Unlike Shinto, which was pragmatic and outward looking, Buddhism stressed the inward nature of humankind. Having diagnosed the self-centred desires of ordinary life as the source of illusion and pain, Buddhism pointed to enlightenment as the goal of austere, disciplined reflection. When the religion arrived in Japan it did so in the specific version of Mahayana Buddhism which stressed that enlightenment was widely available to those who acknowledged any one of a spread of lesser deities and who recited appropriate prayers or sutras. In the period from the sixth to the seventeenth century Buddhism spread throughout much of Japan and the temples became centres of power and learning. As noted above, the Tokugawa rulers brought religion under control and the influence of Buddhism began to decline. However, in time Buddhism in Japan took on a range of pastoral duties which served the local people, even if they had little to do with the original teachings (thus burial services, aiding the sick, finding a bride, safety from traffic accidents). Several austere forms emerged which were oriented to enlightenment, for example, Zen Buddhism. Overall, in contemporary Japan, Shinto and Buddhism operate as background beliefs, whereas Confucianism works more as a set of rules of behaviour or moral precepts (Hunter, 1989: 185).

In the fifth century BC a minor Chinese official, Confucius, attempted to provide a scheme for good government at a time of civil wars. The proposal he made was for an hierarchical society in which all knew their role and dutifully fulfilled it by offering obedience upwards and extending protection downwards. The acquisition of the relevant knowledge of system and duties was attained via learning and was a matter of becoming cultured. The overall package is humanist, although it clearly can be presented as a legitimation of a bureaucratically ordered society. In the following centuries both aspects have been variously presented. Confucianism seems to have arrived in Japan in the sixth century when it was used in early state formation (Yamato state). In the medieval period from the twelfth to sixteenth centuries there was extensive warfare and Confucianism was not widely influential, in contrast to Buddhism. However, in China there was a revival of the original humanist side of the doctrines and these subsequently did have some influence. In the Tokugawa period these ideas were once again picked up as they offered justifications for elite-led bureaucratic rule, but once again the doctrines were not very influential or widely disseminated. After the Meiji Restoration Confucianism faded away, only to be quietly revived in the early years of this century. In brief, the doctrines seem to be somewhat marginal to the mainstreams of Japanese religion, notwithstanding the borrowings of some of the terminology in respect of hierarchies and filial piety.

Christianity has never been widely influential in Japan. The core doctrines of Christianity – salvation, responsibility, monotheism – did not sit well with the indigenous religious ideas and the stress on personal salvation did not appeal to the Japanese ruling elites who were accustomed to viewing religion as a source of social control. Add to this the link between Christianity and the incoming and unwanted modern world and there is scope for cultural misfit and secular conflict.

Finally, there is a series of 'New Religions' which take the form of large sects (Bowring and Kornicki, 1993: 175). They made their first appearance in the early nineteenth century, then again in the early twentieth century, with a third wave in the post-World War II period. The doctrines of these New Religions, some 3,000 of them, are various but they seem to revolve around an affirmation of 'traditional Japanese values': culture, harmony, filial piety, sincerity, modesty, diligence. The character of these organizations is distinctly oriented towards 'social welfare'. They provide social and educational centres for their members, who are mainly women drawn from the respectable petty bourgeoisie.

It is within the arts that we encounter one area of critical self-reflection which is undertaken by societies (Bowring and Kornicki, 1993: 122–49). In the early periods of history art work was a matter for the secular and divine elites and works of art were often bound up with religious or secular authority. However, as the modern world developed, from around the Tokugawa period, the nature of art changed and became at first more popular and thereafter a mass product. In making this shift, art work became both widely available and oriented to entertainment. On the basis of the arguments of Anderson (1983), all this is part of the process of the constitution by 'print capitalism' of those 'reading publics' which were the basis of subsequent nation formation. In the con-temporary world the role of the arts has been supplemented and maybe superseded by the role of the mass media.

Before the seventeenth century pictorial art was bound up with religion and secular power – hence paintings and poetry in respect of deities and lords. Sculpture was also used by these elites. As peace returned after the establishment of Tokugawa there was a call for genre painting from the new elites to decorate their houses (crowds, fairs, floating world images). Only towards the end of the period was there any exchange with Western art – an exchange that came as a surprise to both parties. In the Meiji period there was much borrowing from the West and a huge demand from Europe and the USA for Japanese art (screens, lacquer boxes, ceramics; Wilkinson, 1991). Over the period there was a slow change as elite exclusivity declined in the face of increasing mass involvement.

Performing art in Japan centres on theatre and there are four classical traditions: noh (fourteenth-century stylized symbolic musical drama); kyogen (fourteenth-century comic dramas made to complement the austere noh plays); bunraku (late seventeenth-century stylized puppet theatre) and kabuki (late seventeenth-century stylized song and dance drama). As Japan moved into the modern world it acquired the usual spread of Western performing arts and more recently film. Over this period we can note, as with pictorial arts, a shift in the centre of gravity of the activities away from the elites and towards the masses.

In Japan traditional music was the province of the elite – often using forms and instruments imported from the mainland. A folk music also existed. As with the pictorial and performing arts, the shift down the centuries sees a broadening involvement and an exchange with the West.

Literature in Japan traces back to eighth-century documents which recorded the lives of local Yamato state rulers: *Record of Ancient Matters, Kojiki* and *Chronicles of Japan, Nihon Shoki*. A third major collection of materials was the late eighth-century *Collection for Ten Thousand Generations, Manyoshu*. In the Heian period, 794–1185, much poetry was produced. However, the key work was Murasaki Shikibu's (1010) *The Tale of Genji* which can claim to be the world's first novel – a detailed story of political and sexual intrigue at court. In the wars of the later medieval period poetry and prose became more austere.

The ways in which a culture explains itself to itself are intimately bound up with conceptions of identity. In the case of Japan we can point to an overarching concern with the nature of Japaneseness in a global system that has been, and in many ways remains, dominated by the West (Wilkinson, 1991). Richie (1987) offers a series of sketches of Japanese artists and intellectuals: the novelist Mishima, the film maker Kurosawa, the actor Mifune, the actress Yamada and the director Oshima. In an afterword the author records that they are fragments accumulated over the years and self-consciously offered as such, rather than elaborated statements, which reveal something of the life of Japan. He offers his commentaries as an alternative to the familiar 'guidebook' approach which uses all the usual clichés. Richie takes the view that the clichés are true only because everyone goes around repeating them – in their place he prefers the ethnographic detail of people's lives.

Little tradition, folk culture and the development of popular culture

In pre-industrial Japan leisure for the masses of the population was mainly time free from the immediate demands of the rhythms of an agricultural economy (Bowring and Kornicki, 1993: 260–4). However, in the late Tokugawa period, as wealth slowly increased, the new urban areas developed with their new ways of life and the idea of leisure began to take hold. In the Tokugawa period the crucial shift to commercial woodblock printing encouraged the development of a large reading public who had access to poetry, fiction and drama.

In the late Tokugawa period the developing urban popular culture took one famous form, the 'floating world', which was to be found in the pleasure areas of a city or town. The idea of the 'floating world' stands a

Buddhist idea on its head – where the Buddhist concept stresses the transience of the world of suffering and enjoins resignation, the reworked version insists that if life is fleeting then it should be enjoyed. A famous story by Asai Ryoi, published in 1661, about the adventures of an ex-priest who strives for enlightenment via the pleasures of urban living, was called *The Tales of the Floating World*. The term thereafter comes to designate the pleasure quarters of the town – the bars, theatres, brothels, and so on.

In Ueda's (1994) analysis of the rise of popular culture in the Edo period and its legacies in contemporary Japan, particular attention is paid to those routine practices which are typical of urban life. The city provides new locations for new patterns of activity. As new economic patterns developed and class relations shifted, the urban masses grew more important and the places where they met, exchanged ideas and gossiped took on significance. It is here that we can see the little traditions and folk culture usually associated with rural areas developing into the popular culture of modern societies: for example, bathhouses, cafes, pachinko and the practice of attending lessons in the arts.

The bathhouse originates in the Edo period. In each neighbourhood of the towns there would be a communal bathhouse which served two purposes: hygiene and recreation – a centre for the exchange of local news and gossip. Over the period from Edo through Meiji down to the present day the bathhouse has seen a variety of styles of bathing and related social provisions (single-sex baths, mixed bathing, health cures, prostitution, and so on). The bathhouses have declined since the mid-1960s as new Japanese houses have baths installed.

In Japan the earliest beverage houses were tea houses. They developed from around the early fifteenth century and were located by popular temples. In the Edo period tea houses multiplied and became diverse. In the Meiji era the habit of coffee drinking was picked up from Westerners. This exotic beverage produced a new urban location, the coffee house: new drinks, new ideas and new places – all a part of the rich urban scene. In recent years competition from American-style 'fast-food' restaurants and the non-exotic status of coffee mean that the numbers of coffee houses are declining. The latest style is the café-bar. Again, these are places to meet and talk.

The pachinko parlour is a Japanese reworking of an American game which existed before World War II but became hugely popular afterwards. The parlours are legal sites of gambling for small stakes and are reputedly controlled by yakuza. There are an estimated 16,000 parlours and the turnover is huge – estimated at 4 per cent of gross national product. The social status of pachinko is ambiguous – not really respectable and another centre for information and gossip.

The lesson culture of Japan derives from the Edo period with the growth in classes given by masters on traditional arts. These classes have continued down to the present and are still given by a master, who will now be a member of the relevant association. The classes involve a series of levels and certificates of achievement are awarded to students. In contemporary Japan these classes are slowly being absorbed into general leisure provisions in local government funded 'culture centres'. Again, they represent a way in which the community afforded its members an opportunity to come together and exchange ideas, information and gossip.

Tokugawa urban leisure patterns were remade in the process of rapid industrialization undertaken in the Meiji period. In the nineteenth century there are the beginnings of mass leisure (Ueda, 1994). The first period was the 1920s, which was cut short by militarization. The second period is the present post-war period and its character varies with age, sex and class. Schoolchildren tend not to have much leisure time away from school but spend what time they do have watching TV, playing video games or reading comic books. Teenagers have more time and disposable cash and spend it on familiar youth culture products and activities. University students enjoy familiar student activities. Young women working as office ladies have greater opportunities with high disposable incomes. Married women have their rounds of coffee mornings, etc. Salarymen have their after-hours drinking and weekend golf – although here the dividing line between work and leisure is not so easy to draw. Old retired people take part in various hobbies. In recent years it has been suggested that a new phase of leisure has emerged with an extensive mass consumerism.

Mass culture, popular culture and consumption in the 1990s

Clammer (1997) looks at consumption in modern Japan. The sphere of consumption is placed centrally within ordinary life, which is taken thereafter to be lodged within urban and wider global structures. It is clear, reports Clammer (1997), that the Japanese pattern of life is both shaped by and sustains a highly productive economy. The everyday life of Japanese people is suffused with consumption behaviour. Class conflict is low and status competition is expressed in a consumerism constrained by continually recreated traditions of aesthetics and community. The behaviour is lodged within wider political-economic changes over the post-war period which have seen the state-directed establishment of a consumer society. However, Japan is not just a borrower of other people's ideas and as Clammer points out:

> Japan is also very much a society of innovation, and much of what is consumed in the rest of Asia and throughout the world is now Japanese in origin – fashions, foods, electronic equipment, cars, television serials, to name just a few. (Clammer, 1997: 7)

Clammer (1997) argues that consumer behaviour must be read as a cultural practice and must be analysed in terms appropriate to its contextual specificity. Mass consumption in Japan dates from late 1960s and has antecedents in late Meiji and Taisho. There was also an urban culture in the Edo period. Japanese consumer behaviour is therefore relatively novel. It is also formulaic. Consumption is constrained by social norms, a 'socialism of fashion' (Clammer, 1997: 12) and consumption behaviour is learned, with gift-giving figuring prominently as a way of creating networks. Much consumption is in the domain of women. These networks are meaning-drenched arenas of cooperation and conflict. Clammer notes that

> Much of Japanese life can be understood . . . in terms of symbolic struggle within the context of a society ideologically committed to the public presentation of itself as organised on the principle of . . . harmony. Gift-giving shares this fundamental ambivalence, combining the ideology, and often the practice, of reciprocity with low level symbolic warfare. (Clammer, 1997: 17)

Overall, it is clear that the sphere of consumer culture overlaps extensively with popular culture and ordinary life. Sets of traditional ideas are recreated and expressed in this context. Clammer (1997: 20) records that 'cultural nationalism in Japan occurs today (though certainly not in the past) through consumer culture . . . In Japan what one sees is a national culture of a strongly centripetal character attempting to maintain itself in the face of globalization.'

The notion of groupism

Many commentators on Japan have suggested that there is a core to the culture of the Japanese which can be found in the notion of 'groupism'. The standard story in respect of Japan stresses that the country has a conformist character and that Japanese people are happiest in groups. It is possible to invoke natural explanations for this groupism. Buckley (1990: 83) offers one version which argues from an urban society with a dense population to the need to avoid excessive confrontation with other people. Buckley also offers a second version by noting a past occasion in the demands of agricultural work for cooperation. The traditional rural focus on the group has thus been passed down to the urban present and is reused in the school, the workplace and politics. Richie (1987: 36–9) offers an example: a young man gains employment as an assistant in a sushi bar and comes under pressure to make a commitment to his workplace group by having a tattoo applied to his back. At first he refuses and is bullied; then he agrees and is made welcome as a new member of this particular little family. This preference for groupism is repeated, it is suggested, at a national level in the stress on the Japanese as a uniquely homogeneous people (and thus all one big group). Buckley (1990: 97–9) notes that this idea is widely accepted and routinely expressed.

However, in social science terms the issue is not so clear. Eccleston (1989) argues that Japanese society does manifest conflict, which is routinely controlled, and that the ideology of groupism – which is offered at levels of individual psychologies and the national – serves as a block to critical reflection. Van Wolferen (1989) argues that the invocation of 'culture' is precisely an ideological cover for the actual practices of Japanese society. The celebration of the uniqueness of the Japanese, including their love of consensus, is the province of a particular burgeoning literary genre. This literature reaches back into Japanese history and offers a nationalist version which takes political-economic, social-institutional and political arrangements to be expressive of 'Japanese culture'. It is also an approach that does have its foreign adherents; for example, all those American authors who have recently suggested that Japan is surpassing the USA at least in part because of 'cultural' factors. It would seem that the construction of this literature owes something to the influence of foreigners, both as an 'other' against which Japanese thinkers in the late Meiji period reacted (Dale, 1986), and after World War II when, more directly, Ruth Benedict (1946) provided a 'culturalist' explanation to encourage another round of nihonjin-ron writing (Yoshino, 1992; Clammer, 1995). It is of course a convenient body of ideas as when, for example, the availability of this literature and its partial acceptance by some foreigners lets the Japanese state offer excuses for inaction (as in the case of US criticism of the government's economic policies). In terms of the classical European tradition, offering culturalist explanations is a poor route into understanding a pattern of life.

Against these arguments Clammer (1995: 103) suggests that the 'philosophical principle underlying most Japanese social thinking is not, as it is so often vulgarly supposed, groupism or its variants . . . but harmony'. The notion is a product of religious traditions, in particular Buddhism, and the historically generated and carefully sustained pattern of life of the Japanese. It can be said that society is prioritized in Japanese culture and the individual is derivative. Clammer (1995: 103) argues that the self is relational (and Western-style individualism is read as selfishness, the cardinal social sin).

Clammer (1995) argues that Japan is neglected in Western social theorizing. Some theorists look to political economy and some offer culturalist explanations, but both are partial. However, an adequate analysis requires changes in the epistemological underpinnings in order to grasp the essence of Japanese life. Clammer (1995: 7) suggests that one key is 'seeing Japanese social project as a huge anti-alienation device and as such a profoundly utopian one. Ideas which seem to lie outside of social theory . . . (the principle of interdependence, the desire for harmony, the centrality of emotion rather than reason, the aestheticisation of life, the search for wisdom in nature and the acceptance of the body) prove to be central.' The Japanese social world is highly ordered (constructed). Clammer argues:

The negotiated reality has to be placed squarely in the context of a society where the historical continuity of certain aspects of social structure, such as emphasis on hierarchy, is very marked . . . It is this that creates a dialectic between the demands of reciprocity at the personal level and the equally insistent demand for stability in social relations in general. Or, put in a slightly different way, a central requirement of Japanese social organisation is to maintain the intimacy of face to face relationships (in the workplace, school, neighbourhood and family) while extending that reciprocity from purely personal interaction to the constitution of the society as a whole. (Clammer, 1995: 8)

The familiar means-end rationality of the West does not exhaust rationality in Japan. Emotion, aesthetics and demands of community also figure. The self has long been decentred in Japan.

The mix of modern industrial capitalism and tradition has caused comment and a recent attempt to grasp these matters, reports Clammer (1995: 13), has been cast in terms of modernity and postmodernity. The contemporary form of urban life in Japan looks postmodernist. Some have argued that it is while others have argued that it always has been. Against these debates, Clammer (1995: 15) points out that postmodernism is a Western notion and comes in many varieties. Applied to Japan it looks odd:

1   Yes, urban culture is full of consumerism, but it is contained within a distinctively Japanese cultural sphere.
2   Yes, the self is decentred, but it is located in patterns of social relations, not the postmodernist realm of freely chosen consumption.
3   Yes, calculative reason is not crucial, but the subjective self thereafter identified cannot be grasped in terms relating to Freud, as is the case in West; rather it points to the realm of emotions.
4   Yes, public grand political metanarratives are absent, but there is a strong sense of 'Japaneseness' in its place which finds concrete expression in formalized aesthetics such as the tea ceremony.

The Japanese decentred self is located in community and everyday life is humanistic. Clammer (1995) reports that the personal is reproduced in other spheres – school, office or club. This is not a society of expressive individualism. There has been no epochal shift, rather as socially constructed cultural practices are continually reworked, enfolding tradition is reaffirmed. In general, therefore, 'Japan has thus neither achieved . . . or overcome . . . the modern: it has by-passed it by establishing and following a project quite unlike that of the Enlightenment' (Clammer, 1995: 23). Indeed, Japan has its own cultural logic. 'Japanese society, unlike the postmodernist image of contemporary society, remains deeply humanist' (Clammer, 1995: 30) and it is unpacking this logic, which binds individual and community, that is key to understanding Japan.

In summary, Clammer (1995: 103) reports:

The project of Japanese society is genuinely utopian: an attempt to create harmony. The theme of harmony, however much empirically contradicted in practice, remains an ideal, another indigenous metatheory of Japanese life, something to be realized as people subordinate selfish goals to collective aims, and as they perceive their dependency on others – children on parents, teachers and peers, sportspeople on their coaches, those who have trained with and on their audiences, and so on. This attitude, reproduced endlessly in daily life . . . makes the Japanese an interesting race of deconstructionists: in the text of the individual there is no author, but a multiplicity of formative forces. No one autonomously writes his own life: it is co-authored by those who form, accidentally or by design, the individual's social universe . . . Human life is accepted as transitory, difficult and often tragic and human beings as weak, confused and eternally living in an environment of moral ambiguity. But the human condition can be, if not totally transformed or transcended, at least alleviated, and this can best be done not by radical individualism or through radical liberty, but through discipline: submission to and mastery of an art, a skill and, at the highest level, of relationships themselves.

Conclusion: a Japanese route to a Japanese modernity

The nature of modern Japan has been vigorously debated. A sharp division among Western commentators has developed where, on the one hand, some argue that nothing special has happened in Pacific Asia save for a process of catching up with the West and, on the other hand, some argue that the Pacific-Asian pattern is quite distinctive. Yet if we analyse the historical experience of Japan in the light of the intellectual resources of the classical European tradition we can identify the sequence of phases whereby Japan has ordered its ongoing shift to the modern world. At the outset, Tokugawa had an agricultural economy, a feudal society, a quasi-monarchical polity and its international relations were shaped by closed country policy. Thereafter, Meiji Japan had an industrial-capitalist economy, a developmental society, an oligarchic polity, and its international relations were shaped by drive to catch up. In the Taisho/Showa phase the process of advance was understood and undertaken in imperialist terms. The subsequent post-war phase has seen the development of a sophisticated modern society. In brief, Japan was a late modernizer and then, disastrously, a late imperialist. The period of recovery following the Pacific War has been achieved under the hegemony of the USA by a conservative polity oriented towards the needs of business. At the present time, Japan is a corporate economy, society and polity. We can now turn to consider the relationship of Japan with its modern neighbours in Pacific Asia.

7

JAPAN AND THE DEVELOPMENT OF PACIFIC ASIA

Trade, Aid and Foreign Direct Investment in the Project of Comprehensive Security

In the course of the 1980s the Japanese economy attained high levels of success. At the same time, there were market-oriented reforms within China, the USSR proposed a series of disarmament measures and US influence weakened. The Cold War in Pacific Asia started to wind down and the question of a new economic and political structure began to emerge.

In Japan it has long been acknowledged that there was a crucial relationship between domestic economic growth and regional security within East Asia. It is a preoccupation which dates from the period of the Meiji Restoration. The initial pursuit of these interrelated objectives was cast in terms of an expansionary colonial empire. After the Pacific War the security of Japan was understood in a restricted sense. The peace constitution forbade Japan any recourse to war as an instrument of policy and in any case the country was locked into a security alliance with the USA. However, in contrast, the Japanese economy prospered. The linkage between economic advance and regional security was represented in the late 1970s and early 1980s when the notion of 'comprehensive security' was adopted (Katahara, 1991: 8; Funabashi, 1994: 33–4). It is within this particular domestic Japanese context that the crucial role of economic advance in the post-war years becomes clear. It is also true, more broadly, that the contribution of Japanese trade, aid and investment to the emergence of a Pacific-Asian regional sphere has been crucial.

In the late 1980s there was considerable political, policy analytical and scholarly interest in the record of the countries of the Pacific Asia region. It was argued that the developing networks of economic, social and political interaction were forging an integrated regional grouping which was quite distinctive within the broader global system (Preston, 1998a). Yet in the wake of the extended Japanese post-bubble recession and the late 1990s Asian financial crisis it has been suggested that the 'Asian miracle' has ended. However, in the context of this study these problems can be regarded as transient. The processes underpinning the success of the region remain in place. As the preoccupations of the Cold War period fade into the background, it is clear both that economic strength as a vehicle of security has been a long-standing concern for Japanese governments and that Japan has come to play the role of the regional core economy.

Japan, Pacific Asia and the global system

In the period of Japan's shift to the modern world in the late nineteenth century an early elite concern was with the interrelated issues of economic development and security. In the late nineteenth century and the early years of this century Japan carved out a colonial sphere of influence in East Asia at the expense of the hitherto key regional power, China, whose influence had diminished as it was drawn into a quasi-colonial relationship with the European and American powers. The justification and rationale of Japanese expansionism included a set of core ideas:

1 Flowing from contemporary ideas of nationstatehood, such that Japan, as a major power, had an interest in securing its position in the region.
2 Flowing from a nationalist ideology, which argued that Japan had a particular role and responsibility within the orient (Tanaka, 1993).
3 Flowing from concerns for economic advance, where the argument was made that as Japan was a resource-poor island it had to secure access to resources and markets.

If we date the start of Japan's shift into the modern world from the period of the Meiji Restoration in 1868, and its arrival as a major power from the date of its first expansionist war against China in 1894–5, then, noting its subsequent expansionism, it is clear that Japan was pre-occupied with 'development and security' for the whole of its pre-Pacific War modern history. It was involved in active expansionism from 1894 to 1945. Iriye (1997) reports that Japanese governments were motivated by a mixture of pragmatism and pan-Asianism which slowly came to be asserted against the USA (with its concerns for an international liberal-market trading system). It was the exchange between a regionally oriented Japan and an obdurate USA which precipitated the Pacific War (Iriye, 1987).

The expansionist phase of Japan's modern history has left awkward legacies; in particular, the memories of war and colonial occupation among the countries of Pacific Asia, and the ways in which the whole period is presented within contemporary Japanese public discussion in a stylized and restricted fashion (Buruma, 1994; Stockwin, 1999: 197). Nonetheless, in the immediate post-war period Japan began making reparations to the countries of Pacific Asia. There was a preference for transfers of goods (rather than grant moneys) and a stress on subsequent self-reliance on the part of recipients. In other words resource transfers were controlled and pragmatic. In the early post-war years resource transfers were relatively slight, but with economic reconstruction and success they grew. They have taken two main forms: official development aid and foreign direct investment. Japanese aid and investment has tended to focus on Pacific Asia and has been taken by many commentators to be a major contributory factor to the economic growth of the region. Japanese aid and investment have also been routinely criticized as being too clearly at the service of Japan's own interests (Rix, 1993b; Koppel and Orr, 1993). At the present time, it is quite clear that contemporary Japan is the premier economy of Pacific Asia. The question of the relationship of the Japanese economy to the other economies within the region has often been answered in a fashion that implies the existence of an ordered grouping. Social theorists have spoken of the Japanese core being surrounded by an 'inner periphery' (the NICs) and an 'outer periphery' (ASEAN), to which a new circle has recently been added in the guise of the reforming socialist bloc (Halliday, 1980; Nester, 1990; Phongpaichit, 1990).

Logics of regionalism

At the outset, as Bernard (1996: 339) points out, it is important 'to recognise that the processes that create regional structures must be seen as both historically constituted and located in the context of broader ongoing historical change . . . there is nothing "natural" or generic about regions'. There are a series of ways of addressing the logic of regionalism within the existing spread of the social sciences (Preston, 1998a: 143–6). In brief they include:

(a) theories about economic systems;
(b) theories about the necessary logics of inter-state relations;
(c) theories about civilizations and societies;
(d) theories about cultural processes;
(e) theories detailing historical structural patterns of development.

All these intellectual resources have been deployed at one time or another to grasp the nature of Pacific Asia and the role of Japan within the region.

The available economic approaches, reports Bernard (1996: 339), include:

1   An ahistorical neo-liberalism which looks at economic transactions between national economies and argues for freeing up exchanges.
2   An ahistorical product cycle theory which looks at slowly evolving regional divisions of labour where a high-tech core slowly offloads outmoded technology which is then passed down to the periphery (flocks of flying geese).
3   An apolitical neo-institutionalism which looks at networks of companies within the region.

The crucial problem, in all these cases, is their ahistorical partiality, such that the complex substance of the sequences of historical phases (with their equally subtle legacies) and the detail of the shifting contemporary patterns are elided in favour of formal approaches so radically simplified as to miss the actual substantive nature of the matters in question. In contrast, Bernard (1996: 339), making an argument redolent of the classical European tradition, looks to 'region formation in terms of a number of complex interrelationships: the way the region is linked to both the global and the local; the social relationships that exist both between and within states; the relationship between the material and the ideational; and the tensions between forces of integration and disintegration in region formation'.

In the main tradition of international relations there are available theories which look to the necessary logics of inter-state relations, in particular realist analyses which look to the ways in which states pursue their interests within the unregulated inter-state system. The strategy of analysis generates the view that global or regional stability requires a hegemonic power. In Pacific Asia the security system which was in place over the long years of the Cold War saw two major powers confronting each other, and thereafter the USA was hegemonic within the richer dynamic market-oriented sphere. In this perspective, the role of the USA has been that of a regional hegemon securing a broad stability which has allowed component elements to prosper. However, it might be noted that a closely related line of argument suggests, in general theoretical terms, that a group of regional states could be expected to come together to establish collective institutions in order to pursue common problems against an outside power. In this context it can be noted that the plethora of acronyms within Pacific Asia rarely seem to acknowledge directly what many would regard as the obvious outside power, namely the USA, although the issue continues to exercise regional governments, as with, for example, the Malaysian proposal for an East Asian Economic Group comprising only the 'Asian ten'. It might be noted also that the European Union has recently begun conversations with the 'Asian ten' under the auspices of ASEM (Gilson, 1998b). Yet, in general, for a variety of intellectual reasons, the utility of these conventional international relations theories is unclear (Hollis and Smith, 1990; Linklater, 1990).

A related spread of theories look to the demands of economic activity. So if realism looks to states reaching intergovernmental agreements then a further line of analysis looks to the functional demands of economic activity and anticipates the slow supranational ordering of otherwise coherent regions. It is certainly true that the area displays considerable regional economic interchange. In the case of Pacific Asia it is possible to point to regional organizations, which often include the USA, that do acknowledge the sphere of economic exchange. A particular debate has developed around the distinction between 'inclusionary' and 'exclu-sionary' regionalism, which repeats the discussion about the proper role of the USA. However, at the present time it would be true to say that the extent of explicit formal regional integration remains slight.

The intellectual territory of theories about civilizations and societies is awkward as it involves making very broad comparisons between cul-tural spheres and claiming for large areas a received cultural coherence. In the case of Pacific Asia there have been many attempts to distinguish the typically Asian from the typically Western. Indeed, these attempts date from the nineteenth century when the driving logic of industrial-capitalist expansion brought European and American traders to Asia (Barraclough, 1964; Said, 1978; Tanaka, 1993; Frank, 1998). In the case of contemporary Pacific Asia it is perhaps worth noting that there is an indigenous line of resistance to Western political ideas expressed via the notion of 'Asian values' which reports that the polities of Asia are more naturally consensual than the individualistic polities of the West and that this finds appropriate expression in disciplined and hierarchical societies and polities. In the same vein Huntington (1993) has presented an influential external view of Asia which has characterized it as a coherent cultural bloc, along with several others, all of which are taken to be potential competitors with the West.

In the related area of cultural analysis Bernard (1996: 346) reports that some commentators 'argue that a region-wide civil society is now emerging . . . [which] constitutes the basis for the region to be a new kind of "imagined community"'. Indeed, it has been suggested, for example, that Japanese popular culture is being widely diffused. However, matters are more complex and it is necessary to look at how local areas are located within regional patterns. The movement towards a common civil society could include:

(a) regionalized urban spaces, such that the cities of the region have increasingly common patterns of production and consumption;
(b) regionalized tourism, for example, intra-regional travel and the passion for golf among newly affluent elites;
(c) the networks of Chinese urban bourgeoisie which stretch through much of the region.

But all this is tentative and speculative. Bernard concludes by recording that there has been a growth in interconnectedness within the region but the prospects for further integration are fraught with difficulties and tensions.

It is clear that regions have existed in myriad historical contexts and taken a variety of forms. An historical structural analysis of Pacific Asia (utilizing elements of the above) would look to the successive ways in which the area has been configured and to the ways in which the peoples of the area understood themselves and thereafter acted. The idea of an Eastern Asian region has existed since its invention by Japanese theorists in the late nineteenth century (Tanaka, 1993; Iriye, 1997; Koschmann, 1997). It was constituted in expansionary Japanese military practice in the years up to 1941 but at the end of the war the region was sharply reconfigured. The new pattern owed much to the USA. The US security structure helped to underpin the region while the economy of Japan provided the core of a regionalized economy and the USA provided an ever-open market. Bernard (1996: 340) states:

> They must be understood precisely as a manifestation of global processes and of the way these processes assume concrete form in a world where power emanates from within historically constituted national social formations. Regions are thus co-determined by processes and social forces that operate transnationally and by the organisation of national communities. (Bernard, 1996: 340)

Overall, it is clear that the Pacific-Asian region does evidence an increasingly self-conscious integration (Preston, 1998a). Nonetheless, in looking at the development of region it is clear also that the logics of regionalism are still unfolding and the present condition and likely trajectory of Pacific Asia are not straightforward matters (Katzenstein and Shiraishi, 1997). A series of more particular problems might be noted:

1 Local production fits into a Japan-centred hierarchy and this creates dependence as Japanese keep control.
2 Regional production has required local political and class patterns be fixed in place and this inevitably creates tensions.
3 There are ethnic tensions within regional production as some groups are seen to be advantaged relative to others.
4 In Japan there are the problems of rich country/poor people.
5 There is also the tension created by the region's exports in particular to USA.
6 There is the question of the growing power of China.

However, for the present, Japan can be treated as the core economy of the region.

An agenda

There is a growing literature on Pacific Asia in relation to the global system. It seems that much of it originates in the USA. One aspect of this material, sometimes overt and sometimes covert, is an anxiety in respect of the position of the USA within the global system where the point is repeatedly and variously made that the USA has to attend carefully to its position in relation to the countries of Pacific Asia. We can note the work which celebrates in positive vein the rise of the Pacific century (McCord, 1991; Gibney, 1992). We can note the work which looks in more critical vein to the economic competition offered to the West by Pacific Asia (Vogel, 1979; Thurow, 1994). We can look to those who speak in paranoid vein of the forthcoming 'clash of civilizations' (Huntington, 1993). Most recently, we can note the work of those who have read the 1997–8 financial crisis as proof of the failure of 'crony capitalism' and relatedly of the triumph of the US economic way (Preston, 1998a). Against this, the work of international political economy has offered a more nuanced discussion of the situation within the region and the relationships of the region to the wider global system (Higgot and Robison, 1985; Higgot et al., 1993; Rodan, 1996). It is this work which recalls the concerns of the European classical tradition of social theorizing with its central preoccupation with elucidating the dynamics of complex change. In this chapter we will consider: the general patterns of trade within the region; the rationale of Japanese official development aid; the nature of Japanese foreign direct investment; and the overall impact of trade, aid and investment within the region.

Patterns of trade in Pacific Asia

It is usual to link together discussions of trade, official development aid and foreign direct investment in order to grasp fully the economic interchanges within a particular area. Japanese trade patterns in Pacific Asia have become significant over the period of the 1980s and 1990s and embrace in particular manufactures and raw material supplies. A second major flow of capital can be identified in the networks of overseas Chinese whose economic activities link China to Taiwan, Hong Kong, Thailand and Southeast Asia. In contrast to the Japanese, these flows of capital have been rather more centred upon services, leisure and real estate, although with the continuing economic reforms within China there is more concern for manufacturing (Cronin, 1992: 24). At the present time, commentators would characterize Japan as the 'core economy' of the region, and this will be the concern of this chapter, but clearly the future development of China might be expected to rebalance regional patterns of economic activity (Taylor, 1996).

The key to understanding the Japanese approach to the region is captured in the metaphor of the 'flying geese', with Japan in the vanguard, and the other regional economies strung out behind in formation. The Japanese ideal is of an integrated and complementary regional division of labour. This division of labour should flow from the putative revealed comparative advantage held by each country; in other words,

Japan is the advanced core and the other countries are variously materials suppliers and providers of lower technology manufactures (Cronin, 1992: 27).

In more general terms, it has been argued that Japan's relationship with the four tigers (Singapore, Hong Kong, Korea and Taiwan) is 'complementary-competitive' (Cronin, 1992: 28). They are relatively advanced and have a trade surplus with the USA and deficits with Japan. Singapore and Hong Kong are largely production platforms for exports to third countries and have very high deficits with Japan. Taiwan and Korea have a broader trade exchange with Japan. Thereafter, Japan's relation with Southeast Asia and China (the regional less-developed countries) is 'skewed but complementary' (Cronin, 1992: 28). Japan traditionally had a trade deficit with Southeast Asia as it imported raw materials but in recent years there has been a surplus as Southeast Asia takes more manufactured imports (some of which are components for products to be exported). Relatedly, in the case of China, exchanges are at a relatively early stage, given historical and Cold War problems, but they are rapidly developing. Finally, Japan's relationship with Australasia is 'complex and multifaceted' as these are both developed countries (Cronin, 1992: 29). Japan takes raw materials from Australia, primary products from New Zealand, and thereafter a range of exchanges with tourism, real estate, and manufactures. Overall, Cronin takes the view that Japanese trade is a force for regional integration (Cronin, 1992: 50). However, the relationship is not static because there is relative movement among the component parts of the region, although it is difficult to imagine any rapid significant change in Japan's core role.

It should be noted, however, that the extent of regional integration (as a result of trade, official development aid and foreign direct investment) is not easy to grasp. There are, as noted, intellectually difficult issues involved in deciding what counts as regional integration. At the same time the relationship(s) of the region with the global system continue, and they continue also to shift and change. However, so far as can be judged, it does seem to be the case that there is a significant element of regional integration (Shibusawa et al., 1992; Dobson, 1993; Abegglen, 1994; Thurow, 1994).

Rationale of Japanese official development aid in Pacific Asia

The Japanese concern for the development of the region can be traced back to the period of Meiji and the interrelated concern for development and security. In the 1970s and 1980s Japanese trade with the region began to expand and after 1985 grew very rapidly and within this context official development aid attained its present significance.

All official development aid programmes have a formal rationale. Yet it is clear that all aid programmes express a complex set of assumptions in respect of their purpose. Such assumptions can be taken to be the product of a mix of factors including, most obviously: historical legacies; contemporary concerns; and projected interests (Preston, 1982, 1998a). It is this spread of assumptions which together make up the effective rationale of aid programmes.

Historical legacies shaping Japanese official development aid

In regard to historical legacies there are a series of relevant factors:

(a) the experience of a donor country in working in overseas countries (colonial holdings or other involvements);
(b) the continuing linkages with areas where the donor countries have experience (the nature of decolonization and the linkages maintained, if any);
(c) the way in which such historical linkages are presently understood (as entailing a responsibility, or not, for example).

In the case of Japanese aid programmes in Pacific Asia an analysis should consider:

(a) the nature of the links in the nineteenth and early twentieth centuries;
(b) the actual nature of the Japanese colonial empire in Pacific Asia;
(c) the implications of the manner of Japanese colonial withdrawal;
(d) the way in which all these episodes are recalled in contemporary Japanese thinking (and thus how Japanese politicians and businessmen present themselves in dealings with Pacific Asia).

MEIJI, ECONOMIC DEVELOPMENT AND NATIONAL SECURITY   The nature of the links of Japan and Pacific Asia in the late nineteenth and early twentieth centuries may be taken to be shaped by the experience of the Japanese in regard to their own shift to the modern world. The Meiji restoration in 1868 saw political power within Japan shift from the controlling family within a land-centred economy and polity which resembled the European feudal system to an oligarchic developmental state. This episode of political-economic change has been famously analysed by Moore (1966) who speaks of a revolution from above. The Meiji state proceeded to borrow from the model of the developed West, in particular Europe. In the late nineteenth and early twentieth centuries the economic development of Japan was very rapid and came to involve diplomatic conflict with the great powers in Europe and the USA, particularly in respect of Japanese colonial activities.

At this period the European powers and the USA were extensively involved in China, whose territory was regarded as a trade resource open to exploitation. It should also be noted that in the nineteenth century nationstates still had routine recourse to war in order to settle disputes. At the same time the late nineteenth century saw the high tide of Western imperialism. It can be said that the Japanese simply took the available model when they turned to order their relationships with their regional neighbours. There was early Japanese activity in the Russian Far East, Korea and China. All these areas were geographically contiguous with Japan and thus, given contemporary notions of empire and inter-state relations, obvious places for the assertion of developing Japanese interests against the concerns of China, Czarist Russia and the European and American great powers.

The Sino-Japanese war of 1894–5 lasted nine months in which time the Japanese armed forces expelled the Chinese from Korea, captured Port Arthur and the Liaotung peninsular. In the peace treaty additionally Taiwan was ceded to Japan. However, the Triple Intervention, by Russia, France and Germany obliged the Japanese to withdraw from Liaotung and Port Arthur. As the Europeans and Americans had at that time very extensive colonial holdings this generated irritation among Japanese ruling circles and popular disapproval (Beasley, 1990). Thereafter, this late nineteenth-century and early twentieth-century colonial-style expansion involved conflict with Russia in respect of spheres of influence in Manchuria and Korea. The Russo-Japanese war of 1904–5 saw success for the Japanese. In general all this seems to have attracted the passive sympathy of the Europeans, and it is said particularly in regard to the naval victory over the Russian navy a strong measure of approval from Asians (Barraclough, 1964).

However, when Japan began to make further demands on China, European and American sympathy rather tended to fade away and Japan came to be categorized as aggressive. It is argued that this early rebuff by the Western powers to Japanese borrowings of the notion of empire had the effect of encouraging an aggressive Japanese nationalism which subsequently modulated into the fascism of the inter-war period. In the 1930s the Japanese invaded China. The Imperial Japanese Army was a key actor in this drama. By the 1930s the army had become the dominant force in Japanese politics (Beasley, 1990). An incident was staged at Mukden on 18 September 1931 and this was the pretext for the seizure of Manchuria. In 1932 Tokyo officially recognized Manchukuo and Henry Pu-yi was made emperor in 1934. A little later a general war was being waged in China. The 1937 incident at the Marco Polo bridge outside Peking was the igniting spark. It would seem that the various elements of the Japanese military could never make up their minds just what were their war aims in China and with whom they might deal at the local level. The upshot was a long drawn-out general war (Beasley, 1990) which proved to be fatal to Japanese military expansion as it was Japanese involvement in China which drew the criticism of the USA and Europeans, and in due course the general

Pacific War began which destroyed the military dominated pre-war Japanese polity.

THE EMPIRE IN ASIA   The development of the Japanes empire in Pacific Asia over the early years of the century involved the seizure of Korea and Taiwan and large areas of China and the creation of a new state in northern China, Manchukuo. Then, in later years, the empire expanded in Indo-China, throughout Southeast Asia and embraced a spread of islands in the Pacific. At its height, in early 1942, the empire covered a vast area of territory.

In the inner periphery a colony was created in Korea. The movement into Korea began in the late nineteenth century as the Japanese attempted to prize the territory away from the influence of China and at the same time to block the advance of Russian influence. The territory was made a protectorate in 1905 and became a formal colony in 1910. During the same period a colony was created in Taiwan where Japanese involvement had begun in the late nineteenth century with the territory becoming a colony after the Sino-Japanese war of 1894–5.

There was continuing war in China from the late nineteenth century when the Japanese borrowed Western ideas of colonial expansion and intervened in China through to the military invasions of the 1930s, and thereafter the long drawn-out warfare that ran until 1945. A temporary dependency created in Manchukuo existed from the late 1930s through to 1945.

In the outer periphery in 1941–2 the Japanese army moved into Vietnam, displacing the colonial French, and then extended its influence throughout Indo-China, including drawing Thailand into the war against the West. The holdings of the Japanese were extended by military conquest in the period 1941–2 when the European and US empires in Southeast Asia were taken over in turn: Malaya, the Dutch East Indies, the Philippines, Burma and many Pacific Island territories.

The historical legacy of Japanese colonialism is complex: in brief, a mixture of long-established colonialism, wartime violence and some political and economic reforms. It took a different character in the various territories. The official ideological rationale of Japanese expansion was the establishment of a co-prosperity sphere which would allow both the Japanese and the peoples of Pacific Asia, now free of their Western colonial masters, to flourish in a cooperative fashion.

In the inner periphery in Korea the colonial episode involved the harsh treatment of the indigenous population. It would seem that there is a legacy of bitterness at the present. Again, while it is initially difficult to see any positive legacy, it was the case that the colonial period saw a measure of industrialization (Beasley, 1990: 194–8; Cummings, 1997). However, at the present time pragmatism and geographical proximity underpin economic linkages (Kim, 1993). In Taiwan the colonial episode was similar to that of Korea (Beasley, 1990: 194–8), but Japanese involvement seems to have been rather more positive in that they occupied a remote and underdeveloped fringe area of the Chinese empire and did develop the territory.

In mainland China, including Manchukuo, one might suppose that the record was one of simple violence, remembered with hostility by the victims today and largely unacknowledged to date by the Japanese government (or people) save for ritualistic apologies. In such a case it would be difficult to see a positive legacy from this episode. However, notwithstanding the continuing disruption of war it seems to be the case that there was considerable Japanese investment in Manchukuo and China and that the wartime legacy included a significant measure of industrialization (Beasley, 1990: 194–8). At the present time contemporary economic links are well established. It would seem that a mix of historical and cultural similarities plus delicacy over World War II provide the base for pragmatic links (Zhao, 1993). The Chinese secure a source of capital and the Japanese markets plus stability.

In Indo-China the eventually successful nationalist resistance movement was the Vietminh, so in this instance the pattern was rather different. An attempt to recreate the status quo ante by the French failed, as did the subsequent US attempt. It is difficult to identify a positive legacy of Japanese colonialism and once again we note the overriding influence of present economic power. With the end of the US boycott announced by President Clinton in February 1994, Japanese firms are investing in Vietnam.

In the outer periphery the record is more ambiguous. In the Dutch East Indies the early period of war and exertion of Japanese control gave way to a measure of cooperation. An army of indigenous people was formed, as was a political representation organization led by Sukarno. In this sense the Japanese had a role to play in fostering an eventually successful nationalist movement (Jeffrey, 1981). In Burma a similar situation held with Aung San's army and political organization. In a rather different way this organization modulated into the independence movement which in due course secured this goal (Orr, 1990). However, in Malaysia the Japanese encouraged Malay nationalism while harshly treating the Chinese. The Japanese interregnum has had a lasting impact on Malaysia in the form of communalist politics, whose occasion may in part be traced to the wartime period. In Singapore the wartime episode was harsh and is remembered as such by the largely Chinese population (Turnbull, 1977). Yet, as with other areas of Pacific Asia there is a pragmatic focus on economic cooperation. Finally, in the Philippines a similar pattern is visible. The Filippino elite cooperated with the Japanese and ideas of independence were floated. However, the return of the USA saw the re-establishment of the status quo ante which led directly to the Huk rebellion (Kerkvliet, 1977) and the establishment of a pattern of American-dependent crony capitalism that culminated in the era of Marcos. It is difficult to identify a positive legacy of Japanese colonialism. Again, the current determinants of the relationship are the pragmatics of economic growth coupled to geographical proximity.

If the above notes the political impact of the period of Japanese colonial rule for the outer periphery, it must be said that the economic impact at this time was severe, but of short duration. These territories were absorbed as materials supplying elements of a war economy that quickly collapsed. Rix, in regard to ASEAN, points to a pre-war Japanese concern for resource security, noting that the 'economic rationale for military domination of the region from 1941 to 1945 was paramount' (Rix, 1993a: 23). It is also quite clear that this continues to be the key interest – trade, investment, resources and security in general for the Japanese. Rix (1993a: 22) characterizes Japanese aid for the ASEAN countries as an 'expensive insurance policy'.

THE END OF EMPIRE   After the arguments of Grimal (1965) it can be suggested that the manner of withdrawal from colonial holdings has an impact on the subsequent relationship of ex-colony and ex-colonial power. In the case of the dissolution of the Japanese empire in Pacific Asia we have an abrupt ejection occasioned by war. The political status of the occupied territories changed with independence and the status of the Japanese occupiers similarly changed by virtue of their occupation by the USA.

The manner of the ejection of the Japanese was quite particular and we can note the following factors:

1 The relatively brief period in which the ejection was accomplished, with military defeat becoming obvious by the middle of 1944 and the Japanese armies defeated by late 1945 and withdrawn shortly thereafter.
2 The relatively ordered nature of the withdrawal of the Japanese from the Southeast Asian and Indo-China regions (in contrast to the general debacle which befell Germany in 1945).
3 The use by Europeans and Americans of Japanese soldiers as 'police' in parts of East and Southeast Asia, and Indo-China for the temporarily re-colonized territories in the interregnum between the collapse of the Japanese empire and either the return of the civilian/military powers of the various pre-war colonial powers or the establishment of post-Japanese colonial era regimes.
4 The relatively limited political-economic and cultural changes made in the US occupation period.
5 The relatively benign US occupation, which was initially distinctly idealistic, thereafter rightwing and arguably broadly inept (Buckley, 1990).
6 The very early rehabilitation and reconstruction of Japan which began in 1950 with the outbreak of the Korean War and the US drive against 'world communism'.

Thereafter, the general business of reordering the global system around its new US centre – with processes of decolonization, the establishment of the Bretton Woods economic settlement, the related founding of the UN system and the pervasively deployed US conservative ideology of anti-Communism – gave the Japanese rulers an umbrella under which to shelter as they rebuilt their economy and, along with this, their links to Pacific Asia. It seems fairly clear, as van Wolferen (1989) argues, that this episode of rebuilding involved a great measure of continuity with pre-war patterns of economy and society.

In brief, notwithstanding that in the wake of World War II the Japanese had to re-establish links with Pacific Asia, it turned out that they had a relatively smooth path to such a re-establishment of linkages. One first contact was via the forerunner of official development aid links, that is war reparations (Rix, 1993b).

CONTEMPORARY JAPAN AND ASIA   In contemporary Japanese thinking we can identify two areas of concern in respect of Pacific Asia: the recent past and the longer history.

In regard to the recent historical context, the episode of war, it seems safe to say, at a very general level, that these years are either ignored or taken as essentially unproblematical in the sense that states are taken to have wars and the Japanese state had one which it happened to lose. The idea that Japan was the aggressor and wrought unparalleled destruction across the area is not widely entertained. In this instance the position of the Japanese political classes, and thereafter population generally, is in stark contrast to the response of the German governments and people where the episode of national socialism has been and continues to be subject to extensive public debate. It has been pointed out that the removal of Hitler and the Nazis left the German people able to acknowledge their responsibility and reach back to a rich cultural history separate from the Nazi era. The SCAP decision to leave the emperor in place, and thus the polity in essentials unchanged, blocked the Japanese people from making this sort of move (Buruma, 1994). They could not reach back beyond a discredited group of wartime leaders because the key symbol (and much practice) of that group stayed in place with US support. The subsequent reluctance of the Japanese political elite to acknowledge the country's history is often cited as one of the reasons why they are not trusted either in the West or Asia. However, with the analyses of van Wolferen this trait can be seen as part of a wider and more profound absence of either a political centre in Japan or a developed public sphere serving a democratic polity.

More broadly, because the history of Japanese involvement with Pacific Asia is longer and deeper than the wars of the twentieth century, an available theme characterizing the relationship generates the view that the unique and gifted Japanese are able to lead the rest of Pacific Asia in development. At this point it would seem that the above-noted historical amnesia modulates smoothly into nationalist myth making. It seems that this is a major source of thinking in regard to Pacific Asia and development aid, thus it is seen as a matter of responsibility and duty and the actual narrowly pragmatic nature of the links is glossed over.

Contemporary concerns with aid programmes

Contemporary concerns in respect of official development aid programmes flow from the way a particular country fits into the wider system of which inevitably it is a part and the way in which significant agent groups construe the business of aid. A rational agenda of enquiry would embrace the political, economic and cultural factors shaping Japanese understanding of aid projects.

An attempt to uncover present political concerns shaping official development aid provision would have to address a set of questions in respect of their rationale: What decisions have been made by relevant agent groups, in what political contexts and with what ends in view? Rix notes that the official rationale for aid is one of helping the less fortunate. It is possible, Rix (1993b: 14) reports, to discern a continuity in respect of the idea of self-help rather than simple charity which runs back to the period of Meiji, but otherwise there is no consistent view of development. Japan's aid programmes are linked to the concerns of the Japanese and there is thus a stress on Pacific Asia. Rix (1993b: 23) notes that 'Asian development was more a means of achieving Japanese objectives than a goal in its own right'.

Rix (1993b: 20) records that trying to grasp the detail of Japanese official development aid motivation is difficult, although one can broadly point to differences in emphasis among the various bureaucratic groupings involved. Hence MITI stresses trade, resources and markets, while MOFA looks to diplomacy and security. Within this general frame, shifts of emphasis in aid provision can be detected and a recent defensiveness has been apparent in respect of the geographical concentration of aid and the donor preference for tied aid and loans. It is suggested that the locus of power in regard to aid provision lies within the bureaucracy and that the programmes undertaken are the outcome of complex bureaucratic manoeuvring, which is where reform will have to start if it is to begin at all.

In terms of the detailed politics of official development aid policy, Orr (1990) also argues that this is largely contained within the bureaucracy, with little impact from other sectors of Japanese society, although as with other matters an element of American influence can be discerned but in this case substantively. Orr (1990) makes clear that aid has been subordinated to concerns for resource security. The oil shock of the early 1970s did change the pattern of Japanese aid disbursements away from an exclusive focus on Asia, but the intention remained constant. It might also be noted that the Japanese pattern of aid disbursement is concerned mainly with matters economic and US concerns about tying aid to political reform or strategic military interests have not been pursued.

It is routinely pointed out that official development aid programmes have linkages with Japanese economic interests in Pacific Asia. The dominant player in the aid game at the Japanese end has been the bureaucracy, rather than politicians or other groups, and the bureaucracy maintains close links to the world of industry. Orr (1990) notes that much of the aid has been infrastructural in nature: dams, bridges, ports, and the like, with Japanese companies as virtually the sole agents. In a similar fashion Dobson (1993: 19) records that the Japanese government has been concerned strategically to foster economic development and that aid has been one instrument deployed to this end. It is noticeable, she remarks, that Japanese aid extends help to Japanese firms.

It seems clear that the drive for official development aid disbursements arises within the bureaucracy where it is seen as an adjunct of the overall development of Japan. However, Rix notes that within Japan there has been a public stress by those in authority on Japan's 'duty' to give aid. This flows in turn from sets of ideas about: Japan's relative wealth; Japan's position between the West and Asia and thus its role as a bridge; Japan's need to be seen as a responsible nation (Rix, 1993b: 29). On this basis official development aid has become something of a public issue, in particular the size of the budget and the periodic scandals that surround its use (Rix, 1993b: 45). It is reported that aid commands broad support among the Japanese people and that it has received government-sponsored publicity and educational backing (Rix, 1993b: 50). Although this support may be rather lukewarm there are signs of a more engaged and critical concern growing (Rix, 1993b: 60–4). In general, remarks Rix (1993b: 140): 'The geographical, cultural and racial entity of Asia is a powerful image for the Japanese mind, and at home Japan's role in Asia is widely accepted, even encouraged.'

In general, Japanese official development aid has been linked to the economic interests of Japan and has been focused on the Pacific-Asian area. In its earliest form aid was presented as war reparations. The Japanese distributed goods rather than money and thus the link of aid and Japanese development was made from the outset. In this way, as Rix (1993a) points out, a measure of continuity with pre-war concerns was maintained. This concentration on development aid as a way of furthering the interests of Japan has been somewhat modified but in essentials continues. In terms of the spread of bilateral aid linkages we can distinguish between inner periphery, outer periphery and the newly open sphere of socialist Pacific Asia. As regards the inner periphery of Korea, Taiwan and Hong Kong, Kim (1993) reports in respect of Korea a mix of security and trade interests, all suffused with deep suspicion. Then, as regards the outer periphery, Rix (1993a) notes that with ASEAN a series of concerns are present – trade, investment, resources and security generally. Rix (1993a: 26–32) reports that recent formal statements, from MITI and MOFA, look to a more effective international division of labour and industrial coordination and involve a tripartite mix of aid, private capital and import promotion in broad pursuit of an export-oriented development for ASEAN. One critic has spoken of an effective absorption into an incipient 'colonial relationship' (Sinha, 1982) as the Japanese draw ASEAN countries ever more closely into their sphere. In regard to socialist Pacific Asia, with China Zhao (1993) reports that the relationship is based on long historical links, yet is coloured by post-World War II suspicion. After 1982, with the economic reforms in China, there was a massive jump in Japanese official development aid disbursements, mostly for infrastructural projects. The developments have thus been in line with Japan's interests, although there is now a yen debt problem (and this applies to much of the area of East Asia). In the other parts of Indo-China there is as yet little Japanese involvement, but it is likely that this will soon alter.

Projected Japanese interests in Pacific Asia

Official development aid is made available to recipients in the light of donor expectations in regard to the future. Such expectations can be varied, ranging from anxieties about the future (for example, will there be a flow of poor immigrants into rich areas), through to optimism for the future (thus a little aid can do much to raise levels of living). The concerns can also be very pragmatic, on the part of governments the desire to secure allies and resources, for example, or on the part of firms the desire to secure markets and reap profits.

Japanese official development aid has focused on the development of Japan's economic position. However, in recent years a newer concern has emerged for the political-diplomatic repositioning of Japan at the centre of the ever more integrated global system. The symbol of this concern is the drive to secure a permanent seat on the UN security council (Dore, 1997).

The continuing growth of the Japanese economy and the burgeoning development of Pacific Asia conjoined with Japanese aspirations in respect of an international political role make it difficult to see how the present programme of official development aid could do other than continue. However, the future and role of Japanese aid and investment are bound up with wider matters relating to the position of Japan within the region and the position of the region within the global system. As Cronin (1992) has pointed out with a trio of 'scenarios', it is clear that debate about aid cannot be left to any narrowly construed sphere of poor country development, but must be seen as an aspect of continuing complex change in Pacific Asia.

Complementary role of foreign direct investment

Cronin (1992: 1) remarks that in the early 1990s Japan overtook the USA as the premier source of foreign direct investment in Pacific Asia. Japanese and NIC investment in Asia had been heavy in the 1980s and intra-regional trade increased to $270 billion so that it exceeded Asian exports to the USA at $206 billion and the EU at $182 billion (Cronin, 1992: 8). In all this, reports Cronin (1992: 8), Japan was the catalyst and the USA the market for the resultant production. The key event seems to have been the 1985 Plaza Accord which revalued the yen upwards against the dollar. The resultant pressure on Japanese manufacturers encouraged them to shift production offshore while the rise in the value of the yen meant that existing yen holdings were upwardly revalued and that continuing flows of exports generated ever greater dollar earnings, which in turn were recycled in the form of aid and investment in Pacific Asia, resulting in the establishment of a series of export-oriented 'production platforms' (Phongpaichit, 1990: 38).

The relationship of Japan with the other Pacific Asian countries is often characterized, as we have noted, with reference to the metaphor of 'flying geese', where Japan is the leader with the other countries following stepped down behind (Cronin, 1992: 27). The ideal relationship implied by this metaphor is one of a regionally complementary division of labour centred on Japan (Cronin, 1992: 28). As noted earlier, Cronin points out that the linkages which Japan has with the countries of the region vary significantly: with the NICs the relationship is complementary and competitive (Cronin, 1992: 29–33); with the developing areas such as China the relationship is one of complementary cooperation skewed in Japan's favour (Cronin, 1992: 33–8); with the advanced economies of Australasia the relationship is complex and multifaceted (Cronin, 1992: 38). Cronin concludes that Japanese official development aid is important in working to integrate the region and that it serves to bolster Japan's own economy as aid is often tied. Relatedly, with its focus on infrastructural projects, it smooths the growth of foreign direct investment (Cronin, 1992: 39; Dobson, 1993: 19). Overall, Japanese official development aid and foreign direct investment have been forces for economic growth and regional integration (Cronin, 1992: 50) and, as Dobson (1993: 67) points out, focusing on the ASEAN case, host governments have welcomed such inward investment.

Phongpaichit (1990) looks at the ASEAN case and argues three broad points:

1 The key issue in respect of foreign direct investment is the matter of the host government securing beneficial control.
2 The wave of investment arose from Japan.
3 The ASEAN countries have actively pursued their own agendas in respect of this flow of investment.

Phongpaichit (1990) notes three areas of debate in respect of foreign direct investment: the work of Western economists focusing on MNCs; the particular arguments of some Japanese scholars; and the view of the ASEAN policymakers.

In regard to the first issue Phongpaichit (1990) notes that work which looked at capital movements within the global system has recently given way to work derived from industrial organization theory and product cycle theory which focuses on the advantages to MNCs of involving themselves in foreign direct investment: advantages in terms of organization and technology allow high profits. Against this line of work, critics working with non-mainstream economics ideas have spoken of exploitative relationships and of the overweening power of the global MNCs. At the same time, figures such as Streeten (1994) have argued that the key issue is how the activities of the MNCs can be ordered to the greater benefit of the host countries. In sum, their role in less developed countries is widely regarded as less than self-evidently generally beneficial.

In the case of Japanese work on these matters, Phongpaichit (1990: 9–10) records that some scholars have tagged liberal-market informed foreign direct investment 'oligopolistic', and by implication exploitative, and suggested that other forms of investment could have more positive effects. Japanese investment, it is said, typically looks to enhance complementary comparative advantage within an ordered international division of labour. It would seem that non-Japanese commentators are sceptical of this characterization, yet at the same time it is the case that Japanese aid and investment are both intertwined and act to generate an integrated regional block, that is, a regional complementary division of labour centred on Japan (Dobson, 1993). The policymakers of ASEAN are reportedly sceptical of Japanese theories and have preferred Western explanations. However, Phongpaichit (1990: 23) argues that all these discussions are flawed by a neglect of host country demand. It cannot be assumed that host country governments and capitals (in the sense of class fractions) are passive for they have their own agendas. Thus, for host governments foreign direct investment generates tax revenues, job creation and export earnings, while for domestic capitals the incoming MNCs are a source of disturbance, opportunity and threat: again, the issue is how to control the impact of the MNCs.

It can be argued that in the late 1980s and early 1990s foreign direct investment in the ASEAN region was initiated by changes in the circumstances of the Japanese economy. In the 1950s through to the 1970s Japanese foreign direct investment expanded slowly and in the pre-1985 period the focus was on raw materials, cheap labour and market access (Phongpaichit, 1990: 29). There was a distinctive pattern of investment with the East Asian NICs favoured, and thereafter some attention to Singapore, with the rest of ASEAN coming behind. However, after the 1985 Plaza Accords investment in ASEAN increased sharply and was focused on export-oriented industrialization (Phongpaichit, 1990: 30). Phongpaichit (1990: 33–8) argues that the underlying reason, notwithstanding the issues of the appreciation of the yen and the Japanese governments desire to be seen to be responding to growing US concerns about trade imbalances, was lodged in Japan's shift from an economy centred on labour-intensive heavy industry to one focused on high technology industrial development. This structural change pushed out investment to offshore production platforms as Japanese capital looked to escape the impact of the high yen and US restrictions via a drive to increase markets and production capacity. In the terms of Hamilton (1983), the Japanese economic space was expanded in Pacific Asia. Phongpaichit records that this expansion has had a large impact on ASEAN and she adds that the recipient states have been active participants.

After the style of the political economists, Phongpaichit (1990) suggests that we can distinguish between domestic capital, state capital and foreign capital and thereafter we can plot the shifting patterns of interest and how these are expressed in response to incoming foreign direct investment. In ASEAN, broadly, there was an early resistance to investment as state and domestic capital prospered. Then in the depression of the early 1980s state capital was in trouble and began to run up significant debt. At this point investment became attractive to ASEAN governments and with the incoming investment the phase of export-oriented industrialization took off. It is clear that each country has had a particular experience of investment assisted industrialization but in each case, Phongpaichit insists, the acceptance of investment must be seen as an expression not of passive acceptance but agency.

At the end of this intriguing analysis Phongpaichit (1990) is clear that the new wave of Japanese foreign direct investment in ASEAN has been driven by structural change in the Japanese economy and that its active reception has been shaped by local political–economic configurations. It would seem that Japanese investment in the ASEAN region can be expected to continue notwithstanding problems of yen denominated debt, conflict among capital fractions and maybe the rise of other sources of investment as the ASEAN economies mature.

Overall impact of Japanese trade, aid and investment

As Shibusawa et al. (1992) note, in recent years there has been some considerable debate about the growth of the Pacific Asia region. It is clear that the English language debate had thus far been dominated by commentators from the USA. At the present time we could perhaps identify four streams of commentary:

(a) an optimistic celebration of the Pacific region, often cast in prospective terms;

(b) an anxious concern for the economic competition and power of Japan;
(c) a rather over-anxious concern for the future of Western civilization in the face of a burgeoning Asia;
(d) a recent crisis-related celebration of the overdue end of 'crony capitalism'.

Shibusawa (1992) discusses the economic growth of the region in terms of trade patterns, investment flows and development aid disbursements. In all three areas it is noted that the statistics record strong growth: there is more trade, more investment and more aid. These spheres of activity show complex interdependencies. Shibusawa notes:

> The picture of the early and mid-1980s is therefore one of growing global – rather than merely regional – economic integration and interdependence. But the regional changes that began to be seen in the late 1980s, often closely associated with FDI flows suggest that the 1990s will see an even more complex network of economic interactions. Inevitably, such heightened economic interplay will not be without political repercussions – both domestic and external. (Shibusawa, 1992: 34)

It has become clear over recent years that it is not enough to understand any development aid programme in simple terms derived from the planning rationale underlying it. In terms of a useful slogan it can be said that what counts as development is locally determined. The way in which aid programmes are received by recipient communities is thus an important matter. However, there are many players and their responses will vary: politicians (linked to the state-regime); bureaucrats; business sectors (industrial, extractive, primary, service); employed urban; semi-employed urban; rural; and the poor, subsistence and marginal figures (Worsley, 1984) As Long (1992) has pointed out, development project work is a complex exchange between a series of players, including donor agencies, local political and bureaucratic machineries and local recipients. The practical outcome of these exchanges is what, after the fact, we label the 'development project'. In a related way, the nature of foreign direct investment has to be analysed in terms of the differing intentions and concerns of those exporting and those receiving capital. These patterns are all shifting as regions are ongoing historical projects and Japan's trade, aid and investment have contributed to the present growth of the Pacific Asia region.

An emerging yen zone?

Within the USA and the European Union there is concern voiced in respect of the tendential evolution of the global industrial-capitalist system, in particular it is argued that the world economy should not be left to fragment into three discrete areas – the dollar, euro and yen zones.

Yet it does seem that there is increasing pressure towards such an arrangement. In other words there are contradictory pressures within the global system: on the one hand the exigencies of geography, history and culture point in the direction of a regionalization of the global system, on the other there is continuing concern to protect the concept of an open trading system and here one instances the Uruguay round of GATT and the decision to establish the WTO.

It would seem to be the case that this debate has been sharpened in the wake of the ending of the Cold War. In this context the significance of the Cold War was multiple:

1 It provided an overarching set of themes which ordered inter-state exchanges both within and between the blocks.
2 It provided the overarching rationale for a split within the Pacific-Asian sphere as between the 'free world' and the 'socialist world'.
3 It provided an overarching framework for Japanese and American relationships, such that the Japanese adherence to the tenets of the Western block overrode any problems with economic exchanges.
4 It provided the occasion for US strategic activity which offered opportunities for economic growth to the countries of the region, in particular in East Asia.

It is clear that with the end of the Cold War long-established ways of reading the political economy of the region are called into question. The matter of the relationships between the various countries of Pacific Asia and with the USA and Australasia are once again being addressed. However, these issues are now raised in a situation radically different from that obtaining in the immediate wake of World War II. In place of a spread of war-ravaged economies and polities we have a series of economically prosperous countries. In other words, where the immediate post-World War II period of confusion and disorder saw the unchallenged establishment of the economic, military and political hegemony of the USA – with socialist Asia locking itself away within an inward looking grouping – the present period of change involves a series of much more equal players.

One way in which this new period of reordering has manifested itself is in a concern for ordering the interstate relationships of the Pacific Asia countries. A series of new organizations has been founded, or old organizations revivified or redirected. In contemporary discussions of the development of Pacific Asia new acronyms abound. It would seem that this concern for groupings in the post-Cold War phase has been prompted by the success of the Europeans in pursuing unification through the EU. Thus the formation of the EU prompted the pursuit of the Asia-Pacific Economic Cooperation (APEC). An alternate notion has been East Asia Economic Caucus (EAEC) promoted by the government of Malaysia. And there are other organizations, with ASEAN Free Trade

Area (AFTA) promoting ASEAN as an integrated market, with NAFTA linking countries in America and most recently with the establishment of Asia Europe Meeting (ASEM), linking the countries of the European Union with the 'Asian ten'.

These political manoeuvrings are responses to fundamental changes within the global economy which in the wake of the end of the Cold War are having to be addressed directly. In brief, there has been both a measure of internationalization in production and exchange (although consumption is still skewed towards the developed countries) and a drift towards regionalization.

The global system is vehicled/ordered through a number of institutions:

(a) the inter-state system of treaties;
(b) formal intra-governmental organizations such as the IMF, World Bank and GATT;
(c) the presence and activities of global economic organizations (MNCs) and practices (the 24 hour financial markets);
(d) the capacities of new technologies of communications and travel.

At the same time the givens of geography and history, coupled to present economic and political imperatives, are pushing the global system towards a set of regional groupings – in brief, the three currency zones noted at the outset.

Cronin (1992) has considered the post-1989 phase of the development of the global system in the Pacific region in terms of three distinct scenarios: the constructive globalization of Japan; a heightened rivalry between the USA and Japan; and the emergence of an Asia-Pacific region dominated by Japan. In the first scenario Japan builds links with the USA and Pacific Asia so as to develop further an open market Asian region and the impetus to this flows from reform within Japan in line with the underlying logics of economics (Cronin, 1992: 107–9). In the second scenario, of heightened rivalry, the Japanese continue to build up their own position, thereby fostering conflict as other economies respond to protect themselves (Cronin, 1992: 111–14). This thesis is affirmed by those who analyse Japan as being neo-mercantile. In the third scenario, a Japan-dominated Asia Pacific, the provision of more official development aid and foreign direct investment coupled to greater access to the Japanese market for Asian exports, result in the formation of a yen zone (Cronin, 1992: 115–18). Cronin adds that given that export success is a matter of the USA importing these goods, it is difficult to see such an outcome coming to pass, and he draws a distinction between a core economy and a yen zone (Cronin, 1992: 117). Overall, Cronin (1992: 133) looks to a period of reordering in the Pacific area, but argues that Japan's room for manoeuvre is constrained by the USA and historical legacies. Yet in the wake of the collapse of the bubble and the Asian financial crisis it might be appropriate to add a fourth scenario, the slow development of an 'internationalized yen zone', which sees Japan continuing to develop its distinctive economic system, advancing its role as the regional core economy and slowly enhancing its regional and global political role.[1]

The bubble and the crisis

The collapse of the Japanese bubble economy in the early 1990s generated both real domestic problems (in dealing with an overhang of bad debts within the financial system) and became the occasion for domestic and foreign criticism of the Japanese government (for its alleged lack of action) and the Japanese political-economic system in general (where local commentators joined outsiders in arguing after the fashion of neo-liberals for deregulation in the expectation that this was the sovereign remedy for the ills of the economy, polity and indeed wider society). In the event the domestic financial crisis has been addressed piecemeal and there is little sign that this will or ought to alter. The domestic problems and the consequent debates were overtaken by further events in the late 1990s.

The 1997–8 financial crisis in Pacific Asia has been the subject of considerable debate. At one extreme advocates of the US-style, market-liberal system have blamed the political and business elites of the region. In reply, regional advocates of the particularity of the development experience of Asia have spoken of a Western conspiracy to undermine Asia's success. Yet, in contrast, the focus of the classical European tradition on elucidating the dynamics of complex change suggests that the crisis has its roots in post-Cold War and post-Bretton Woods inter-regional adjustment within the increasingly integrated global system. In respect of the former element, the reorientation of American thinking from geo-strategy to geo-economics has made the pattern of economic exchanges between Asia and the USA much more problematical. The USA is evidently no longer prepared to offer a market of last resort to Asian countries in exchange for declarations of support in a Cold War competition with Communism. In respect of the latter it is clear that the Asian financial crisis was but an instance of a wider global crisis as the old regimes of the Bretton Woods system gave way in the context of an emergent tripolar system. It is clear that the rules of the new global system are in doubt and a set of rules will have to be agreed, which clearly will not be easy.

The future of Japan within the region of Pacific Asia is now, therefore, bound up within wider debates about the modes of regulation of an integrated tripolar global system. It is unlikely that the necessary formal rules and agreed routine practices will be established quickly, or without intense political manoeuvring.

Conclusion

It does make some sort of sense to speak of Pacific Asia becoming a coherent unit within the ever more integrated global system. The Pacific-Asian countries increasingly trade among themselves and invest in each other's countries. The role of Japanese official development aid and foreign direct investment are encouraging the formation of an integrated economic space. The Pacific-Asian countries have established a set of international forums where they can meet and order their interactions (all the acronyms). Nonetheless this cannot be seen as an exclusionary regionalism since the area is embedded within the global industrial-capitalist system (thus much of the recent economic expansion of Pacific Asia rests on US and EU absorption of its exports); nor can it be seen as inclusionary regionalism as the area shows no signs of having determined upon a course of action which would see it submerged within a global liberal-market system.

It does make some sort of sense to speak of Pacific-Asian political economies, societies and political cultures as distinctive. A summary characterization can be made in the following fashion:

1   The economy is state directed.
2   State direction is oriented to the pragmatic pursuit of economic growth (that is, it is not informed by explicit or debated political-ideological positions).
3   State direction is top-down style and pervasive in its reach throughout the political economy and culture.
4   Society is familial and thereafter communitarian (thus society is non-individualistic).
5   Social order is secured by pervasive control machineries (sets of social rules and an extensive bureaucratization of everyday life) and a related hegemonic common culture (which enjoins submission to the demands of community and authority).
6   Political debate and power are typically reserved to an elite sphere (and political life centres on the pragmatic pursuit of overarching economic goals).
7   Political debate and action among the masses are diffuse and demobilized (thus there is no 'public sphere').
8   Culture comprises a mix of officially sanctioned tradition and market sanctioned consumption.
9   Culture stresses consensus, acquiescence and harmony and eschews open conflict (Preston, 1998a).

In sum, we can note that the model is distinct from received models of Western society (both Anglo-Saxon and European social democratic) and that the pattern sketched is undoubtedly coherent and effective. These are not countries aspiring to and failing to achieve the standard model of the West (Gray, 1998). However, these countries are diverse and any idea of regionalism must be handled carefully – the notion points to arrangements within the global system rather than separate from the system (regionalism is not old-style autarchy writ large). It is also clear that for the foreseeable future Japan will be the core economy of Pacific Asia.

Note

1 The scenario is a broad brush synthesis of aspects of the work of Sheridan (1998b), Dore (1997) and Preston (1998a). It will be pursued in Chapter 8.

8

JAPAN, PACIFIC ASIA AND THE TRIPOLAR GLOBAL SYSTEM

The Regional Context of Contemporary Political-Cultural Projects

The situation of Japan has most recently been debated within a particular double context: first, the movement towards an integrated Pacific-Asian regional block (within a tripolar global system including the USA and EU); second, the parallel movement towards an interdependent global system. The character of the Japanese involvement with Pacific Asia within the context of a regionalized global system has become a key issue. A series of scenarios have been posited:

1   Internal Japanese reforms in line with logic of the liberal-market model leading to a harmonious development future for Pacific Asia and its trading partners.
2   A mercantilist Japanese strategy leading to the strengthening of its position at the cost of endemic conflicts with trading partners.
3   The partial reform of Japan to allow Pacific-Asian countries relatively open access to the Japanese market leading to the de facto creation of a Pacific-Asian block within a tripolar global system.
4   The further deepening of the regionally integrative economic role coupled to a more internationalist political stance, leading to a more open variant of the yen zone.

Relatedly, a key issue, cutting across geo-economic concerns, is the geo-strategic issue of security in Pacific Asia, where the partial withdrawal of the USA, the emergence of China and the role of Japan are all presently debated within a novel post-Cold War context. These are complex matters and in this chapter a series of restricted reflections will be offered, dealing with, in turn: the outline of a tripolar global system; the routes to the modern world taken by the countries of Pacific Asia; the changing identities within the region; and the role of Japan within the developing project of the region.

The new context: a tripolar global system

The classical European tradition is concerned with elucidating the dynamics of complex change in the ongoing shift to the modern world. It is an interpretive, critical and reflexive tradition. The arguments of social theorists are influenced by the changing social environments within which they work. In the wake of the end of the 'short twentieth century' (Hobsbawm, 1994) and the related collapse of the received certainties of the Cold War which had shaped and obscured the understandings of European and American thinkers, it has become clear that a new global industrial-capitalist system is taking shape. The system shows a number of cross-cutting tendencies: first, to integration on a global scale, with a financial system that is integrated across the globe and with increasingly de-nationalized MNC/TNC operations; second, to regionalization within the global system, with three key areas emerging where intra-regional linkages are deepening; third, to division on a global scale, with areas of the world apparently falling behind the regionalized global system. Hobsbawm (1994) argues that this is an unstable system which recalls the equally unstable situation in the latter years of the 'long nineteenth century'.

New global patterns

These arguments point to new patterns within the global system. Agent groups will have to read and react to these structures as they order their various political projects. The ways in which inhabitants of territories within the global system understand themselves as ordered collectivities will determine the overall direction of their particular political-cultural projects. The nature of the forms of life within the tripolar global system are divergent. It has been argued that the pattern of the European Union presents a social-market system, while the pattern of the USA should be characterized as liberal market, and both are to be distinguished from Pacific-Asian developmental capitalism (Thurow, 1994; Preston, 1997; Gray, 1998).

In the post-World War II period the peoples, organizations and government machines of Europe understood themselves within the overall framework of Cold War bipolarity. In Eastern Europe matters were cast in terms of the achievement of a socialist polity and in Western Europe they were understood in terms of the notion of the free world. The East was ordered according to the tenets of Soviet state socialism and became an autarchic region within the global system. The West was ordered at the macro-structural level in terms of the ideas, institutions and power relationships established by the Bretton Woods agreement which made the USA the core economy of an open liberal trading region. However, as the post-World War II settlement began to weaken following the confusions of the early 1970s the countries of Europe moved to adjust to the new circumstances.

The countries of Western Europe slowly moved towards a closer union and found an available mechanism in the European Community (EC), itself a development of the European Economic Community (EEC) which had been founded back in the early 1950s. These ideas and institutional mechanisms were in place when the extent of structural change finally became unequivocally clear with the 1989–91 collapse of the USSR. At Maastricht the idea of the European Union (EU) moved to the fore and it is now the overarching political project around which European political life revolves. Overall, the project of European unification which began in the wake of World War II shows no sign of faltering. Notwithstanding tensions and confusions the established institutional machineries look set to provide the vehicle for a distinctive European region.

In this context, the key elements of the European economy, society and culture could be said to include:

(a) a political economy in which state and market interact, with the state having a directive role;
(b) a social-institutional structure which affirms an idea of the importance of community and sees economy and polity acknowledging the important role of the community;
(c) a cultural tradition which acknowledges established institutions, a broad humanist social philosophy and a tradition of social-democratic or christian-democratic welfare politics.

World War II saw the emergence of the USA as the premier power within the global system. Its economic power was used to establish and underpin the Bretton Woods system within the sphere of the West and its military and economic power were central to confrontations with the socialist bloc. There was a period of US hegemony during the 1950s and 1960s but in the 1970s the system came under great pressure. The following factors contributed to the decline: the financial implications for the USA of the war in Vietnam and the end of the Bretton Woods system in 1971; the oil price shocks of 1973; the rise of the EU and the Japanese sphere in East Asia; and the partial and uneven globalization of the industrial-capitalist system. In addition in the 1980s the USA was the major sponsor of the doctrines of market liberalism which have further undermined the order of the global system.

The upshot of all these changes over the period 1973–91 has been a movement into an unstable, insecure and novel tripolar global industrial capitalist system. The end of the Cold War has seen the USA continuing to press for an open global trading system but these arguments are now made within the context of a tripolar system. The influence of the Washington-based International Monetary Fund (IMF) and World Bank are extensive in promoting liberal free trade and recent expressions of these concerns have been the establishment of NAFTA and APEC which link the USA to Latin America and Pacific Asia respectively. A link to the Europeans is secured via the security mechanism of NATO and the routine conversations of the G7 economic group. A key element of US policy is the objective of a series of multilateral open trading areas whose institutional structures have a common locus in the USA.

In the context of an increasingly regionalized global system the key elements of the US economy, society and culture might be taken to include:

(a) commitment to an open market economy;
(b) a strong preference for individualism and a tradition which celebrates the achievements of ordinary people;
(c) a cultural tradition of liberal individualism along with a public commitment to republican democracy.

It is on the basis of these established cultural resources that the USA will seek to deal with the peoples of the other regions.

The Pacific region over the post-World War II period has been divided by Cold War institutions and rhetoric into a Western-focused group and a socialist bloc. The Western-focused group has been subject to the military, economic and cultural hegemony of the USA. However, it is undergoing considerable change and in brief this may be summarized as the beginnings of a political-economic, social-institutional and cultural emancipation from the USA. At the same time the countries of the socialist bloc which had spent decades following autarchic state-socialist development trajectories are now opening up to the Western-focused group. Japan is the core economy in the Pacific-Asian region. In the years following the Pacific War patterns of trade, aid and foreign direct investment have worked to integrate the region and a series of spheres can be identified (Halliday, 1980). The countries of the inner periphery of East Asia have prospered over a long period of economic development in the political and military shadow of the USA and the economic shadow of Japan. Thereafter the countries of the outer periphery of Southeast Asia have recently reoriented themselves towards the economic model of Japan. Relatedly, we can note the turn of the countries of Australasia towards the Pacific-Asian economies. Finally, we have the ongoing process of the reorientation of China and Indo-China in the wake of Deng Xiaping's reforms and the 1985 Plaza Accords which generated a flood of yen for foreign investment. Overall, the region has been undergoing considerable structural change since the late 1970s and there is now a significant measure of regional trade, integration and acknowledged cultural commonality (Preston, 1998a).

A speculative illustration of the economy, society and culture of Pacific Asia would include the following points:

1 The economy is state directed and oriented to the pragmatic pursuit of economic growth.
2 State direction is top-down style and pervasive in its reach.
3 Society is familial and thereafter communitarian.
4 Social order is secured by pervasive control machineries and a related hegemonic common culture.
5 Political debate and power are typically reserved to an elite sphere and debate and action among the masses are diffuse and demobilized.
6 The culture stresses consensus, acquiescence and harmony and eschews open conflict.

Global and regional dynamics

The global industrial-capitalist system shows a number of cross-cutting tendencies. The movement towards economic and financial integration on a global scale continues and may be read as the most recent expression of that dynamism which Marx originally identified as the product of the core logic of capitalism. At the same time, there is movement towards regionalization within the global system, with three key areas emerging, and the issues of the nature of this regionalization within the system (inclusionary/exclusionary) and the extent of any internal integration remain open. It is here that commentators begin to speak of divergent models of industrial-capitalist development. Finally, it is clear that there is increasing division on a global scale with areas of the world apparently falling behind the regionalized global industrial-capitalist system.

Pacific Asia: routes to the modern world

The modern history of Pacific Asia centres on the nature of the shift of the region to the modern world. In schematic terms this can be taken to include in turn: first, the precontact period and process of absorption within the Western colonial system; second, the post-colonial pursuit of effective nationstatehood; third, the rise of Pacific Asia centred on Japan. It is the complex pattern of exchanges between Japan and its Asian neighbours, on the one hand, and the region and global system, on the other, with Japan as the key country, which have shaped the modern history of Pacific Asia.

Form of life of the modern world

Worsley (1984) argues that the modern world can be understood as a particular cultural form. The cultural form of modernity comprises the general celebration of the power of human reason, the extensive development of natural science and an economic system dedicated to material progress via science-based industry. This cultural form developed in

Europe over the period 1500 to 1900. During this time it refined itself internally, that is, it became better organized and penetrated deeply through the social world, and expanded externally, that is, it grew geographically. It can be described as a process of absorption and reconstruction during which existing cultural resources are more or less radically remade in line with the expectations and demands of modernity.

The general characteristics of the pre-contact forms of life of the peoples of Pacific Asia can be seen to have taken two broad forms. On the one hand, the East Asian sphere was typified by the closed bureaucratic feudal agrarian society of imperial China, with a similar society in Japan. On the other hand, the Southeast Asian sphere was typified by the riverine agrarian empires of Indo-China and the maritime trading empires of Southeast Asia. It should also be noted that Asia's third major cultural area, South Asia, centred on India, has exerted considerable influence on the other two areas, for example, with Islam, Hinduism and Buddhism (Evans, 1993: 9). It was this spread of long-established civilizations and the multiplicity of simpler peasant forms of life lodged within their bounds which the carriers of the expanding global capitalist system encountered in the sixteenth century (Grimal, 1978).

The expansion of European- and American-based capitalism moved through a series of phases: first, the early trade journeys involving very few traders and specializing in exotic luxury goods; second, the later linkages involving relatively settled factories whereby the trade in luxury products was regularized, albeit still at a very low level of numbers of traders and quantities of goods; third, the shift towards much more extensive trade links as the competing incomers looked to establish exclusive spheres; fourth, the shift towards colonial holdings; finally, the establishment of colonial holdings alongside the new schedule of demands made upon the resources and peoples of the region by industrial capitalism. In the case of Pacific Asia, the European traders had little impact on existing societies in the early years of contact. In the mid-sixteenth century when these traders first arrived they did so in small numbers and with trade expectations confined to small quantities of exotic and luxury products. This pattern of exchange persisted and slowly expanded through the seventeenth and eighteenth centuries.

It was in the nineteenth century that the depth of the involvement of the Europeans and Americans in the territories of Pacific Asia deepened significantly, when as a result of the dynamics of metropolitan industrial capitalism the schedule of demands for trade goods in the region expanded, and at the same time the rapidly increasing technological superiority of the West in respect of the ruling regimes of the region allowed them to insist that their requirements be acknowledged. The upshot was a slow but steady movement to take control of areas within the region in order to facilitate their integration within the industrial-capitalist system. The final stage of this process involved the imposition of formal colonial regimes on large parts of the region, the quasi-colonization of China and the effective resistance of Japan. In the twentieth century it was against the empire systems that the nationalists of the colonized territories were to organize their resistance as the political-cultural resources of the colonizers were turned back against themselves (Barraclough, 1964; Anderson, 1983).

The shift to the modern world

The nature of the shift to the modern world effected by Japan was conditioned by two sets of anxieties on the part of the Japanese political elite: the first concerned their relationship with the technologically superior Western powers whose concerns for trade and colonial expansion represented direct threats to Japanese autonomy; and relatedly, their relationship with the countries of East Asia, whose weakness in the face of Western expansion represented a broad threat to Japanese interests. The Japanese ruling Tokugawa shogunate was unable to formulate a response to these twin problems and it was overthrown in the 1868 Meiji Restoration which saw political power shift from the controlling family within a land-centred economy and polity which resembled the European feudal system to an oligarchic developmental state, and a project of national development inaugurated. In the late nineteenth and early twentieth centuries the economic development of Japan was very rapid. A key aspect of this ordered and rapid renewal was a deep anxiety in respect of the possible further intrusive demands of the West. The authoritarian modernization from above was undertaken within the context of this real anxiety and as success was achieved it found expression in imperialist terms taken from the West. The Japanese saw a legitimate sphere of interest in Northeast Asia within which they could remedy some of the resource-poor aspects of their domestic economy. The Japanese elite pursued the project of empire in Asia. In the early phases this project had the sympathy of the West. However, an early rebuff to Japanese hopes in respect of China had the effect of encouraging a Japanese nationalism which subsequently modulated into the fascism of the inter-war period. It was involvement in China which drew the criticism of the USA and Europeans and in due course lead to the Pacific War (Ienaga, 1978; Thorne, 1986).

The slow decline of the Chinese Qing Dynasty as a result of internal decay and European and American incursions accelerated over the second half of the nineteenth century in the wake of the Opium Wars of 1840–2 and the resultant treaty port system which acknowledged and firmly established the European and American trading presence. Inside the Chinese ruling class there was considerable debate about the appropriate strategy of response to these incursions. The established Chinese world view placed the Imperial Court at the centre and ranged all others in circles of descending importance around this core. The culture was

inward looking and disinclined to begin the business of learning from
outsiders. However, the military defeats of the Opium Wars and the
routine evidence of European and American commercial vigour did
encourage the pursuit of modernization by some groups within China.
But they received no support from the Imperial centre, indeed they were
discouraged and overall, reports Moise (1994), there was little real grasp
of the extent of changes required within China if the country was to
respond positively to the arrival and demands of the Europeans and
Americans.

In 1899 the forces of the Boxer Rebellion, which had the tacit support
of the Empress, laid siege to the foreign legations in Beijing. The rebellion
was quickly suppressed and the Qing Dynasty finally began a serious
programme of modernization. Moore comments: 'The pattern of her [the
empress dowager] actions strongly suggests that her real goal was the
establishment of a strong centralised bureaucratic government over
which she would be able to exercise direct personal control, roughly
along the lines of a Germany or a Japan' (1966: 184). However, in 1911
the Qing Dynasty central government experienced one more crisis (over
railway construction), there was a widespread revolt among provincial
gentry and two-thirds of the country quickly fell into the hands of Sun
Yat Sen's revolutionaries who declared him President in the provincial
city of Nanjing.

However, the Qing authorities asked the regional army commander,
General Yuan, to suppress the rebels and in the ensuing confusion both
the Dynasty and the newly established republic gave way first to the
brief rule of General Yuan and subsequently a series of regional warlords. Thereafter, up until 1937, there was a battle for power between
the KMT, Sun's nationalist party, led since 1925 by Chiang Kai Shek, the
CCP, which had been founded in 1921, and the still powerful regional
warlords. Chiang Kai Shek slowly broadened his power and established
a unified Chinese state with a military government in Nanjing in 1927.
Moore (1966: 188–201) regards the KMT government with its landlord-
ism, gangsterism, opportunistic commercial factions, backward-looking
nationalism and its militarism as a variant of the familiar European
model of fascism. Further, the effective collapse of central authority in
China, and the political and social chaos which followed, left the country
open to the demands of foreign powers. The Western colonial powers
expanded the spheres of influence they had established in the late nineteenth century and the Japanese became involved, with open warfare
raging from 1937. The Sino-Japanese war, in turn, was subsumed within
the wider Pacific War.

Overall, in this process of industrial-capitalist expansion, the demands
made by the system deepened and the territories were slowly remade
in line with the schedule of needs of the metropolitan centres. The
upshot was the pre-1941 situation of colonial Asia where the Dutch and
British controlled Southeast Asia, the French ruled in Indo-China, the

Americans occupied the Philippines, the Japanese occupied Korea and Taiwan, and all these powers competed for advantage in China. At this point the entire sphere of Pacific Asia had been drawn one way or another into the Western-centred industrial-capitalist system.

The military victories of the Japanese armed forces in 1941–2 destroyed the European and American colonial power structure and out of the chaos of the period laid the basis for the post-war independence throughout the region. The disruption of familiar economic, social and political patterns left a space open for indigenous nationalist movements. The post-war formal withdrawal of the colonial powers was accomplished relatively quickly, although in many cases it was attended by violence.

Rise of Pacific Asia in the years following the Pacific War

The Japanese empire did not survive the wartime exchange with the USA and its allies. However, the occupation of Japan by the USA was distinctly idealistic, somewhat rightwing, arguably inept and relatively benign (Buckley, 1990). The occupation powers made relatively limited changes to the political-economic, social-institutional and cultural structures of Japan and the rehabilitation and rapid reconstruction of the country began with the outbreak of the Korean War in 1950 and the US drive against world Communism. Thereafter, the general business of reordering the global system around its new US centre, with decolonization, the establishment of the Bretton Woods settlement, the related founding of the UN and the pervasively deployed US conservative ideology of anti-Communism, gave the Japanese a framework within which they could rebuild the economy and, along with this, their links to Pacific Asia.

It seems fairly clear that the episode of post-war reconstruction involved a great measure of continuity with pre-war patterns of economy and society (Johnson, 1982; van Wolferen, 1989). More broadly, because the history of Japanese involvement with Pacific Asia is longer and deeper than the wars of the twentieth century, an available theme within Japanese commentaries characterizing the relationship generates the view that the unique and gifted Japanese are able to lead the rest of Pacific Asia in development (Rix, 1993b). It seems that this is a major source of thinking in regard to Pacific Asia and development aid. Thus it is seen as a matter of responsibility and duty and the actual narrowly pragmatic nature of the links is glossed over (Orr, 1990). Nonetheless the ideas are available and help underpin the role of core regional economy.

The question of the relationship of the Japanese economy to the economies of Pacific Asia remains crucial and has often been answered by non-Japanese commentators in a fashion which implies the existence of an ordered grouping. These social theorists have spoken of the Japanese core being surrounded by an inner periphery (the NICs) and an outer periphery (ASEAN) to which a new circle has recently been added in the guise of the reforming socialist bloc (Nester, 1990; Phongpaichit, 1990; Cronin, 1992). It is clear that the history of modern Pacific Asia can be told in terms of the series of exchanges between Japan and the territories of Pacific Asia on the one hand and the exchanges of the region with the Western dominated global system on the other.

Contemporary change in Pacific Asia

A central theme within the classical European tradition is the analysis of complex change and one aspect of this general concern is the matter of identity. The ways in which individuals and groups understand themselves is taken to be a matter of reading changing circumstances in the light of available ideas and presently urgent problems. In the post-Cold War period, with the comfortable certainties of confrontation gone and Japan ever more obviously the regional core economy, the issue of identity can be raised in the context of Pacific Asia. In particular, it can be asked whether the ideal of a Pacific Asia region, which would inevitably centre on Japan, could offer the disparate countries of the area an overarching theme around which more local identities could be ordered.

The Pacific-Asian region over the post-World War II period has been divided by Cold War institutions and rhetoric into a Western-focused group and a socialist bloc. The Western-focused group has been subject to the economic, political and cultural hegemony of the USA. The countries of the socialist bloc have spent decades following autarchic development trajectories. However, the Western-focused group in Pacific Asia is undergoing considerable change and, in brief, this may be summarized as the beginnings of a political-economic and cultural emancipation from the hegemony of the USA. At the same time the socialist bloc in Pacific Asia is undergoing rapid change and in the period since the early 1980s there have been economic, social, political and diplomatic changes which, in total, may be summarized as an opening up to the global industrial-capitalist system.

The central role of Japan in Pacific Asia is now clear. The Plaza Accord of 1985 which revalued the yen upwards against the US dollar had the unforeseen consequence of further accelerating the development of the Japanese presence in the countries of Pacific Asia as home industries were relocated to low-cost parts of the region. The region now displays a significant measure of internal integration and new questions have emerged in respect of the depth of such integration and the likelihood of the Japanese assuming an overt leadership role. In all, the deepening particularity of the Pacific-Asian region within the tripolar global system is evident and now commands increasing scholarly and policy analytic attention.

The relationship of Japan and the countries of Pacific Asia is coloured by memories of Japanese colonial expansion and war. The historical legacy of Japanese colonialism in Pacific Asia is complex and involves a mixture of long-established rule, wartime violence and some political and economic reforms. One theme which runs through the available discussions of Japan's role in Pacific Asia is the matter of leadership. Commentators ask whether Japan wishes to exercise leadership and if so whether it is able to exercise leadership. All agree that this implies reforms within Japan and the following issues are often mentioned: reforms to Japanese politics; reforms to the Japanese economy; reforms to Japanese society; plus reforms to Japanese culture; and an extensive reworking of Japan's relationships with Pacific Asia, in particular via reforms to Japanese ODA programmes.

A general diagnosis of Japanese politics is given by Buckley (1990) who notes that there are problems with political and business corruption, a pork-barrel style of local politics, a secretive and powerful bureaucracy and most broadly a general inability of the political system effectively to articulate and thereafter deal with a spread of domestic and international policy problems. Similarly, van Wolferen (1989) argues that the political system centred on the bureaucracy is 'results focused' by which he means that it attends not to matters of principle and policy but to the pragmatic resolution of immediate problems. Within a dominating over-all commitment to economic expansion, problems are tackled on an ad hoc basis. This means that the system is hugely successful within its own terms and that it is unable to formulate responses to problems which fall outside its routine frame of expectations. In stronger terms van Wolferen argues that strictly speaking the system is so flexible and pragmatic that it amounts to an absence of a formal state. Instead there are shifting patterns of alliances between the various important players in the bureaucracy, business and politics and in this it recalls the system established at the time of the Meiji Restoration. It is a system running mostly out of the control of its beneficiaries and victims.

The general nature of the criticism of the Japanese economy is that the system is in some way a victim of its own success and that reform is urgently needed to redirect its energies away from production and the expansion of production towards consumption, in particular both private and public consumption for the benefit of the ordinary people of Japan. Eccleston (1989) notes that the state is routinely interventionist and works in a corporatist fashion. It takes no large equity shares because it does not have to in order to secure control. The state invests in industry and infrastructure. The state holds down social consumption (of schools, hospitals, transfer payments and the like). The state encourages savings and uses them for economic development. The state oversees business activity with MITI offering 'administrative guidance', and in any case the line between administration and business is blurred (thus civil servants retire and shift into the private sector). In all, Japan has a corporatist developmental state and all this generates a series of issues that are hotly debated and involve: first, the nature of the role of the state, where debate revolves around the costs and benefits of such interventions (World Bank, 1993); second, the nature of the economic structure, where debates revolve around the costs and benefits of the dual structure with a large firm sector and a small firm sector; third, the nature of employment patterns, where debate revolves around costs and benefits of life-time employment and small sector employment; fourth, the nature of the costs and benefits accruing to the Japanese consumer of the present system, for example, the controlled retail sector; finally, the costs and benefits of the production focus of the system to Japan's trading partners.

The schedule of reforms canvassed in respect of polity and economy is lengthy and their interactions various, and the proposals all have widespread implications for the nature of Japanese society. The practical problems which are routinely cited include poor housing, poor public facilities, long hours of work (and commuting), inequality between genders, excessively examination centred schooling, a lack of leisure time for families, overstressed habits of conformity and the problems of an aged population. In all, the Japanese people are presented as the unwitting victims of the successful corporatist system which they have created and from which they restrictedly benefit. Thereafter, if we consider the Western commentators, excluding the over-anxious nationalists, then theorists of the right propose the liberalization of the Japanese economy in the expectation that consumer benefits will follow, while commentators of the centre-left propose a more consumer friendly democratic system. In this way one can see a broad similarity in the approaches of the two groups as both are concerned to enhance the position of the Japanese consumer at the expense of currently dominant producer interests. Yet if we consider the debate among Japanese, Sheridan (1993: 3) notes 'there still has been surprisingly little popular public debate in Japan about the future directions of economic development and national purpose'.

After an exhaustive review of the development experience of Japan, which recalls the story told above, Sheridan (1993) argues that while Japanese have become rich there are problems with long working hours and long commuting times, very expensive housing costs and a lack of adequate social capital (or infrastructure). Sheridan (1993) notes that over the 1960s and 1970s there was some improvement both in quality of life (for example, with environmental standards) and a declining inequality in wealth, but the 1985 revaluation of the yen triggered speculation on the back of asset inflation and this has done great damage (especially via land prices which may be expected to feed through into higher housing costs). However, Sheridan (1993) does see reasons for hope in the signs that the Japanese people are beginning to shift from a politics of fear to a politics of utopias (that is, away from reactive positions towards prospective stances). Relatedly, the system does allow collective effort in respect of communal goals. Sheridan (1993) argues that the system could be shifted away from its preoccupation with economic expansion towards the provision of the social capital necessary to improve people's lives. Sheridan (1993) points out that the Japanese state is an effective activist state and a future oriented to quality of life could be envisioned. Sheridan (1993) then goes on to unpack this overall proposal in terms of a series of policies designed to enhance the position of women, improve local and neighbourhood life, reduce inequalities and reform the land market. All of these goals are to be pursued with a Japanese strategy which would draw on the established strengths of country for coopera- tive collective hard work. However, any reform strategy is dependent upon action from the centre, and here the myths of marketeers and the state's prejudices against welfare spending would have to be overcome. In all, change is likely to be slow.

Japan in Pacific Asia

The relationship of Japan and Pacific Asia is bound up with trade, official development aid and foreign direct investment. The official rationale of Japan's aid is helping the less fortunate. Self-help by recipients is stressed, otherwise there is no consistent view evidenced. There are cultural antecedents in Meiji ideas of self-help and charity is not stressed. Rix (1993b: 20) notes that trying to grasp Japanese motivation is not easy as MITI stresses trade, resources and markets while MOFA looks to diplomacy and security, and there are shifts and changes in emphasis over time. The focus on Asia and the stress on responsibility is noticeable and Rix comments that 'Asian development was more a means of achieving Japanese objectives than a goal in its own right' (1993: 23). In a similar fashion Yasutomo (1986) deals with the diplomatic rationale of Japanese aid and is clear that it is a matter of national self-advancement. The role of aid is lodged within a concept of 'comprehensive national security' which urges that this depends upon regional security, and in turn is helped by economic growth in the area. Yasutomo argues that the Japanese govern- ment pursues five interrelated goals with its aid programmes: 'economic well being'; 'national prestige'; 'domestic support'; 'peace diplomacy'; and 'national security' (1986: 112). Overall, the Japanese aid programme is relatively loosely organized and that while it needs revising so as to encompass a Japanese aid leadership role, this is unlikely to happen. The present system serves many vested interests and all seem content with the status quo. However, as the Pacific-Asian region integrates there are wider implications for the global system.

Sketching the future

Cronin (1992) argues that Japan can constitute the core of the region. However, the export dependency of the region on the consumer markets of the USA means that it cannot become a closed block. The enquiry is pursued through the presentation, as noted earlier, of a series of 'scenarios' for the future.

The first scenario is of the competitive globalization of Japan. Cronin argues that this 'would have Japan interacting with Asia as an increasingly open economy, partially supplanting the United States as an export market for Asia-Pacific countries, while at the global level using its financial resources to undergird the present system' (1992: 107). A wider spread of concerns in respect of ODA might also be anticipated, including 'greater participation by non-Japanese firms and more emphasis on human resources development . . . investment projects would involve more participation by local subcontractors, transfer more technology, and be more oriented to the Japanese market' (1992: 107). Cronin suggests that this scenario is close to the optimistic reform position within Japan and would find support in the USA. It would mean Japan 'using its growing economic power to support the current global trading system' (1992: 107). On optimistic analyses the result would be an expanding global economy and a stable international environment. Cronin reports that an 'important theoretical basis for this scenario is the premise that Japan cannot suspend indefinitely the operation of what many see as universal economic laws' (1992: 109), and that liberalization will have to take place. However, he immediately adds that support within Japan for globalization remains 'shaky at best' (1992: 110). In sum, this scenario involves Japan building on established links with the USA and Pacific Asia in order further to develop the open markets of the region as the closed Japanese system bows to economic market logic and opens up to the global system.

The second scenario sees 'Japanese aid and investment in Asia as primarily acting to increase the competitive position of Japanese companies in world markets vis-à-vis the fast rising NIEs, while Japan's own markets remain relatively closed' (1992: 111). Cronin speculates that this is an unstable line of advance as trading partners might react against the lack of reciprocity. Over the longer term the Japanese relationship with the USA could wither away and such an eventuality would call into question many currently taken for granted ideas in respect of order in Pacific Asia. A school of thought has now emerged, reports Cronin, which holds that Japan 'will not significantly abandon its neo-mercantilist policies' (1992: 112) and there are many problem areas that could tip the Pacific system towards protectionism (for example, the issue of the US trade deficit). In sum, the second scenario is one of heightened rivalry as Japan continues to build up its own position, thereby fostering conflict as other states respond to protect their economies. The implication is one of various patterns of breakdown of the established global order.

The third scenario sees 'Japanese aid and investment, and increasing access to the Japanese market by Asian exporters, as producing a Japan centred Asia-Pacific economy' (Cronin, 1992: 115). Cronin comments that this scenario could develop in a beneficial way for most non-US countries or could turn into a second co-prosperity sphere. In both 'variants of this scenario, Asia-Pacific countries would become increasingly dependent on Japan for capital flows (both aid and investment) and increasingly tied to Japan by trade links, whole US domestic manufacturers and multinationals would face increased competition both in Asian and in the US market [as would the EU]' (1992: 115). One condition required by this scenario is that the Japanese market supplant that of the USA as the regional core – able to draw in the region's imports and fuel the region's need for new capital and technology. Cronin notes that there is no agreement at present on how the system is moving and that there are arguments for and against the notion of an emerging yen zone. However, Cronin takes the role of the USA as market and investment location to be of continuing importance, and thus the emergence of a yen bloc looks unlikely. In sum, the third scenario is a Japan-dominated Pacific Asia where more ODA and FDI plus trade access for Asians to the Japanese market result in the creation of a yen bloc. However, cutting against this possibility is the general extent of global integration and the particular links which Japan has with the USA.

A fourth scenario can be posited. In the wake of the collapse of the bubble and the Asian fiancial crisis it is appropriate to revisit the analysis of the dynamics of the region, in particular the role of Japan, and consider new possible routes to the future. At the outset it seems clear that the Japanese economy will continue to develop according to its own distinctive logic. Against the enthusiasts of market liberalism it should be noted that there is no rational warrant for any expectation of rapid change. It is similarly clear that the role of the Japanese economy within the regional economy will continue to be crucially important. It might also be noted that the trans-Pacific security and trade relationship with the USA are likely to be sustained. In addition, it can be suggested that the slow internationalization of Japanese foreign policy might be expected to continue. The upshot could be an 'internationalized yen zone'. This would embrace a series of factors: first, the continuing development of the distinctive Japanese domestic political-economic system: second, the further promotion of the Japanese role as the regional core economy; third, the continuation of links with the USA; fourth, the slow enhancement of the Japanese political role wihin both the region and the global system.

Inner periphery of East Asia

The expansion of the Japanese state into the area of East Asia began in the late nineteenth century and came to involve large holdings in Manchuria, colonies in Korea and Taiwan and extensive interests in China. All this may be tagged 'late imperialism'. In due course the war against China

precipitated the Pacific War. In the early period of successful expansion
the Japanese government looked to the formation of a Greater East Asia
Coprosperity Sphere, an area of mutually beneficial economic activity.
However, in the post-World War II period the colonies of South Korea
and Taiwan were taken from Japanese control and prospered under
American protection. Halliday (1980) characterizes their extensive economic links with Japan in terms of their constituting an 'inner periphery'.
Nonetheless the relationship at both popular and governmental levels is
somewhat fraught as ever-present historical memory continues to haunt
otherwise successful economic exchanges.

South Korea constitutes, according to Shibusawa, a 'near-perfect
example of a developmental state' (1992: 69) as the circumstances of
independence plus the dominant role of the military fed into an
authoritarian pattern of development. Yet after some 30 years of post-
war success the political economy, society and culture advanced to the
point of rejecting the authoritarian aspects of the system. A series of
distinct groups can be identified within society, each with its own
interests, which include the world of business, an educated middle class
and an energetic working class. In recent years there has been an extensive political liberalization. At the same time South Korea has attempted
to shift the focus of its development away from Japan and the USA in
order to embrace a wider spread of Pacific-Asian and OECD partners.
The relationship with the USA which was forged in the post-World War
II period of aggressive anti-Communism has been crucial to South Korea.
It has always been viewed with doubt by sections of the population in
Korea and in the USA (with a recent episode of 'Korea bashing' on
economic grounds) and it must be expected that it will change in the
wake of the end of the Cold War. In contrast the relationship with Japan
is both historically long established, close in practical terms and deeply
difficult. There is an historical memory of the colonial period in Korea
and a routine discrimination against Koreans in Japan.

Relatedly, we should note that a similar situation holds in respect of
Taiwan whose economic record is if anything even more remarkable
than that of South Korea. In the late 1980s a process of reform from above
was begun in the political sphere and in recent years attempts have been
made to redirect the linkages of the economy with the global system. In
this case it is a matter of winding back dependence on the USA and
Japan in order to look to the region and the countries of the OECD.
However, in the case of Taiwan a major economic linkage is developing
with mainland China. In terms of patterns of identity it would seem that
as Pacific Asia changes it is the link to China which will dominate
Taiwanese thinking for the foreseeable future.

Overall, at the present time in respect of the East Asian view of the role
of Japan within the growing Pacific-Asian region we can point to a
mixture of historical memory, post-World War II economic success and
a regional situation which is slowly changing in the post-Cold War

period with the relative eclipse of the USA and the rise of China. As the USA slowly reconfigures its relationship with the countries of the region in the wake of the ending of the Cold War, the inner periphery faces the task of maintaining a continuing relationship with Japan where the burgeoning economy and political instability of China constitute a further and developing relevant context.

Outer periphery of Southeast Asia

The relationship of Japan with the other Pacific-Asian countries is often characterized with reference to the metaphor of 'flying geese', where Japan is the leader with the other countries following stepped down behind (Cronin, 1992: 27). The ideal relationship implied by this metaphor is one of a regionally complementary division of labour centred on Japan. Cronin points out that the linkages which Japan has with the countries of the region vary significantly and with the developing areas such as China and most of Southeast Asia the relationship is one of 'complementary cooperation' (1992: 33) skewed in Japan's favour. Overall, Japanese ODA and FDI are a force for economic growth and regional integration and, as Dobson (1993) points out, focusing on the ASEAN case, in recent years host governments have positively welcomed such inward investment.

It can be argued that the recent wave of foreign investment in the ASEAN region was initiated by changes in the circumstances of the Japanese economy. In the 1950s through to the 1970s Japanese FDI expanded slowly and in the pre-1985 period the focus was on raw materials, cheap labour and market access (Phongpaichit, 1990: 29). There was a distinctive pattern of investment with the East Asian NICs favoured, and thereafter some attention to Singapore, with the rest of ASEAN coming behind. However, after the 1985 Plaza Accords investment in ASEAN increased sharply and it was now focused on export-oriented industrialization. Phongpaichit argues that the underlying reason, notwithstanding the issues of the appreciation of the yen and the Japanese government's desire to be seen to be responding to growing US concerns about trade imbalances, was lodged in Japan's shift from an economy centred on labour-intensive heavy industry to one focused on high technology industrial development. This structural change pushed out FDI to offshore production platforms as Japanese capital looked to escape the impact of the high yen and US restrictions via a drive to increase markets and production capacity (Phongpaichit, 1990: 33). The Japanese economic space within Pacific Asia expanded. Phongpaichit records that this expansion has had a large impact on ASEAN and she adds that the recipient states have been active participants.

In Malaysia (Kahn and Loh, 1992) the government instituted an explicit 'look east' policy in the early 1980s which took Japan as the model for Malaysian development. Khoo (1992) argues that this was the policy of a group of modernizing technocrats surrounding the Prime Minister, Dr Mahathir, and that the drive for development has overriden other more traditional groups within Malaysian society. It has been a policy conducive not merely to economic growth but also to extensive social conflict which found partial expression in politically charged debates about the nature of 'Malayness'. In a similar fashion the increasing prominence of the Japanese sphere within the global economy has been noted in Singapore, where Japan is a major trading partner. The government has recently promulgated a policy which acknowledges Singapore's 'double role' as partner to the Japanese and as a long-established nexus in the global system in terms of the goal of the status of 'regional hub economy'. Thereafter, relatedly, in the resource-rich areas of Southeast Asia, that is Thailand and Indonesia, MacIntyre argues that there have been 'remarkable economic developments' (1993: 250) in both countries and that there are increasing signs that the East Asian NIC model of export-oriented development is being repeated. MacIntyre comments that there is 'little doubt that their economies have been profoundly influenced by Japan and the four NICs' (1993: 261) and that both countries have benefited from being located in a rapidly growing region. In the future it is likely that the key problems will not be economic, rather they will be political and social as the broader impacts of the recent phase of outward directed growth work themselves through the societies of Indonesia and Thailand (MacIntyre, 1993: 267).

Phongpaichit (1990) suggests that we can distinguish between domestic capital, state capital and foreign capital and thereafter we can plot the shifting patterns of interest and how these are expressed in response to incoming foreign direct investment. In ASEAN, broadly, there was an early resistance to investment as state and domestic capital prospered. Then in the depression of the early 1980s state capital got into difficulties and began to run up significant debt. At this point investment became attractive to ASEAN governments and with the incoming investment the phase of export-oriented industrialization takes off. It is clear that each country has had a particular experience of investment-assisted, export-oriented industrialization, but in each case Phongpaichit insists that the acceptance of investment must be seen as an expression not of passive acceptance but agency. In these terms, the actions of Southeast Asian state-regimes over the late 1980s can only be read as a knowing acquiescence in the dominance of the region by Japan.

China and Indo-China

Against an historical backdrop which included both centuries of exchange, where Japan was the cultural borrower, and a post-Meiji series of antagonism culminating in the war of 1937–45, the linkages of the recent decade have been dominated by the pragmatics of economic expansion.

Shibusawa (1992) reports that the 1978 reforms initiated by Deng Xiaping looked to secure the 'four modernizations' (agriculture, industry, science and defence) in order to achieve by the turn of the century a modest level of development in China. The story thereafter is one of burgeoning success coupled to internal social and political stress. The reforms in the rural areas were initially successful and the farmers launched a variety of industrial activities. Shibusawa notes that the impact of these reforms on the images of China held in the region were positive – China looked as if it were becoming another developmental state. However, the reform process in the industrial sector turned out to be much more problematical. These industries were long established and closely integrated in the party and state apparatus. In this sector reform was difficult and slow and indeed the failure of attempts to secure change coupled to the avoidance of political reform to the party and state machinery can be taken to have led to the political tensions which culminated in the Tiananmen Square debacle.

It is clear that the reform process inaugurated by Deng Xiaping has led to significant economic advance. However, in recent years in addition to the tensions noted above, there have been two key features which commentators now routinely address:

1 The pronounced regional nature of the economic changes with coastal regions experiencing rapid growth and apparently signifi- cantly enhanced regional powers at the expense of Beijing, while the inner agricultural regions are rather left behind.
3 The increasingly visible and vital linkages of the burgeoning coastal regions of China with the Pacific-Asian region in general.

In the future, commentators anticipate that the outward directed devel- opment of China will continue. Indeed it is said to be running somewhat out of control and that social and political change are almost inevitable. A key issue for the future will be the way in which China orders its relationships with the Pacific region in general, and that region's core Japanese economy in particular (Gipouloux, 1994). Finally, we might note that in Indo-China a similar story can be sketched out. The key aspect was the resolution of the Cambodian problem and relatedly the removal of the American veto on foreign direct investment and multilateral development agency assistance to Vietnam, now with its own marketization programme. The region is now rapidly reorienting itself to the global capitalist system in general and the Japanese regional core in particular.

Australasia joins Pacific Asia

In the 1980s the governments of both Australia and New Zealand have had explicit policies which point to the future of these countries within the developing Pacific-Asian region. In the case of New Zealand the accession of the UK to the EEC caused great damage to the local economy and a process or reorientation began. In the 1980s a series of New Right governments continued the marketization and regionalization of the New Zealand political economy and with it a shift to an Asia-sensitive multiculturalism in regard to identity. Relatedly, in the case of Australia we find a long-running concern with the issue of identity, and indeed many of the terms of debate pre-date the rise of Pacific Asia (Whitlock and Carter, 1992).

Walter (1992) recalls the invention of a 'British Australia' around the turn of the twentieth century where before there had been only colonies looking to the UK. These ideas of Australia were informed by notions of 'British stock' making up an immigrant community who had, given their pattern of economic life, a particular affinity with 'the bush'. The invention of this tradition can be traced to particular groups of intellectuals and journalists (White, 1992). The native people of the continent, the Aboriginals, were simply written out of the story. However, in the post-World War II period the story itself was revised and a notion of the 'Australian way of life' emerged in the context of a general Western anti-Communism. This view of Australia was implicitly anti-immigrant in line with ideas of a 'White Australia' (White, 1992). Overall, this general record forms the background to the deliberate 1980s turn towards Asia which has seen an explicit 'multiculturalism' in the domestic sphere linked to a concern to locate Australia in its wider geographical context of Asia. Many of the arguments which have been adduced to support this reorientation point to the economic linkages of the country with Pacific Asia, yet against this it has been argued that the economic policies of the 1980s were deeply flawed and that the economic linkages to Asia have been wildly oversold (Byrnes, 1994).

An integrated Pacific Asia

It is possible to identify broad political-economic, social-institutional, political and cultural similarities among the various countries of Pacific Asia. It is also possible to point to recent economic growth and suggest that available similarities are proving to be the basis for practical exchanges which in due course might be expected to find political expression. However, two points need to be kept in mind: first, that the region is presently dependent on the USA as a market for the consumption of its exports; second, that the region is very large and diverse (in terms of economies, societies and cultures). However, we can conclude by recording that it does make some sort of sense to speak of the distinctiveness of Pacific-Asian political-economic, social-institutional and cultural structures. Overall, it seems clear that some sort of distinctive developmental capitalism is in the process of formation in Pacific Asia.

Conclusion

In Pacific Asia the elite-level response to the withdrawal of long familiar Cold War ways of understanding the world has been an interest in the ideal of a Pacific-Asian region. The enthusiasm is evident in the plethora of acronyms which now abound. However, there is a structural occasion for the elite-level discourse and it resides in the changing patterns of economic power within the global system. It is on this structural basis that we might look to the ideal of Pacific Asia as an ordering theme for the countries of the region.

As elite groups respond to these slowly changing structural circumstances by advancing an idea of Pacific Asia – a response made more vigorous by the collapse of the available strategy of understanding vehicled through the essentially American rhetoric of Cold War – one might expect the emergent new identities to find both institutional and popular expression in new patterns of political linkages, new patterns of economic activity and new patterns of political-cultural understanding.

It would seem that a broad commonality in political economy, society and culture could be further deepened around the energetic expansion of the regional core economy of Japan. It is to the possible future role of Japan that we turn in the concluding chapter.

9

CONTEMPORARY JAPAN

Crisis, Disputed Understandings and Readjustment

In the Pacific Asia region in the 1990s a series of interrelated problems have confronted political actors and social science analysts. In Japan the rapid growth of the late 1980s developed into an economic bubble which was fuelled by cheap money and asset price inflation. However, the economy turned down in the early 1990s. The government has made repeated efforts to stimulate new growth but the economy has continued to record very low growth rates. The Japanese recession has also been drawn into the wider regional financial crisis. The devaluation of the Chinese renmimbi in 1994 by approximately 20 per cent shifted the balance of export advantage within the region against those countries with established export-oriented growth strategies, and in 1997 foreign speculation against the Thai baht proved overwhelming. The resultant collapse of the currency was the trigger for the wider Asian crisis. The Asian financial problems subsequently modulated into a global financial crisis involving Russia, Latin America and the USA, which thereafter, recalling the European Union's 'exchange rate mechanism' crisis of 1992–3, came to be seen as systemic. It has been within this sequence of crises that the future of Japan in Pacific Asia and the wider global system has come to be discussed (Preston, 1995, 1998b).

The crises of the 1990s

There have been three overlapping crises in the 1990s which have impacted severely upon the hitherto smooth path of Japanese advance:

1 The domestic experience of the collapse of the speculative bubble economy in the early 1990s.
2 The regional financial crisis which swept through Pacific Asia in the late 1990s.

3   The wider and deeper instabilities and uncertainties running through the global industrial-capitalist system in the years following the end of the Cold War.

Collapse of the bubble economy

Sheridan (1998b: 9) argues that the Japanese economy in the early 1990s 'underwent a period of chaos following the collapse of the speculative boom'. A further series of related problems included the shift of production overseas, the costs of an extensive government machinery with consequent high taxes and the related loss of choices over spending personal incomes.

The speculative boom which had gathered pace from the mid-1980s finally came to an end in 1990. Henshall (1999: 170) reports that the trigger was the decision of the Bank of Japan to increase interest rates. The economy fell into a severe and prolonged recession. The price of land which had contributed to the long economic boom fell sharply, as did the values recorded on the stock market. The collapse of land and stock values caused great difficulties for companies which had used these holdings as collateral for loans and the banks discovered they held a wealth of bad debt. The bad debt of the banks in turn, undermined their positions. The collapse of the bubble led, therefore, to a crisis in both the real productive economy and the financial system.

The economic crisis spilled over into the social world. Firms cut back on labour and unemployment rates climbed to unfamiliar levels (though still much less than European or US rates) causing consequent damage to ordinary family life (in turn reacting on the economy as consumer confidence drained away) and the political world, where the ruling LDP party lost office after many years in power (Stockwin, 1999: 81). In the following years there was an electoral reform and further party political instability.

The response of the Japanese governments to the crisis was widely regarded, domestically and internationally, as unsatisfactory. A series of Keynesian style attempts to reflate the economy proved unsuccessful. The government's efforts to deal with the bad loan problem of the financial sector moved ahead only very slowly. At the same time the Japanese government came under increasing pressure from outside the country, in particular from the USA. It was argued that radical action was needed and this was understood, broadly speaking, in terms of a rapid movement towards a more liberal-market system (Gibney, 1998). Nonetheless, in the event, the scope of government ameliorative action and the extent of systemic reform were both modest. Overall, Sheridan (1998b: 9) argues that by 'mid-1996 the situation had been brought under control, but industries and households have been left with the task of trying to recover their financial losses. All this has fuelled the general public's anxiety about the economic management of the country and the future prospects of society.'

Sheridan (1998b: 10) comments that while these anxieties are familiar within advanced countries 'what sets Japan's case apart is the sudden appearance of this fear about the future prospects of the economy in the population in general'. Sheridan adds (1998b: 11) that while it is true that the Japanese face the task of reordering their economy (as a consequence of the effects of the bubble and also because the economy has shifted from capital poor and labour rich to capital rich and labour poor), a rational debate is presently pre-empted by 'a simplistic nationwide cry for deregulation of the economy, as if the removal of public control and guidance will create market competition which will then act as a panacea for the country's economic ills'.

Against this current enthusiasm for market liberalism, Sheridan considers the historical process of the construction of the Japanese pattern of industrial activity and social organization, with its preference for social harmony, and insists that it is with reference to this historical legacy that future options for Japan might best be considered. In which case it is clear that the distinctive pattern of relationships between the state, industry and working population has developed over the long post-Meiji period. Sheridan (1998b: 13–22) recalls the concern for national development which typified Meiji, the post-World War I development of paternalistic industrial relations, later deepened into a broad social mobilization in the context of the Pacific War, and the activities following the Pacific War which reworked the cooperative ethos in the context of national recovery. Sheridan (1998b: 23–8) argues that the Japanese government missed an opportunity in the late 1960s as the economy prospered and failed properly to advance the interests of ordinary working people. An overwhelming commitment to national economic growth led to domestic consumption being relatively neglected and left at a lower level than other highly developed economies. Sheridan (1998b: 26–8) reports that there was a growing unease about the direction of economic development among the population which was not assuaged over the period of asset price inflation in the late 1980s. The domestic system thus manifests great success and a relative neglect of the interests of the ordinary Japanese. Sheridan (1993, 1998b) is clear that the system has great strengths, in particular the ability to respond collectively and work towards common goals. It is within this broad context that current discussions about the future course of Japan are taking place.

The Asian financial crisis

The Japanese economy was further stressed as the Asian financial crisis unfolded. The financial crisis of 1997–8 in Pacific Asia has been the subject of acrimonious debate. At one extreme advocates of an American-style liberal-market system have blamed the political and business elites of the region. In reply, regional advocates of the particularity of the development experience of Asia have spoken of a Western politico-financial conspiracy to undermine Asia's success. The Japanese government has been blamed for not taking action and at the same time proposals for Asian-based support packages have been vetoed by the USA (Higgott, 1998). However, the roots of the crisis lie in post-Cold War and post-Bretton Woods inter-regional adjustment within the increasingly integrated global system. In this sense the Asian crisis represents an acute expression of what is likely to prove to be a deeper and more intractable problem, that is, the process of mutual adjustment between three powerful regions as the major elements of the economic and political architecture of the post-Cold War, post-Bretton Woods global system, including institutions, law and customary norms and procedures, are assembled.

A new scholarly and policy analytic agenda has emerged in the period following the end of the Cold War as scholars, policy analysts and political actors have turned away from 'geo-strategy' towards the 'geo-economics' of the tripolar global system. In recent years increasing social scientific effort has been turned to the question of the operation of the global system and argument strategies derived from the classical European tradition allow the dynamics of complex change, their scale, differing rhythms and break points to be discussed.

The historical development experience of the broad area of Pacific Asia can be grasped in terms of a series of phases whereby the diverse indigenous civilizations of the region are drawn into the modern world as an interrelated group of nationstates. At the outset, in the first pre-contact period, there were a series of forms of life having distinctive political economies, social-institutional structures and cultures. The key civilization within the region was China. Thereafter, the second major period of the area saw the reconstruction of indigenous forms of life in line with the demands of industrial capitalism, a process expressed in formal colonial empires. Following this, in the third period, after the Pacific War, the territories of the area travelled through the process of decolonization and nation building while simultaneously becoming lodged within the bipolar Cold War division of the region. After the end of the Cold War, in the current phase, the area becomes ordered as Pacific Asia. In this period the forms of life of the region with their particular political economies, social-institutional structures and cultures come to have an increasing interdependence and distinctiveness within the global system. In general the region has taken shape over the last ten or 15 years and the key episodes would include:

(a) the American–Chinese rapprochement of 1971;
(b) the process of market reforms in China which were started in 1978 by Deng Xiaping;

(c) the 1985 Plaza Accords which revalued the yen upwards and occa-
    sioned a flood of Japanese investment in Asia;
(d) the period 1989–91 which saw the dissolution of the USSR and its
    system of socialist allies.

The importance of the region has led to a debate about its boundaries
and character. There are a series of definitions of the regions and what is
at issue is the nature of the region and its links with the wider global
system. A series of debates are running:

(a) regionalism in general, that is, the extent of economic, social and
    cultural/political unity;
(b) regionalism as contested, that is, whose definition of the region is to
    be granted priority (EAEC, ASEAN, AFTA or APEC);
(c) regionalism within the global system, that is, the relationship of the
    region with the wider system, where recent debate has revolved
    around the distinction between closed versus open regionalism.

It is clear that the relatively recent recognition of the Pacific-Asian region
has occasioned fraught political, policy analytical and scholarly debate.
The immediate availability of these areas of contemporary argument,
confusion and anxiety have provided the backdrop to the debates about
the financial crisis in Asia. A series of interrelated lines of commentary
can be presented which concern: the scale of long-term structural
dynamics; the diversity of rhythms within any social formation; and the
routine nature of change.

   Against the market-liberal economic orthodoxy, which extrapolates
from contemporary, that is, immediate, trends to a diversity of conclusions (for example, East Asian collapse or Chinese great power
dominance, or to globalization and so on), the materials of the classical
European tradition point to the explanatory importance of long-term
structural dynamics of change, where we can distinguish: (a) stable
patterns of economic, social and cultural life; (b) processes of reconfiguration; and (c) more or less abrupt breaks (Moore, 1966; Strange,
1988). What is at issue is whether or not the financial crisis is an historical
break, or a significant regional reconfiguration, or whether, alternatively,
it is merely a transient episode within the historical development of a
fundamentally stable pattern of life. Many Western commentators, in
particular American, have argued that we are seeing an historical break
which will issue in either (a) the radical reorganization of the region
along Western-specified, market-liberal lines or (b) a process of collapse,
disintegration and regression to the Third World. Yet, the standard
agency data show that the Pacific Asia region has experienced rapid
economic growth over the last 25 years and now has an aggregate gross
national product of a magnitude similar to that of the USA or the EU. In
the context of the historical development experience of the region it

seems unlikely that the 1997–8 crisis will be other than transient. The alternative lines of speculation seem deeply implausible and the key issue arising from the current crisis would seem to be the nature of the future development of the region and its relations with the wider global system.

The current debate surrounding the crisis in Pacific Asia is symptomatic of deeper processes of inter-regional post-Cold War, post-Bretton Woods adjustment. In this context it is clear that an interrelated tri-regional global system is in process of formation, rather than any general process of globalization. However, it can be noted, first, that the machineries which might order this system are not in place (and current discussions, by default, are conducted among the developing intellectual and policy analytical ruins of the Bretton Woods system). Second, the USA has long been a key player in Pacific Asia and remains committed not merely to the pursuit of a global market-liberal, political-cultural project but, as Sachs (1998: 23) remarks, to its achievement 'on the cheap'. More critically, Gray (1998) argues that the project is futile and its pursuit damaging. It seems clear, therefore, that the present situation will inevitably involve the countries of Pacific Asia in conflicts with the USA. Thus, it can be noted, in the context of the crisis in Asia, that the actions of the IMF have come under intense critical scrutiny. Wade and Veneroso (1998) review the actions of the IMF in the recent crisis and note that the organization has acted not merely to deal with transient financial problems but has gone on to propose reforms oriented to US-style market liberalization and market opening which are both wholly outside its traditional remit and reveal a radical misunderstanding of the nature of the East Asian 'developmental capitalism'. Wade and Veneroso (1998) suggest that the economic and social costs of the demands of the IMF, which they lodge within the politico-institutional context of the 'Wall Street–Treasury–IMF complex', are likely to fuel a political reaction within Asia against the self-serving interference of the USA. Thereafter, more broadly, Wade and Veneroso (1998) argue that the free movement of capital, which is routinely affirmed as a policy objective by the Wall Street–Treasury–IMF complex, can, in the wake of the Mexican, East European and now Asian crises, be seen to be radically destabilizing. They add that calls for a new Bretton Woods conference cannot any longer be dismissed as far-fetched.

The proponents of a market-liberal future for the region are guilty of an intellectually illegitimate affirmation of the priority of the model of American industrial capitalism. It is clear that there is no single model of industrial capitalism. At the same time it would seem that the regional advocates of a radically different Pacific Asia captured, familiarly, in terms of a summary notion of Asian values, are overstating their case. Against these claims, the classical European tradition, with its preoccupation with elucidating the dynamics of complex change, would posit a slow process of incremental regional integration and read the current crisis as symptomatic of the deeper changes within the global system. Overall, it is clear that:

1 Globalization is not a plausible characterization of present global dynamics and does not represent an inevitable global future.
2 Liberalization and deregulation are not self-evidently desirable, nor are they inevitable.
3 Acquiescence in a situation whereby the metropolitan financial market tail wags the entire global economic, social and political dog is not rational.

Now clearly all these points can be presented as flowing from the logic of analysis. Any more positive practical action could only be initiated by local agents and possible lines might include:

(a) upgrading existing regional institutional mechanisms to coordinate a regional response;
(b) the use of the yen as a regional currency;
(c) ASEM might increasingly look like a useful counterbalance to the US-dominated APEC.

Most generally, any debate about a new economic and political global architecture must be explicit as there is no intellectual warrant for these matters to be discussed, as they are presently, within the framework of expectations lodged within the disintegrating US-centred Bretton Woods system. Indeed, the likely future development of the global system would seem to be some mixture of national economies lodged within developing regional spaces, with the broad global system developing only as a result of continuing processes of partial and intermittent internationalization.

Financial crises and systemic failure

The financial crisis in Asia was one of a run of such episodes, including:

(a) the collapse of the European ERM;
(b) the Asian crisis;
(c) the severe problems of the Russian financial system;
(d) the near collapse of the American LTCM hedge fund;
(e) the pressure on Latin American economies.

It is clear that the 1980s hegemony of neo-liberal ideas is now in doubt. Any further calls by the proponents of deregulation in pursuit of globalization are likely to meet with resistance in Europe and Asia.

The run of crises has led to widespread discussion of the idea of a broad systemic crisis. The optimistic financial deregulation urged upon states by neo-liberals in the 1980s has come to be seen to be problematical. In particular the mixture of deregulation and advancing technology has meant that large sums of capital can be moved around the global system very easily. The weakening or removal of national restrictions on capital movements has ushered in a period of routine and massive international flows of capital. The system has thus become more unstable. At the same time the processes of deregulation have left states with fewer means to control or manage the deleterious effects of unhindered capital movements. One consequence of the financial crises of the 1990s has been a sharp rise in interest in the ways in which the global financial system is controlled, both at a national level in terms of the regulations promulgated by individual states and at an international level through the residual machineries of the Bretton Woods system (Higgott, 1999).

The sequence of interlinked crises effects a reworking of the context within which reforms to the Japanese economy might be engineered. Sheridan's (1993, 1998a) arguments rejecting neo-liberalism in favour of a distinctively Japanese route to the future have been strongly reinforced. It is also clear that the internal political dynamics of Japan favour continuity rather than abrupt changes. Nonetheless, it is also clear that the sequence of crisis has re-ignited debate about the nature of the global system in general and the Pacific-Asian region in particular.

Pacific-Asian model of development revisited

The debates around the case of Japan and the broader Pacific-Asian model of development are extremely tangled and there are diverse scholarly, policy analytic and political lines of argument. By way of a schematic review of these debates, many of which have been discussed throughout this text, we can ask three interrelated questions: what are the key elements of the model; which groups of theorists, policy analysts and political agents are concerned about the model; and what are the implications, if any, of any conclusions which we might reach about the Pacific Asian model?

Key elements of the Pacific-Asian model of development

The debate that has swirled around the Pacific-Asian model since the middle 1980s has a series of overlapping centres:

1 The contested claim that the area is more than a geographical territory and by virtue of developing economic, social and political networks constitutes a region.
2 The contested claim that the region is both discrete (that is, separate from other regions in the overall global system) and particular (that

is, has its own distinctive character, or economic, social and political logics).
3 The contested claim that theorists, analysts and political agents will have to seek to understand and act within a multipolar global system.

In brief, the core claim is that a Pacific Asia region has emerged and that it is home to a distinctive variant of industrial capitalism.

THE CLAIM TO THE EXISTENCE OF A REGION   At the outset in these debates there is a contested claim that the area is more than a geographical territory and that by virtue of developing economic, social and political networks the area constitutes a region. There are a series of ways of addressing the logic of regionalism. In a schematic fashion we can identify, in brief:

(a) theories about economic systems;
(b) theories about the necessary logics of inter-state relations;
(c) theories about civilizations and societies;
(d) theories about cultural processes;
(e) structural theories detailing historical patterns of development. All these intellectual resources have been deployed at one time or another to grasp the nature of Pacific Asia.

   (a) Economic analyses   Bernard (1996: 339): reports that the available economic approaches include:

1 An ahistorical neo-liberalism which looks at economic transactions between national economies and argues for freeing up exchanges.
2 An ahistorical product cycle theory that looks at a slowly evolving regional divisions of labour where a high-tech core slowly offloads outmoded technology which is then passed down to the periphery (flocks of flying geese).
3 An apolitical neo-institutionalism which looks at networks of companies within the region.

However, Bernard (1996: 339) looks to 'region formation in terms of a number of complex interrelationships: the way the region is linked to both the global and the local; the social relationships that exist both between and within states; the relationship between the material and the ideational; and the tensions between forces of integration and disintegration in region formation'.
   (b) International relations analyses   In the main tradition of inter-national relations there are available theories which look to the necessary logics of inter-state relations, in particular realist analyses which look to the ways in which states pursue their interests within the unregulated inter-state system (Hollis and Smith, 1990). The strategy of analysis

generates the view that global or regional stability requires a hegemonic power. In Pacific Asia the security system which was in place over the long years of the Cold War did see two major powers confronting each other and the USA hegemonic within the richer dynamic market-oriented sphere. If realism looks to states reaching inter-governmental agreements then a related line of analysis considers the functional demands of economic activity and looks to the slow supra-national ordering of regions. Once again the line of analysis concludes that regional integration requires a hegemonic power. In the case of Pacific Asia it is possible to point to regional organizations such as APEC which acknowledge the sphere of economic exchange. However, it would be true to say that the extent of formal regional integration remains slight and sharply contested. The continued security role of the USA and the economic role of APEC are both in question (Akaha and Langdon, 1993; Higgott, 1998).

(c) *Analyses of civilizations*   Theories about civilizations involve making very broad comparisons between cultural spheres and claiming for large areas a received cultural coherence. It is a problematical area insofar as it can quickly take on the guise of ideological myth making (Said, 1978; Tanaka, 1993). In the case of Pacific Asia there have been many attempts to distinguish the typically Asian from the typically Western. In the case of contemporary Pacific Asia there is an indigenous line of resistance to Western political ideas expressed via the notion of 'Asian values' which reports that the polities of Asia are more naturally consensual than the individualistic polities of the West and that this finds appropriate expression in disciplined and hierarchical societies and polities (Mahathir and Ishihara, 1995).

(d) *Cultural analyses*   In the related area of cultural analysis which is concerned with the sets of ideas affirmed in routine social life (Inglis, 1993; Jenks, 1993), the familiar reflections upon the commonality of the broad cultural resources of the region (religion, language and 'ethnicity' (Evans, 1993)) have been supplemented in recent discussions by materials which deal with novel aspects of extant patterns of life, in particular those which work to construct a popular idea of Pacific Asia. Bernard (1996: 346) reports that some commentators 'argue that a region-wide civil society is now emerging . . . [which] constitutes the basis for the region to be a new kind of "imagined community"'. The movement towards a common civil society could include:

(a) regionalized urban spaces, having increasingly common patterns of production and consumption;
(b) regionalized tourism, for example intra-regional travel;
(c) the networks of Chinese urban bourgeoisie which stretch through much of the region.

(e) *Historical structural analyses*   The classical European tradition of social theorizing is concerned with elucidating the historical structural dynamics of complex change. The contemporary approach of structural international political economy offers a similar strategy (Strange, 1988). It is clear that regions have existed in myriad historical contexts and have taken a variety of forms. An historical structural analysis of Pacific Asia would look to the successive ways in which the region has been configured and to the ways in which the peoples of the region understood themselves and thereafter acted. The idea of an Eastern Asian region has existed since its invention by Japanese theorists in the late nineteenth century. It was constituted in expansionary Japanese military practice in the years up to the Pacific War but thereafter the region was sharply reconfigured. The new pattern owed much to the USA. The US security structure helped to underpin the region while the economy of Japan provided the core of a regionalized economy and the USA provided an ever-open market.

In general, we can note that the Pacific-Asian region does evidence an increasingly self-conscious integration. However, it is clear that there are also problems:

1 Local production fits into a Japan-centred hierarchy, which creates dependence.
2 Regional production has required local political and class patterns be fixed in place, which creates tensions.
3 There are ethnic tensions, as some groups are seen to be advantaged relative to others.
4 In Japan there are the problems of rich country–poor people.
5 There is the tension created by region's exports to the USA.
6 There is the question of the growing power of China.

THE CLAIM TO THE DISTINCTIVENESS OF THE REGION   The claim that the region is both discrete (that is, separate from other regions in the overall global system) and particular (that is, it has its own distinctive character or economic, social and political logics) is contested. It is in this area of debate that we meet three interrelated ideas: (a) that there are a diversity of instances of the generic pattern of industrial capitalism; (b) that the global system has become tripolar; and (c) that Pacific Asia is a distinctive region with its own version of industrial capitalism.

(a) A diversity of instances of industrial capitalism   Gray (1998) sets up this debate in terms of a distinction between European and American Enlightenment aspirations to universality in social scientific thinking, in which case there is only one version of industrial capitalism and rational policymaking dictates that lines of action be ordered accordingly. In its contemporary variant Gray (1998) argues that this position finds expression in the 'Washington consensus', orchestrated by the American government, the IMF and the World Bank, which celebrates the market-liberal project. The upshot, argues Gray (1998), is that the discrete tradition and culture-bound versions of industrial capitalism which are evident around the planet are all subject to American-sponsored lines of unitary policy advice and the practical consequence is the routine degradation of local cultures.

The intellectual vehicle of these sorts of arguments can be found, contra Gray's sweeping dismissal of the tradition of the Enlightenment, within the ambit of the resources of the classical European tradition of social theorizing with its concern to produce emancipatory elucidations of the political-economic, social-institutional and cultural dynamics of complex change in the ongoing shift to the modern world. In brief, a mixture of structural analysis conjoined to the anthropological, sociological and cultural analysis of the patterns of understanding and action of agents can be used to produce substantive analyses of current situations (Preston, 1996, 1997).

In this perspective, a key concern of social science is with the business of how people pursue their 'livelihoods', in which case it is clear that economic activity is routinely embedded within social institutional patterns of life. In turn these patterns are lodged within the cognitively and ethically rich contexts of discrete cultural little traditions. In turn the whole ensemble is subject to rational self-inspection in terms of the resources of discrete great traditions. In this context, the familiar claims of American market liberalism, to the naturally given nature of individualistic competitive acquisitiveness oriented to expressive consumption, represent merely one more local tradition (Gudeman, 1986; Dilley, 1992; Preston, 1994).

(b) A tripolar global system   The collapse of the received certainties of the Cold War left many commentators in Europe and the USA confused. The intellectual resources deployed to theorize the bipolar Cold War global system were inadequate to the new situation. A series of responses were made including the affirmation of the ethico-political end of history and the declaration of a new global order. However, in time a useful distinction was made between geo-strategy and geo-economics. A new discourse emerged which revolved around the dynamics of globalization, regionalization and local political-cultural projects. It was at this point, as we have seen, that commentators were able to speak of the sphere of the USA, the development of the European Union and the emergence of Pacific Asia.

World War II saw the emergence of the USA as the premier power within the global system. The economic power of the USA was used to establish and underpin the Bretton Woods system within the sphere of the West. The military and economic power of the USA was central to the confrontation with the socialist bloc. There was a period of US hegemony in the 1950s and 1960s. However, in the 1970s the system came under great pressure. The following factors contributed to the decline:

(a) the financial implications for the USA of the war in Vietnam and the end of the Bretton Woods system in 1971;

(b) the oil price shocks of 1973;
(c) the rise of the EU and the Japanese sphere in East Asia;
(d) the partial and uneven globalization of the industrial-capitalist system.

In addition in the 1980s the USA was the major sponsor of the doctrines of market liberalism which have further undermined the order of the global system. The upshot of all these changes over the period between 1973 and 1991 has been a movement into an unstable, insecure and novel tripolar global industrial-capitalist system.

The end of the Cold War has seen the USA continuing to press for an open global trading system but these arguments are now made within the context of a tripolar system. The influence of the Washington-based IMF and World Bank is extensive in promoting liberal free trade and recent expressions of these concerns have been the establishment of NAFTA and APEC which link the USA to Latin America and Pacific Asia respectively. A link to the Europeans is secured via the residual Bretton Woods machineries, the security mechanism of NATO and the routine conversations of the G7.

(c) The Pacific-Asian model   One key contemporary public issue concerns the arguments to the effect that the pattern of change in Pacific Asia is such that we can talk about a Pacific-Asian model of development where this is taken to be a particular variety of industrial capitalism distinct from the American or European models. It is true that the Pacific-Asian region is more accurately grasped as a series of complex economic, social and cultural processes but the simplification of the notion of a model does allow a clear perception of the particularity of the ongoing historical development experience of the region. The Pacific-Asian model has a series of key features, together encompassing the political-economic, social-institutional and cultural spheres:

1   The economy is state directed.
2   State direction is policy-pragmatic (not ideological except for an overriding commitment to economic expansion).
3   State direction is top-down style.
4   Society is familial and thereafter communitarian.
5   Society is non-individualistic.
6   Politics is typically restricted to an elite sphere.
7   Political thinking among the population is diffuse and demobilized.
8   Political life is pragmatic and not centred on a public sphere.
9   Culture comprises a mix of officially sanctioned tradition and market sanctioned consumption.
10 Culture stresses consensus and harmony and eschews conflict.

In the work of the orthodox liberal-market theorists there is nothing special about the Pacific-Asian political economy. As Krugman (1994b) has it, the region is simply playing catch-up and in due course will achieve a normal Western level of modernization. Gray (1998) would characterize such analyses as symptomatic of American Enlightenment hubris. In contrast, all sophisticated readings of the important Japanese variant of the Pacific-Asian model call attention to the active role of the state. In this perspective, to simplify, the development experience of Japan is read in terms of the exchange between an oligarchic ruling class (involving the bureaucracy, business, politicians and in earlier versions the military) determined to secure the position of a late-developer within the expanding global system, and the structures of that system, which flowed from the activities of the other major participants and players. In the post-World War II period this drive to achieve position and security has evidenced itself in a strategic concern for economic expansion. Japan has a capitalist developmental state (Johnson, 1982; Appelbaum and Henderson, 1992).

It is often argued that the political-economic success of the countries of Pacific Asia is due to the character of local societies. In particular, Pacific-Asian society is held to be familial and communitarian rather than individualistic on the model of the West (a model dominated by the experience of the USA). Relatedly, Pacific-Asian society is held to be disciplined and ordered unlike the West which is taken to be riven by the unfortunate consequences of excessive individualism (again with the image of the USA to the fore). It is clear that in the territory of Pacific Asia there are enormous differences in patterns of life (Evans, 1993). The general nature of the social system of Pacific Asia centres on family and kin. Thereafter, the family lodges itself within the wider group, either village, urban area or extended kin network, within which it operates. In other words the focus is on family group and local community. This pattern is different from the situation obtaining in the West where the position of the individual is more central to social philosophical thinking. In classical liberal terms there are only individuals and families and the social world is thereafter a realm of contract. The distinction can be made positively (Pacific Asia is lucky to have escaped the trials of Western individualism), or negatively (Pacific Asia is mired in an anti-individualist traditional culture). A related theme in the positive literature which deals with the model of Pacific Asia is the continuance of social discipline and order in contrast to the West. Proponents of the model of Pacific Asia point to traditions of respect for family, for elders and for those set in authority. All this is contrasted with the individualistic, ill-disciplined and declining West.

There is much to say in regard to the culture of the Pacific-Asian model. Yet Evans (1993: 6) comments: 'The use of the term Asia can be extremely misleading if it is used to denote some sort of cultural uniformity throughout the geographical area.' However, the strategy of looking to broad historical-cultural areas points to regions inhabited by peoples who have over the years developed cultural traits which can somehow be taken to be typical. This strategy of characterization points to patterns of life, language groups, physiology (race) and common experience. The best we can say in respect of broad historical-cultural areas in Pacific Asia is that there are three main cultural streams: the Indian, flowing into Southeast Asia; the Southeast Asian, which originates in that area; and the Chinese, which originates in that area and which has spread throughout the region as a whole. With this in mind we can note that on the standard characterizations there is a familial, communitarian and non-individualistic pattern of life in Pacific Asia.

The political-cultural life of the countries of Pacific Asia has routinely diverged sharply from the model of the West. The state-directed pursuit of economic growth has often simply overridden any discussion among the wider population. Indeed, generally the peoples of the region have no historical experience of open debate within the public sphere which forms at least in principle the core of Western democratic political life. The detail of these processes within the Pacific-Asian countries is complex. However, within this general sphere of the political culture of Pacific Asia we can note that local theorists are speaking now of a Pacific-Asian model of democracy. It is clearly both an affirmation of local models of political practice and a counter-statement directed to critical outsiders usually from the West.

Held (1987) makes it clear that democracy comes in several varieties. The American-style representative democracy has a written constitution, separation of powers, open debate and interest groups, and is theorized typically via notions of liberal political pluralism. In contrast European social democracy has written constitutions, clearly dispersed patterns of power, open debate and active and involved citizens (Anderson, 1992). In terms of the overall political-economic, social-institutional and cultural package it might be possible to speak, after the style of Macpherson (1966), of models of democracy, including the Northwest European, the North American and a Pacific Asian. On this last, we can note the arguments from Chan (1993) where we meet an idea of communitarian democracy, and she suggests tentatively that the Pacific-Asian model of democracy involves the following: communitarian rather than individualistic; deferential rather than competitive; having a dominant party system; and a strong state. It seems to be increasingly widely granted that there is something in these arguments, notwithstanding elements of elite excuse making, and it is certainly the case that democratic polities are ongoing historical achievements.

CLAIM TO THE IMPORTANCE OF THE NOTION OF MULTI-POLARITY   The claim that theorists, analysts and political agents will have to seek to understand and act within a multipolar global system is contested. On the one hand, we find the proponents of the evident centrality of the historical experience of the West, the continued vitality of the ideas of the Enlightenment and the universality of their social science and the policy advice derived therefrom, whereas, on the other hand, we find the advocates of the particularity of extant forms of life who insist on the cultural context boundedness of analysis and advice (Bauman, 1987; Gray, 1998). There are two aspects to these debates: (a) substantive, the question of how the world is ordered; and (b) formal, the question of how the world might be apprehended in the available terms of social theoretical traditions.

(a) The substantive issue   The end of the Cold War in Pacific Asia was a phased process. A series of dates might be indicated: the decision in 1971 to float the US dollar; the start of market reforms in China in 1978; the Plaza Accords of 1985 which revalued the yen; the 1989–91 dissolution of the USSR. As this slow reordering advanced and reached its climactic moment, a series of established global structural changes found more explicit acknowledgement in public discourse. As commentators turned to consider the new global situation, it was clear that Pacific Asia constituted a nascent regional block within a distinctly tripolar global system. In the new context analysts confronted three general issues: the extent of integration within the global system; the nature of regionalism; and the linkages between global, regional and local levels of activity.

Overall, it is clear that the debate about regionalism within the global industrial-capitalist system has become more urgent as the incipient tripolarity of the global system has been abruptly acknowledged. The debate in respect of the logic of regionalism points to a series of necessary elements:

(a) an economic base in productive activity, intra-regional trade and financial flows;
(b) an institutional structure which acknowledges and orders economic activity;
(c) a common cultural pattern which allows otherwise disparate nations to come together in interdependent economic activities and institutional structures;
(d) a common elite political recognition of the value of interdependence and thereafter a disposition to foster integration;
(e) a measure of broad support for integration amongst relevant populations.

(b) The formal issue   The presumption of the centrality of the historical experience of the West and the general applicability therefore of its social scientific traditions have both been called into question by recent changes within the global system. It is clear that the claim to the substantive centrality of the historical experience of the West is untenable. A revision to substantive theories about patterns of global change is necessary and is in process of achievement in the work of a range of scholars who have granted this point (Frank, 1998).

A rather more awkward debate surrounds the claim to the context-bound nature of received Western traditions of social theorizing. One strategy is to insist upon the universality of science in general, and the scientificity of the received Western tradition of social science in particular. However, this seems a deeply implausible strategy. Gray (1998) identifies the USA as the sole remaining Western country where the hubris of the Enlightenment continues to be affirmed.

There are alternatives: to acquiesce in the apparent givenness of diverse intellectual traditions and to affirm the notions of contingency, irony and solidarity, thus we make the best of things in a piecemeal, optimistic and non-dogmatic fashion (Rorty, 1989); to restate the materials of received tradition in order to distinguish the legislative and interpretive roles of social science, the better to see that in the (post)modern world only the latter allows us to make any sense of our circumstances (Bauman, 1987); or to restate the materials of received inhabited tradition in order to represent the classical European tradition of social theorizing (Preston, 1996).

Concerns of theorists, policy analysts and political agents

Those who are concerned about the Pacific-Asian model include scholars, policy analysts and political actors as familiar political and intellectual agendas are recast in the light of the notion of 'regions'.

SCHOLARS   The contested claim that the area is not mere geography but is a region has opened up a debate about the nature of regions. There are a number of theories of regions and they have been variously applied to the territory of Pacific Asia.

The contested claim that the region is discrete has opened up a related debate about the relationship of the global system, regions, nations and sub-national units (Albrow, 1996; Gamble and Payne, 1996; Hirst and Thompson, 1996; Zysman, 1996).

The contested claim that the region is particular has opened up a debate about the diversity of routes to the modern world (Moore, 1966; Albert, 1993).

The contested claim that theorists, policy analysts and political agents will have to learn how to act within a multipolar global system has (re)opened a related debate about the limits of received traditions of social scientific reflection as well as the related substantive issue of handling the diversity of extant forms of life (Dore, 1987; Fallows, 1995; Johnson, 1995; Fay, 1996; Wade, 1996; Wade and Veneroso, 1998).

POLICY ANALYSTS   There are a series of policy analytic debates: economic exchanges (trade and financial links); social exchanges (patterns of migration and travel); security issues (patterns of treaty obligations and the balance of forces within the region); and cultural issues (the implications of trans-national or trans-regional patterns).

POLITICAL ACTORS   In the wake of the end of the Cold War and the shift in political and policy scientific interest from geo-strategy to geo-economics the familiar political agendas of the countries of the area (internal and international politics) are reorienting to embrace the shifting patterns of political-economic power within the region, and between the region and other regions.

Implications of acknowledging the particularity of the Pacific-Asian model

A series of lessons might be drawn from the (ongoing) debate about the Pacific-Asian model. In the territory of scholarship we are reminded of a clutch of awkward problems: that social scientific analysts inhabit discrete cultural and intellectual traditions; whose conceptual vocabularies are the basis for exercises in argument making; where such arguments are oriented to a variety of tasks (as Cox (1995) has it, arguments are always arguments on someone's behalf). In summary, a necessary condition of scholarship is reflexive self-embedding (Preston, 1985). It seems to me that this implies, (for Europeans and those working with reference to these materials) a return to the resources of the classical tradition as the basis for new analyses of shifting patterns of complex change.

In the territory of policy analysis we are reminded: that the economic interchange between discrete regions is a matter of negotiating 'deep access' (Zysman, 1996); that the ill-advised and disruptive US drive to secure its Enlightenment project of a global liberal-market system has not been discontinued (Gray, 1998); that as the region develops the issue of dealing with inter-regional and trans-regional social networks becomes more important; and that in the sphere of cultural exchanges we are reminded that the assumptions to the priority of the West, which have been familiar in the recent past, are now untenable.

In the realm of political life we are reminded that competition between powerful political actors will continue to define and order the future of the region and its relations with other regions within the global system.

Role of Japan in the Pacific-Asian region

It is clear that the Asian financial crisis has caused extensive problems. However, revisiting the debate on the Pacific-Asian region recalls the concerns of scholars, policy analysts and political actors with the detail of complex processes of long-term structural change. At the present time these processes of change continue to operate within the broad territory of Pacific Asia. It is difficult to imagine any significant alteration to what has been, by common consent, a long period of success. Nonetheless, the role of Japan within the region remains a key question.

Drifte (1998) points out that while Japan is the premier economic power in Pacific Asia there is little sign that the Japanese elite are anxious to embrace a wider role. The matter of leadership is a theme which runs through the discussions of the role of Japan in Pacific Asia. A series of commentators have asked whether Japan is able to exercise leadership and, if so, to what end? It is clear that the assumption of any leadership role would imply a lengthy schedule of reforms:

(a) reforms to the Japanese political economy;
(b) reforms to Japanese society;
(c) reforms to Japanese politics;
(d) reforms to Japanese culture;
(e) a reworking of Japan's relationships with Pacific Asia, in particular via reforms to Japanese aid;
(f) the identification of a plausible Japanese political-cultural project within Pacific Asia.

It is unlikely that these reforms will be put into practice in the foreseeable future. Nonetheless, the simple economic power of Japan within the region will remain and questions will continue to be asked about the position of the country within the wider region.

Reforms to Japanese political economy

The core of critical commentary is that while the Japanese economy is hugely productive the lives of the people who run this productive machine are relatively narrow and impoverished. Thereafter the line of argument varies. Reading (1992) argues that the system is running out of control and the elite whose power and inactivity are responsible do not seem to notice the damage done to either the local population or the economies of other countries, and that political reform is needed to redirect the system into economically rational and socially equitable directions. In a similar fashion Sheridan (1993, 1998a) argues that the power of the system to order its developmental route to the future should not be abandoned to 'market forces' but instead should be turned to the service of those who actually work the machinery. Against these lines, market-liberal theorists such as Ohmae (1987) look to a future of multinational firms operating within a borderless world in the expectation that a liberal-market system would maximize human benefits.

At the outset it should be noted that the debate about the economy of Japan has a particular history. Eccleston (1989) notes that the Japanese economic experience in the 1960s and 1970s was mainly studied by Third World development theorists who were interested in the speed of the economic recovery of the post-war period. However, since the mid-1980s there has been a strong 'learning from Japan' literature, especially among business writers in the West, which has looked to borrow the lessons of success so as to reinvigorate Western economies. The genre concerned with learning from Japan has grown in the USA, with Ezra Vogel as one key early figure. Eccleston notes that US work has tended to dominate the English-language literature and this is unfortunate as the material has tended to study Japan in terms of how it diverges from the US model rather than directly. Eccleston (1989) notes that many Western commentators explain Japanese success in terms of harmony and consensus (a cultural explanation). However, the observable 'harmony and consensus' are not simply given but derive from episodes and practices lodged in the development history of Japan. Thereafter, Eccleston (1989) notes that Western economists committed to the stories told by the market-liberal orthodoxy usually look to explain the success of the Japanese economy directly in these terms. Moreover, the Japanese are also happy to speak in these terms, either because it frees them from attacks on trade deficits, etc. where they suggest that the real economic problem lies with the USA, or because they are professionally committed to the same ideology. The US market-liberal theorists have had a further occasion to read Japanese success in terms of the market because acknowledging that other explanations could be offered, and perhaps were better, would have undermined their position in domestic policy debates. Against all this, Eccleston (1989) argues that it is important for theorists to attend directly to the detail of the Japanese case. The key to the Japanese political economy lies in the routine involvement of the state in the pursuit of economic development. All this generates a series of issues that are hotly debated.

In respect of the matter of the role of the state, the issue cuts directly to the heart of contemporary debates in Western social science in respect of the nature of the economic sphere and the appropriate role of the state within that sphere. In the tradition of neo-classical, market-liberal theory, which has been emphatically represented in the 1980s and 1990s, the state has only a minimal rule-setting role in a system that centres on an otherwise self-regulating market. An essentially liberal model of state and market is affirmed. However, in the case of Japan it is quite evident that the role of the state is much broader than the simple business of rule setting, and moreover Japan has had a remarkable record of success in the post-World War II period. It is at this point that commentators such as Johnson (1995) or Dore (1986) begin to speak of a 'capitalist developmental state'. However, it should be noted that there are legions of free market dogmatists ready to argue that the role of the state in post-war recovery and success of the Japanese economy has been marginal at best. A further move in this line of reaction is the refusal of commentators to grant that there might be anything special from which others could learn in the Japanese model. Indeed one right-wing Western business magazine recently argued, somewhat bizarrely, but all too familiarly, that Japan was converging on the US model (*Economist*, 1994).

In the standard neo-classical model of the self-regulating liberal market there are no broad structural discontinuities. The marketplace is an essentially homogeneous economic space within which firms and consumers move. An economy which diverged from this ideal homogeneity would necessarily be taken to be operating inefficiently. However, it is clear that the Japanese economy is dualistic and comprises a core of modern large-scale mass production-oriented firms, the realm of the salaryman, which dominate the activity of the economy, and a large spread of small-scale firms which service the larger firms and, in the form of an elaborate consumer distribution system, the community as a whole. It is also clear that the system both works and is successful. In debates on the structure of the Japanese economy a series of issues are addressed:

(a) the nature of the organization of the large firms both internally (how they order their workplace relations) and externally (how they order their links with sources of finance, sources of supply and consumers);
(b) the nature of the organization of small firms (internally and externally);
(c) the ways in which the two sectors interact (a mixture of large firm support and exploitation of small firm in manufacturing, plus small firm labour absorption in the service sector);
(d) the implications of this pattern for the overall performance of the Japanese political economy (which is made very productive), the Japanese society (which is made very cooperative) and the Japanese culture (which is made very consensual).

In the model of the neo-classical market theorists there is no life-time employment. The market for labour is like a market for dead fish (Hutton, 1994) – if the price is right the market will clear and any interference with the market mechanism can only result in economic inefficiency. However, as Hutton notes the market for labour is embedded with complex social rules. This is a general truth. In Japan, as Dore (1983) has shown, the key is not open market 'spot contracting' but instead 'relational contracting'. In the Japanese system exchanges are between people who have an expectation of a long-term relationship. People do not deal with each other in terms of the immediate price that can be realized in a spot market. In the Japanese system life-time employment works. It is widespread in the modern manufacturing and service sectors. In the small-scale sector things are not quite the same as family firms and small firms may operate in terms of relational contracting, but do not have the economic strength to run life-time employment strategies. Dore (1983) suggests, rather pointedly, that perhaps relational contracting is the product of a process of civilizing which, by implication, the West has yet to undertake.

The costs and benefits to the Japanese manufactured goods consumer can be detailed in terms of a trade-off between short-term higher prices

and long-term social harmony. The system as a whole is hugely productive yet the Japanese consumer of manufactured goods pays a high
price for a distribution system that soaks up large amounts of labour.
More broadly, a debate can be made around the general level of living
enjoyed by the ordinary Japanese in the light of the very productive
system which they inhabit. It is much harder to judge the trade-offs
made when the question is pitched at this general level. However,
commentators are agreed that the system demands more than is war-
ranted by the returns accruing to individuals. Against those who would
argue for a schedule of market-liberal reforms, the issue now becomes
one of identifying an apposite Japanese schedule of reforms in respect of
an apposite Japanese goal (Sheridan, 1993, 1998a).

The costs and benefits of the system to Japan's trading partners are
widely debated. The position of Japan within the Pacific-Asian region
and thereafter the role of that region within the global system have
exercised commentators ever since the 1985 Plaza Accord revalued the
yen and occasioned a flood of Japanese capital to the countries of Pacific
Asia. Against those market-liberal theorists who argue, simplistically, for
'free trade' and who thereafter generate an elaborate schedule of consequent necessary reforms for the Japanese system, we must assert that the
logics of the slowly evolving regional and global systems are matters of
some complexity. It is clear that the Japanese economy is presently the
core of Pacific Asia. It is also clear that patterns of social change are slow.
It might therefore be more useful to set the slogans of the market-liberal
theorists aside in order to detail the real processes at work in the region.
It is only on the basis of reliable knowledge that specific patterns of
reform can safely be the subject of policy argument.

The intensity of the debate among social scientists schooled in the
traditions of the West can be noted around the issue of state and market.
Johnson (1995) remarks that those who analyse Japan in terms of the self-
regulating free market are in the same position as those who a few years
ago used to analyse the situation of the economy of the Soviet Union in
terms derived from Marxism-Leninism. Johnson (1995) argues that Japan
is best read as an 'Asian Venice', which is to say that it is an oligarchic
trading state running a mercantilist policy. Johnson (1995) argues that
the key decisions taken in setting up this system date back to Meiji, a mix
of received tradition and borrowed theory as the vehicle for catching up
with the West. The theory which the Japanese borrowed and which has
informed their practice was German Historical School national
economics. It has been and is successful.

Johnson (1995) goes on to suggest that the USA has recognized this but
not widely acknowledged it as the demands of Cold War alliances
required the convenient untruth that Japan was a liberal democracy
(with the corollary that the 1930s militarism was an aberration). A
further aspect of this systematic untruth is the claim that Japan's economy operates according to the rules of neo-classical market economics.

Johnson (1995) argues that American economists are key players in the promulgation of the convenient untruth. If their claims to scientific status are taken at face value, then the only judgement available is that they are wrong. Johnson (1995) argues broadly in favour of substituting inconvenient truth for convenient untruth: in the realm of scholarly analysis of Japan, where the truth is that a developmental state presides over a mercantilist economy; and in the realm of policymaking in respect of US relations with Japan, where reason suggests that the USA treat Japan as Japan treats the USA (managed trade). Johnson thinks two things are driving a preference for truth: scholarly work, which makes the received tale look ever more implausible; and the end of the Cold War, which means that the original geo-strategic reason for the convenient untruth is now removed. It might be added that Johnson's preference for inconvenient truth might well be broadened to include all those concerned with bilateral and multilateral post-Bretton Woods arrangements; thus, the countries of Pacific Asia and the European Union.

Reforms to the social-institutional order of Japan

The schedules of reforms canvassed in respect of economy and polity are large, and their interactions various, and the proposals all have widespread implications for the nature of Japanese society. The problems which are routinely cited include:

(a) poor housing;
(b) poor public facilities;
(c) long hours of work (and commuting);
(d) inequality between genders;
(e) schooling which is excessively examination centred;
(f) lack of leisure time for families;
(g) habits of conformity are overstressed;
(h) the problems of an aged population.

In all, the Japanese people are presented as the unwitting victims of the corporatist system which they have created and from which they benefit – it is a paradox of relatively limited lives among one of the world's most productive economies.

If we consider the Western commentators then theorists of the right propose the liberalization of the Japanese economy in the expectation that consumer benefits will follow, while commentators of the centre-left propose a more consumer friendly democratic system. In this way one can see a broad similarity in the approaches of the two groups as both are concerned to enhance the position of the Japanese consumer at the expense of currently dominant producer interests. In contrast, a rather different position is advanced by Clammer (1995, 1997) who argues against reading the experience of Japan and the Japanese in terms of the conceptual machineries of Western social science, rather the historically generated particularity of the society should be acknowledged. Clammer (1995) argues that the fundamental Japanese social project is, in fact, a deeply lodged humanism which looks to order the celebration of individuality within an ordered, risk-averse social whole. The theme of the particularity of Japan's dealings with the modern world is echoed by Sheridan (1993: 3), who does, however, note that 'there still has been surprisingly little popular public debate in Japan about the future directions of economic development and national purpose'.

Sheridan (1993: 1–8) offers a distinctive view and begins by noting that Western commentators on Japan often cite three reasons for the development success and these are the culture, the role of the government, and the neglect of welfare. Proposals for reform follow directly from this diagnosis and commentators argue that the government should redirect the system's attention towards consumption (public and private) and should do so by withdrawing from its routine and extensive involvement in the system in favour of a greater role for market forces. Sheridan (1993) takes the view that this is poor advice for there is no particular reason to privilege the marketplace, notwithstanding the standard stories told by economists about the maturation of economies, and that to do so would only in reality privilege the economically powerful. In contrast, she argues that the state is routinely involved in the economy and society and that in place of a withdrawal there should be a redirection of involvement away from the single-minded pursuit of economic expansion towards a social-democratic concern for the quality of life of the Japanese people.

Sheridan (1993: 220–3) notes that over the 1960s and 1970s there was improvement in the quality of life (for example, with environmental standards and less inequality), but the 1985 revaluation of the yen triggered speculation on the back of asset inflation and this has done great damage. However, reason for hope is identified in the signs that the Japanese people are beginning to shift from a 'politics of fear' to a 'politics of utopias' (that is, away from reactive towards prospective stances). Relatedly, the system does allow collective effort in respect of communal goals. The system could be shifted away from its preoccupation with economic expansion towards the provision of the social capital necessary to improve people's lives. It is clear that the Japanese state is activist and effective. If the myths of the marketeers are set aside (plus some of the prejudices against social spending of the Japanese government) then a future oriented to quality of life could be envisioned. Sheridan (1993: 228–42) goes on to unpack this overall proposal in terms of a series of policies: to enhance the position of women; to improve local and neighbourhood life; to reduce inequalities; and to reform the land market. She suggests that all of these goals are to be pursued with a 'Japanese strategy' which would draw on established strengths of cooperative, collective hard work.

In a later text Sheridan (1998b: 29) revisits the debate and identifies four scenarios for the future of Japan:

(a) a continuation of established trends, with only modest reforms, such that the economy becomes ever more prosperous and able to support a larger non-working population;
(b) an extensive schedule of reforms in order to shift the economy towards a deregulated American-style economy;
(c) a modification to established trends to enhance through traditional organizational means the welfare of the population;
(d) a shift to a high-tech, post-industrial society.

Sheridan (1998b: 39) considers these options and rejects the path of deregulation in favour of some mix of those strategies which retain the cooperative workplace-based ethic of the Japanese form of life.

Reforms to Japanese politics

A discussion of the problems of Japanese politics is presented by Buckley (1990). A series of particular problems are cited: political and business corruption; a pork-barrel style of local politics; a secretive and powerful bureaucracy; and a general inability of the political system effectively to articulate and thereafter deal with a spread of domestic and international policy problems.

The problem of corruption is widespread within Japanese politics and takes the form of patterns of collusion between business groups and politicians in respect of public plans, permits, contracts and the like. In exchange for their favours the politicians receive large cash contributions to their political expenses which in turn allow them to shower their constituents with personal gifts (for a family wedding or funeral, for example). It is suggested that at election time envelopes with cash in them are passed around. Overall, it is alleged, the present pattern of Japanese politics requires large amounts of cash to keep it running and these flow in from the routinized corruption of the link between politics and business (van Wolferen, 1989; Stockwin, 1999).

The role of the parliamentary representative centres on pork-barrel politics. A successful local politician will act as a line of communication between constituents and the decision makers in Tokyo. A politician is expected to show his value to the local area by securing government resources for local development projects – roads, bridges, public buildings and the like. As with electioneering, the routine life of the parliamentarian revolves around money – securing it and then spending it. There seems to be little of the Western-style notion of representing the voice of the constituents within the public sphere. It is generally taken to be the case that power within the Japanese political system resides primarily with the bureaucrats of the state machine. These are the people whom constituents must access for permissions, licences, grants and money. The parliamentary politician must have an appropriate network of contacts. It is within the confines of the bureaucracy that politicians, business men and bureaucrats come together and it is from this location that decisions emerge. It is not a system that is open to public scrutiny. Van Wolferen (1989) argues that the political system centred on the bureaucracy is 'results focused' by which he means that it attends not to matters of principle and policy but to the pragmatic resolution of immediate problems. Within a dominating overall commitment to economic expansion, problems are tackled on an ad hoc basis. It means both that the system is hugely successful within its own terms and that it is unable to formulate responses to problems that fall outside its routine frame of expectations (hence the growing criticisms of the relatively poor lives of the Japanese people and the growing criticisms of Japan's burgeoning trade surplus with the rest of the world). In stronger terms van Wolferen argues that strictly speaking the system is so flexible and pragmatic that it amounts to an absence of a formal state. Instead there are shifting patterns of alliances between the various important players in the bureaucracy, business and politics, and in this it recalls the system established at the time of the Meiji Restoration.

In respect of the general issue of political life there seems to be widespread agreement on two general points and very little agreement on a third practical point. The first two points are the necessity for political reform in Japan and the remote possibility of such reform. On the third point, the nature of the ongoing upheavals in Japanese party politics, which began in 1993–4, there is little agreement as to the nature of the changes or whether they will in the end amount to anything (Stockwin, 1999: 201). The position of most commentators seems to be that there is a genuine drive to secure political reform, in the guise of a shift to a two-party system in place of the old LDP dominant party system. However, it is at least as plausible to characterize present manoeuvring as merely an open faction fight in place of the earlier more discreet faction fighting. It is certainly the case that the cooperation of the bureaucracy and industry continues, apparently quite happily, in the absence of direction from the realm of party politics.

We can try to get behind the surface debate by looking at the various structural analyses of the Japanese political system that are usually invoked. There seem to be three main lines of analysis. First, the optimistic modernization theory approach takes Japan to have successfully shifted to the modern world with the Meiji Restoration and considers the period of military dominance and war to be essentially a catastrophic interlude which came to an end in 1945 when the normal development path was resumed. In this case Japan is a liberal democracy and any requirement for reform is rather minor. Second, there is the rather more sceptical version of this which sees much less evidence of an early shift towards liberal democracy and notes much greater continuity of the post-war period with the pre-war era. In this case Japan appears to be politically semi-developed and the liberal democracy is mostly a super-ficial cover for a rather more nationalistic, expansionist, neo-mercantile country. In this case the requirements for reform are rather extensive and moreover are unlikely to be forthcoming without considerable outside pressure. Finally there is a line of political economic analysis which looks to treat the Japanese case in its own terms, in line with the analytic concerns of the core European tradition of social theorizing, in which case both the optimistic liberal democrats and the sceptics are rather off target. The Japanese system is read as a state-directed, developmentalist, political-cultural project fashioned in response to global system circum-stances. There are two sub-varieties of this position: the optimistic, which sees a harmonious communitarian system having little need for exten-sive reforms (and none for US-sponsored liberal-market agendas) (Sheridan, 1998a; Clammer, 1995, 1997); and the pessimistic, which sees a domineering elite and a powerless obedient mass and concludes that while there is a strong need for reform little will be done (van Wolferen, 1989).

Reforms to Japanese culture

A series of commentators have made the point that the pattern of life of the ordinary Japanese is suffused with references to the distinctiveness of Japanese culture. A nationalistic ideology of control is often diagnosed (Dale, 1986; Yoshino, 1992). However, against these critics it is also possible to point to patterns of cooperative action which are deep seated and valuable (Clammer, 1995, 1997).

On this matter Clammer (1995) argues that the Japanese historical development experience should be confronted directly. A series of points are made. First, Western social science, whether the high road of Enlightenment inspired reasoning or the lower road of post-World War II American professionalized disciplines, typically fails to access the core economic, social and cultural logics of Japan. Second, the historical development experience of Japan, as the only non-Western country effectively to establish an autonomous industrial economy and society, ought to be a matter of compelling interest for Western social scientists, as it points to the necessity of a genuinely comparative social theory. Third, more substantively, the Japanese political-cultural and social projects are deeply humanist:

1   Persons are taken to be lodged within social contexts and natural contexts (a humanistic de-centring of self which recalls the core ideas of classical European sociology).
2   Persons are taken to have reason, emotion and aesthetic sensibilities, and routinely and inevitably to be limited in skills and fallible in practice.

3   The social world is taken to revolve around overlapping networks of personal relationships, including family, group and organization.
4   A reasonable aspiration is for individual achievement within these multiple social contexts (and that, in contrast, standard market-liberal Western notions of rational calculative expressive consumption and self-agrandizement, individualism in short, look deeply foolish and self-defeating).

Clammer (1995: 7) suggests that the key is 'seeing the Japanese social project as a huge anti-alienation device and as such a profoundly utopian one'. The Japanese social world is highly ordered (constructed) but 'the negotiated reality has to be placed squarely in the context of a society where the historical continuity of certain aspects of social structure, such as emphasis on hierarchy, is very marked' (Clammer, 1995: 8). Clammer argues:

> It is this that creates a dialectic between the demands of reciprocity at the personal level and the equally insistent demand for stability in social relations in general. Or, put in a slightly different way, a central requirement of Japanese social organization is to maintain the intimacy of face to face relationships (in the workplace, school, neighbourhood and family) while extending that reciprocity from purely personal interaction to the constitution of the society as a whole. (Clammer, 1995: 8)

Clammer (1995: 13) notes that the mix of modern industrial capitalism and tradition has caused comment. A recent attempt to grasp these matters has been cast in terms of modernity and postmodernity. But postmodernism is a Western notion, and comes in many varieties. Applied to Japan it looks odd. This is not a society of expressive individualism. The Japanese 'decentred self' is located in community; everyday life is humanistic and the personal is widely reproduced (in school, office or club). There has been no epochal shift, rather as socially constructed cultural practices are continually reworked, enfolding tradition is reaffirmed. Clammer (1995: 23) suggests that 'Japan has thus neither achieved . . . or overcome . . . the modern: it has by-passed it by establishing and following a project quite unlike that of the Enlightenment'. Japan has its own cultural logic. Japanese society remains humanist and it is unpacking this logic, which binds individual and community, that is key to understanding Japan.

Overall, one might point to two broad occasions of change in Japanese culture. Japan's involvement with the global system entails accepting pressures which impinge ever more acutely on received patterns of life in Japan (either through 'messages' from the outside coming into Japan or, what is already happening, increasing numbers of Japanese travelling outside Japan and finding new ideas and experience as a result). There is a drive for political reform within Japan where this is taken to be the key to a further spread of economic and social reforms – all of which, both process and programmes, will challenge received ideas and practices. Yet, against these pressures, it remains the case that the Japanese have successfully remade their inherited hierarchies and sustained a widely articulated commitment to harmony over all the long years since the Meiji Restoration moved them decisively and distinctively into the modern world.

Reforms to linkages with Pacific Asia

The relationship of Japan and Pacific Asia is bound up with trade, official development aid and foreign direct investment linkages. It is a familiar claim that aid is designed to secure a broad regional economic integration around a core role for Japan. If we focus the discussion on the role of aid we can cut through the material in a number of ways: (a) the ethical critique of aid (Rix, 1993b); (b) the diplomatic analysis of aid in Pacific Asia (Yasutomo, 1986); (c) the role of aid and investment in regionalism in Pacific Asia (Phongpaichit, 1990); and (d) the resultant place of Pacific Asia within the wider global system (Cronin, 1992).

Rix (1993b) looks at the philosophy, organization and intentions of Japan's official development aid and asks how is it linked into a 'leadership' role in East Asia. In this way Rix (1993b) draws on rather conventional discourses of development within the West where, at least in principle, a disinterested ethical imperative drives involvement with matters of development. Rix (1993b: 23) investigates the situation in Japan, discovers a lack of similar purpose, notwithstanding official statements of intention, and comments that 'Asian development was more a means of achieving Japanese objectives than a goal in its own right'. It is likely that Asia will remain the focus of Japanese aid activities and that this effort will remain loosely oriented to securing Japanese economic advantage in the region.

Rix (1993b), in sum, argues that the Japanese official development aid programme is relatively loosely organized and that while it needs revising so as to encompass a Japanese aid leadership role this is unlikely to happen. The present system serves many vested interests and all seem content with the status quo. The role of aid seems to be that of assisting the further creation of a Japanese economic sphere. There will be Japanese activity but little leadership. However, Yasutomo (1986), who deals with the diplomatic rationale of Japanese official development aid and who is clear that it is a matter of national self-advancement, suggests that rather more is being achieved. The role of aid is lodged within a concept of 'comprehensive national security' which urges that national security depends upon regional security, and in turn this is helped by economic growth in the area. Yasutomo (1986: 112–14) argues that the

Japanese government pursues five interrelated goals with its aid programmes: (a) 'economic well being'; (b) 'national prestige'; (c) 'domestic
support'; (d) 'peace diplomacy'; and (e) 'national security'. Yasutomo
(1986) suggests that the 'manner of giving' is such that an integrated
regional bloc, which is to the benefit of all participants, is now in the
process of forming.

The role of trade, aid and foreign direct investment in the constitution
of an integrated Pacific-Asian bloc is considered by Phongpaichit (1990)
who argues, in brief, that the post-1985 wave of Japanese investment in
the region was driven by structural changes in the Japanese economy (as
it moved to higher value added activities) and was shaped by the actions
of governments and firms in the recipient countries. Phongpaichit (1990)
expects this pattern of regional development around Japanese aid and
investment to continue in the future, even if there are problems such as
the 'hollowing out' of the Japanese economy and a build-up of 'yen debt'
among recipient countries.

As the Pacific-Asian region integrates there are wider implications for
the global system. As we have seen, Cronin (1992) offers a series of three
'scenarios' for the future, to which, in the wake of the financial crisis, we
can add a fourth. The first scenario is of the competitive globalization of
Japan. Cronin (1992: 107) argues that this 'would have Japan interacting
with Asia as an increasingly open economy, partially supplanting the
United States as an export market for Asia-Pacific countries, while at the
global level using its financial resources to undergird the present system'.
The second scenario sees 'Japanese aid and investment in Asia as
primarily acting to increase the competitive position of Japanese
companies in world markets vis-à-vis the fast rising NICs, while Japan's
own markets remain relatively closed' (Cronin, 1992: 111). The third
scenario sees 'Japanese aid and investment, and increasing access to the
Japanese market by Asian exporters, as producing a Japan centered Asia-
Pacific economy' (Cronin, 1992: 115). The fourth scenario can be posited
in the wake of the collapse of the bubble and the Asian financial crisis. At
the outset it seems clear that the Japanese economy will continue to
develop according to its own distinctive logic. It is extremely unlikely
that the crises of the 1990s will occasion the 'third opening' of Japan
(Gibney, 1998: 4). Against the enthusiasts for market liberalism it should
be noted that there is no rational warrant for any expectation of rapid
change. It is similarly clear that the role of the Japanese economy within
the regional economy will continue to be crucially important. Indeed, in
the context of developing regional patterns of consumption, it has been
suggested that Japanese popular culture is being widely diffused through
Pacific Asia (Clammer, 1997). In contrast, it might also be noted that the
trans-Pacific security and trade relationship with the USA is likely to be
sustained. In addition, it can be suggested that the slow internationalization of Japanese foreign policy might be expected to continue (Dore,
1997). The upshot could be, so to say, an 'internationalized yen zone'.

This would embrace a series of factors: first, the continuing development of the distinctive Japanese domestic political-economic system; second, the further promotion of the Japanese role as the regional core economy; third, the continuation of links with the USA; fourth, the slow enhancement of the Japanese political role within both the region and the global system.

Yet overall it would seem from the commentators that the prospects for change in Japan are relatively limited. One additional point must be made for, as Buckley (1990) reminds us, while Japan's economic strength works quietly to its advantage in a global system dominated by economic concerns (rather than military), the key external relationship for the Japanese government is with the USA. It is difficult to envision any significant changes in the role which Japan plays within the global system being made without the link to the USA first being reworked. This would require a considerable political departure from established patterns on the part of the government of Japan.

Finally, it might be noted that these reflections open up a wider issue, namely, the developing shape of the global system itself. In the wake of the end of the short twentieth century and the related collapse of the received certainties of the Cold War which had shaped the understandings of European and American thinkers, it has become clear that a new integrated global industrial-capitalist system is taking shape. On Hobsbawm's (1994) arguments this is an unstable system which recalls the equally unstable global system of the latter years of the long nineteenth century. At the present time the global industrial-capitalist system shows a number of cross-cutting tendencies: (a) to integration on a global scale, with a financial system that is integrated across the globe and extensive increasingly de-nationalized MNC/TNC operations; (b) to regionalization within the global system, with three key areas emerging where intra-regional linkages are deepening; and (c) to division on a global scale, with areas of the world apparently falling behind the regionalized global system. In these matters it is the second issue, regionalization, which is most immediately relevant. In the light of the resources of the classical European tradition, structural arguments point to the emergence of new patterns within the global system to which agent groups will have to respond as they order their various projects. The analysis points to the differences in the ways in which inhabitants of territories within the global system understand themselves. The results of such enquiry have been anticipated in broad terms in recent polemical debate on the divergent nature of the forms of life of the peoples living within the three regions of the tripolar global system (Thurow, 1994). It has been argued that the pattern of the USA should be characterized as liberal market, while the pattern of the European Union presents a social-market system, and both are to be distinguished from Pacific-Asian developmental capitalism. In this context, the future of Japan within the developing global system becomes a matter of general concern.

Japan in the future

If one reviews the broad sweep of the history of Japan it is evident that deep-seated structural change in the economy, society, polity and culture is slow. It could be argued that this is the case for all countries. It is certainly the case that within the classical European tradition of social theorizing, which is concerned with the issue of complex change, that patterns of change are identified which run over long periods of time:

(a) structural change within an economic system as new patterns of production and exchange develop;
(b) structural change within a political system as new groups emerge in the economic system and come together to formulate, lodge and secure political changes;
(c) deep-seated change in society as the detail of patterns of life and institutional arrangements adjust to new political-economic conditions;
(d) subtle changes within the cultural sphere as new experiences and arrangements are self-consciously read back into the social world.

None of this denies that complex change can be fairly abrupt, as witnessed in the shift of Japan to the modern world, or that in some social spheres there can be a rapid sequence of changes (in all sorts of fashions, for example). It might also be accepted that the development experiences of countries are typically episodic and combine periods of stability with periods of faster change. However, it seems to me that all these lines of commentary are in the end dealing with patterns of change whose proper context is historical; in other words, social change is typically slow.

It is clear that this position contradicts directly not only popular opinion in the West, or at least their media, which routinely speaks of the increasing rate of change of society, but also the recently fashionable postmodernists, who have announced that the world has entered a new consumer driven age, where all are free to choose their own life-styles, and thus selves, in an endlessly fluid system. In my view popular opinion is simply wrong and the postmodernists are peddling a quietist (or, indeed, defeatist) intellectual fad belonging to the over-consumptionist late 1980s (Woodiwiss, 1993). Against these views I would suggest that it is better to regard structural social change as slow. If this is indeed the case one would not expect much change in Japan over the next few years.

Conclusion

The rapid growth of the late 1980s in Japan developed into an economic bubble. As the economy turned down in the early 1990s and began to record very low growth rates, questions about the nature of the Japanese system and its future were raised. However, these debates were overtaken by events in 1997 when the collapse of the Thai currency triggered the Asian financial crisis, which subsequently modulated into a systemic global financial crisis. It has been within this sequence of crises that the future of Japan, Pacific Asia and the wider global system has come to be discussed (Preston, 1995, 1998a).

In this new context the familiar American arguments for neo-liberal deregulation within Japan and the wider Pacific-Asian region are not likely to be successful. The future direction of Japan is likely to be incrementally determined by the internal dynamics of Japanese politics. Yet, as Japan is now the regional core economy a greater political role might be anticipated but it is unlikely to emerge quickly. As many commentators have noted, the Japanese government and people have been successful over the long period since Meiji and they are unlikely to revise radically their established patterns of life.

REFERENCES

Abegglen, J. (1994) *Sea Change*. New York: Free Press.

Akaha, T. and Langdon, F. (eds) (1993) *Japan in the Posthegemonic World*. Boulder: Lynne Rienner.

Albert, M. (1993) *Capitalism Against Capitalism*. London: Whurr.

Albrow, M. (1996) *The Global Age*. Cambridge: Polity.

Anderson, B. (1983) *Imagined Communities*. London: Verso.

Anderson, P. (1992) *English Questions*. London: Verso.

Appelbaum, R.P. and Henderson, J. (eds) (1992) *States and Development in the Asian Pacific Rim*. London: Sage.

Aston, T.H. and Philpin, C.H.E. (eds) (1985) *The Brenner Debate*. Cambridge: Cambridge University Press.

Axford, B. (1995) *The Global System*. Cambridge: Polity.

Barraclough, G. (1964) *An Introduction to Contemporary History*. Harmondsworth: Penguin.

Bartley, R.L. et al. (1993) *Democracy and Capitalism: Asian and American Perspectives*. Singapore: Institute of South Asian Studies.

Bauman, Z. (1976) *Culture as Praxis*. London: Sage.

Bauman, Z. (1987) *Legislators and Interpreters*. Cambridge: Polity.

Bauman, Z. (1997) *Globalization: The Human Consequences*. Cambridge: Polity.

Beasley, W.G. (1990) *The Rise of Modern Japan*. Toyko: Tuttle.

Beasley, W.G. (1991) *Japanese Imperialism: 1894–1945*. Oxford: Clarendon.

Benedict, R. (1946) *The Chrysanthemum and the Sword*. Boston, MA: Houghton Mifflin.

Berger, P. and Hsiao, H.M. (1988) *In Search of an East Asian Development Model*. New York: Transaction Books.

Bernard, M. (1996) 'Regions in the global political economy', *New Political Economy*, 1 (3).

Billig, M. (1995) *Banal Nationalism*. London: Sage.

Borthwick, M. (1992) *Pacific Century*. Boulder, CO: Westview.

Bourdieu, P. (1984) *Distinctions*. London: Routledge.

Bowring, R. and Kornicki, P. (eds) (1993) *The Cambridge Encyclopedia of Japan*. Cambridge: Cambridge University Press.

Brenner, R. (1977) 'The origins of capitalist development: a critique of neo-Smithian Marxism', *New Left Review*.

Buckley, B. (1990) *Japan Today*. Cambridge: Cambridge University Press.

Buruma, I. (1994) *Wages of Guilt*. London: Cape.

Byrnes, M. (1994) *Australia and the Asia Game*. Sydney: Allen and Unwin.

Chan, H.C. (1993) 'Democracy: evolution and implementation', in R.L. Bartley (ed.), *Democracy and Capitalism: Asian and American Perspectives*.

Chan, S. (1990) *East Asian Dynamism: Growth, Order and Security in the Pacific Region*. Boulder, CO: Westview.

Chen, P. (ed.) (1983) *Singapore Development Policies and Plans*. Oxford: Oxford University Press.

Cherry, K. (1997) *Womansword: What Japanese Words Say About Women*. Tokyo: Kondansha.

Clammer, J. (1995) *Difference and Modernity*. London: KPI.

Clammer, J. (1997) *Contemporary Urban Japan: A Sociology of Consumption*. Oxford: Blackwell.

Cox, R. (1995) 'Critical political economy', in B. Hettne (ed.), *International Political Economy: Understanding Global Disorder*. London: Zed.

Crisman, L. (1995) 'The physical and ethnic geography of East and Southeast Asia', in C. Mackerras, *Eastern Asia*. London: Longman.

Cronin, R.P. (1992) *Japan, the United States and the Prospects for the Asia-Pacific Century*. Singapore: Institute of Southeast Asian Studies.

Cummings B. (1997) *Korea's Place in the Sun*. London: Norton.

Dale, P. (1986) *The Myth of Japanese Uniqueness*. London: Routledge.

Deyo, F.C. (ed) (1987) *The Political Economy of the New Asian Industrialism*. New York: Cornell University Press.

Dilley, R. (ed.) (1992) *Contesting Markets: Analysis of Ideology, Discourse and Practice*. Edinburgh: Edinburgh University Press.

Dobson, W. (1993) *Japan in East Asia: Trading and Investment Strategies*. Singapore: Institute of Southeast Asian Studies.

Dore, R. (1983) 'Goodwill and the spirit of market capitalism', *British Journal of Sociology*.

Dore, R. (1986) *Flexible Rigidities*. Stanford, CA: Stanford University Press.

Dore, R. (1987) *Taking Japan Seriously*. Stanford, CA: Stanford University Press.

Dore, R. (1997) *Japan, Internationalism and the UN*. London: Routledge.

Downer, J. (1996) *Japan in War and Peace: Essays on History, Culture and Race*. London: Fontana.

Drifte, R. (1998) *Japan's Foreign Policy for the 21st Century*. London: Macmillan.

Duiker, W.J. (1995) *Vietnam: Revolution in Transition*. Boulder, CO: Westview.

Eccleston, B. (1989) *State and Society in Post-War Japan*. Cambridge: Polity.

Economist (1994) 'Oriental renaissance: A survey of Japan', 9 July.

Evans, G. (ed.) (1993) *Asia's Cultural Mosaic*. Singapore: Prentice Hall.

Fallows, J. (1995) *Looking at the Sun*. New York: Vintage.

Fay, B. (1975) *Social Theory and Political Practice*. London: Allen and Unwin.

Fay, B. (1987) *Critical Social Science*. Cambridge: Polity.

Fay, B. (1996) *Contemporary Philosophy of Social Science*. Oxford: Blackwell.

Frank, A.G. (1998) *Reorient: Global Economy in the Asian Age*. Berkeley: University of California Press.

Franks, P. (1992) *Japanese Economic Development*. London: Routledge.

Funabashi, Y. (1994) *Japan's International Agenda*. New York: New York University Press.

Gadamer, H.G. (1960) *Truth and Method*. London: Sheed and Ward.

Gamble, A. and Payne, T. (1996) *Regionalism and World Order*. London: Macmillan.

Gellner, E. (1964) *Thought and Change*. London: Weidenfeld.

Gellner, E. (1983) *Nations and Nationalism*. Oxford: Blackwell.

Gibney, F. (1992) *The Pacific Century*. Tokyo: Kondansha.

Gibney, F. (ed.) (1998) *Unlocking the Bureaucrat's Kingdom*. Washington: Brookings.

Giddens, A. (1979) *Central Problems in Social Theory*. London: Macmillan.

Giddens, A. (1982) *Profiles and Critiques in Social Theory*. London: Macmillan.

Giddens, A. (1984) *The Constitution of Society*. Cambridge: Polity.

Giddens, A. (1987) *Social Theory and Modern Sociology*. Cambridge: Polity.

Giddens, G. (1979) *Central Problems in Social Theory*. London: Macmillan.

Gilson, J. (1998a) 'Japan's pragmatic role in the Asia-Europe meeting'. Paper presented at the British Association of Japanese Studies Conference. Cardiff, April.

Gilson, J. (1998b) 'Creating "Asia" through ASEM: closing the gap between two regions?'. Paper presented at the Third Pan-European International Relations Conference and Joint Meeting with the International Studies Association. Vienna, September.

Gipouloux, F. (ed.) (1994) *Regional Economic Strategies in East Asia*. Tokyo: Maison Franco-Japanaise.

Gray, J. (1998) *False Dawn: The Delusions of Global Capitalism*. London: Granta.

Grimal, H. (1965) *Decolonization: The British, French, Dutch and Belgian Empires 1919–1963*. London: Routledge.

Grimal, H. (1978) *Decolonization*. London: Routledge.

Gudeman, S. (1986) *Economics as Culture*. London: Routledge.

Habermas, J. (1971) *Towards a Rational Society*. London: Heinemann.

Habermas, J. (1989) *The Structural Transformation of the Public Sphere*. Cambridge: Polity.

Halliday, J. (1980) 'Capitalism and socialism in East Asia', *New Left Review*, 124.

Hamilton, C. (1983) 'Capitalist industrialization in East Asia's four little tigers', *Journal of Contemporary Asia*, 13.

Hawthorn, G. (1971) *Enlightenment and Despair*. Cambridge: Cambridge University Press.

Held, D. (1987) *Models of Democracy*. Cambridge: Polity.

Henderson, J. et al. (1988) 'Deciphering the East Asian crisis', *Renewal*, 6 (2).

Henshall, K.G. (1999) *A History of Japan*. London: Macmillan.

Hewison, K., Robinson, R. and Rodam, G. (eds) (1993) *Southeast Asia in the 1990s*. St Leonards: Allen and Unwin.

Higgott, R. (1996) 'Ideas and identity in the international political economy of regionalism: the Asia Pacific and Europe Compared'. Paper presented at the ISA-JAIR Joint Convention. Makuhari, Japan.

Higgott, R. (1998) 'The Asian economic crisis: a study in the politics of resentment', *New Political Economy*, 3 (3).

Higgott, R. (1999) 'Economics, politics and (international) political economy: the need for a balanced diet in an era of globalization', *New Political Economy*, 4 (1).

Higgott, R., Leaver R. and Ravenhill, J. (eds) (1993) *Pacific Economic Relations in the 1990s*. St Leonards: Allen and Unwin.

Higgott, R. and Robison, R. (eds) (1985) *Southeast Asia: Essays in the Political Economy of Structural Change*. London: Routledge.

Hirst, P. and Thompson, G. (1996) *Globalization in Question*. Cambridge: Polity.

Hobsbawm, H. (1994) *The Age of Extremes: The Short Twentieth Century*. London: Michael Joseph.

Hollis, M. and Smith S. (1990) *Explaining and Understanding International Relations*. Oxford: Clarendon.

Holub, R.C. (1991) *Jurgen Habermas: Critic in the Public Sphere*. London: Routledge.

Honda, K. (1993) *The Impoverished Spirit of Contemporary Japan*. New York: Monthly Review Press.

Howe, C. (1996) *The Origins of Japanese Trade Supremacy*. London: Hurst.

Hunter, J. (1989) *The Emergence of Modern Japan*. London: Longman.

Huntington, S.P. (1993) 'The clash of civilizations', *Foreign Affairs*.

Hutton, W. (1994) *The Weekly Guardian*, 31 July.

Ienaga, S. (1978) *The Pacific War: World War II and the Japanese, 1931–1945*. New York: Pantheon.

Inglis, F. (1993) *Cultural Studies*. Oxford: Blackwell.

Iriye, A. (1987) *The Origins of the Second World War in Asia and the Pacific*. London: Longman.

Iriye, A. (1997) *Japan and the Wider World*. London: Longman.

Ishihara, S. (1991) *The Japan That Can Say No*. New York: Simon and Schuster.

Jeffrey, R. (ed.) (1981) *Asia: The Winning of Independence*. London: Macmillan.

Jenks, C. (1993) *Culture*. London: Routledge.

Jessop, R. (ed.) (1988) *Thatchersim: A Tale of Two Nations*. Cambridge: Polity.

Jessop, R. (1990) *State Theory*. Cambridge: Polity.

Johnson, C. (1982) *MTU and the Japanese Miracle*. Stanford, CA: Stanford University Press.

Johnson, C. (1995) *Japan: Who Governs?* New York: Norton.

Kahn, J.S. and Loh, F.K.W. (1992) *Fragmented Vision: Culture and Politics in Contemporary Malaysia*. Sydney: Allen and Unwin.

Katahara, E. (1991) *Japan's Changing Political and Security Role*. Singapore: Institute for Southeast Asian Studies.

Katzenstein, P. and Shiraishi, T. (eds) (1997) *Network Power: Japan and Asia*. New York: Cornell University Press.

Kerkvliet, B. (1977) *The Huk Rebellion: A Study of Peasant Revolt in the Philippines*. Berkeley: University of California Press.

Kerr, C. (1973) *Industrialism and Industrial Man*. Harmondsworth: Penguin.

Kim, H. (1993) 'Japanese ODA policy in the Republic of Korea', in B.M. Koppel and R.J. Orr (eds), *Japan's Foreign Aid: Power and Policy in a New Era*. Boulder, CO: Westview.

Khoo, K.J. (1992) 'The grand vision: mahathir and modernization', in J.S. Khan and F.K.W. Loh (1992) *Fragmented Vision: Culture and Politics in Comtemporary Malaysia*. Sydney: Allen and Unwin.

Kodansha, (1993) *Japan: An Illustrated Encyclopedia*. Tokyo: Kodansha.

Kolko, G. (1968) *The Politics of War*. New York: Vintage.

Koppel, B.M. and Orr, R.J. (eds) (1993) *Japan's Foreign Aid: Power and Policy in a New Era*. Boulder, CO: Westview.

Kosaka, M. (ed.) (1989) *Japan's Choices: New Globalism and Cultural Orientations in an Industrial State*. London: Pinter.

Koschmann, J.V. (1997) 'Asianism's ambivalent legacy', in P. Katzenstein and T. Shiraishi (eds), *Network Power: Japan and Asia*. New York: Cornell University Press.

Krugman, P. (1994a) *Peddling Prosperity: Economic Sense and Nonsense in the Age of Diminished Expectations*. New York: Norton.

Krugman, P. (1994b) 'The myth of Asia's miracle', *Foreign Affairs*.

Large, S. (1997) *Emperors of the Rising Sun*. Tokyo: Kodansha.

Lim, K.W. (1988) *Hidden Agenda*. Petaling Jaya: Limkokwing.

Linklater, A. (1990) *Beyond Realism and Marxism: Critical Theory and International Relations*. London: Macmillan.

Long, N. (ed.) (1992) *Battlefields of Knowledge*. London: Routledge.

McCord, W. (1991) *The Dawn of the Pacific Century: Implications for Three Worlds of Development*. New Brunswick: Transaction.

MacIntyre, A. (1962) 'A mistake about causality in social science', in P. Laslet and W.G. Runciman (eds), *Politics, Philosophy and Society Second Series*. Oxford: Blackwell.

MacIntyre, A. (1971) *Against the Self-Images of the Age*. London: Duckworth.

MacIntyre, A.J. (1993) 'Indonesia, Thailand and the Northeast Asia connection', in R. Higgott, R. Leaver and J. Ravenhill (eds), *Pacific Economic Relations in the 1990s: Cooperation or Conflict*. St Leonards: Allen and Unwin.

Mackerras, C. (1995) *Eastern Asia*. London: Longman.

Macpherson, C.B. (1966) *The Real World of Democracy*. Oxford: Oxford University Press.

Macpherson, W.J. (1987) *The Economic Development of Japan*. London: Macmillan.

Mahathir, M. and Ishihara, S. (1995) *The Voice of Asia*. Tokyo: Kondansha.

Marx, K. (1852) 'The eighteenth brumaire of Louis Bonaparte' (first published in *Die Revolution*), New York.

Meyer, A. (1981) *The Persistence of the Old Regime*. New York: Croom Helm.

Mills, C.W. (1959) *The Sociological Imagination*. Harmondsworth: Penguin.

Moise, E. (1994) *Modern China*. London: Longman.

Montes, M.F. (1998) *The Currency Crisis in Southeast Asia*. Singapore: Institute of Southeast Asian Studies.

Moore, B. (1966) *Social Origins of Dictatorship and Democracy*. Boston, MA: Beacon.

Morris-Suzuki, T. (1995) 'Japanese nationalism from Meiji to 1937', in C. Mackerras (ed.), *Eastern Asia*. London: Longman.

Nairn, T. (1988) *The Enchanted Glass*. London: Hutchinson Radius.

Nakane, C. (1970) *Japanese Society*. Tokyo: Tuttle.

Naya, S. and Takayama, A. (eds) (1990) *Economic Development in East and Southeast Asia: Essays in Honour of Professor Shinichi Ichimura*. Singapore: Institute for Southeast Asian Studies.

Nester, W.R. (1990) *Japan's Growing Power Over East Asia and the World Economy*. London: Macmillan.

Nester, W.R. (1992) *Japan and the Third World*. New York: St Martin's Press.

Ohmae, K. (1987) *Beyond National Borders: Reflections on Japan and the World*. Tokyo: Kondansha.

Orr, R.M. (1990) *The Emergence of Japan's Foreign Aid Power*. New York: Columbia University Press.

Overbeek. H. (1990) *Global Capitalism and National Decline*. London: Allen and Unwin.

Ozawa, I. (1994) *Blueprint for a New Japan*. Tokyo: Kondansha.

Pempel, T.J. (1982) *Policy and Politics in Japan: Creative Conservatism*. Philadelphia, PA: Temple University Press.

Phongpaichit, P. (1990) *The New Wave of Japanese Investment in ASEAN*. Singapore: Institute of Southeast Asian Studies.

Pollard, P. (1971) *The Idea of Progress*. Harmondsworth: Penguin.

Preston, P.W. (1982) *Theories of Development*. London: Routledge.

Preston, P.W. (1985) *New Trends in Development Theory*. London: Routledge.

Preston, P.W. (1986) *Making Sense of Development*. London: Routledge.

Preston, P.W. (1987) *Rethinking Development*. London: Routledge.

Preston, P.W. (1994) *Discourses of Development: State, Market and Polity in the Analysis of Complex Change*. Aldershot: Avebury.

Preston, P.W. (1995) 'Domestic inhibitions to a leadership role for Japan in Pacific Asia', *Contemporary Southeast Asia*, 16 (4).

Preston, P.W. (1996) *Development Theory*. Oxford: Blackwell.

Preston, P.W. (1997) *Political-Cultural Identity: Citizen and Nation in a Global Era*. London: Sage.

Preston, P.W. (1998a) *Pacific Asia in the Global System*. Oxford: Blackwell.

Preston, P.W. (1998b) 'Reading the Asian crisis: history, culture and institutional truths', *Contemporary Southeast Asia*, 20 (3).

Reading, B. (1992) *Japan: The Coming Collapse*. London: Orion.

Richie, B. (1987) *Geisha, Gangster, Neighbour, Nun*. Tokyo: Kondansha.

Rix, A. (1993a) 'Managing Japan's foreign aid: ASEAN', in B.M. Koppel and R.J. Orr (eds), *Japan's Foreign Aid: Policy and Power in a New Era*. Boulder, CO: Westview.

Rix, A. (1993b) *Japan's Foreign Aid*. London: Routledge.

Robison, R. (ed.) (1996) *Pathways to Asia*. St Leonards: Allen and Unwin.

Robison, R. and Goodman, D. (eds) (1996) *The New Rich in Asia*. London: Routledge.

Robison, R., Hewison, K. and Higgott, R. (eds) (1987) *Southeast Asia in the 1980s*. St Leonards: Allen and Unwin.

Rodan, G. (ed.) (1996) *Political Oppositions in Industrializing Asia*. London: Routledge.

Rorty, R. (1989) *Contingency, Irony and Solidarity*. Cambridge: Cambridge University Press.

Sachs, W. (1992) *The Development Dictionary*. London: Zed Books.

Saga, J. (1987) *Memories of Silk and Straw*. Tokyo: Kondansha.

Said, E. (1978) *Orientalism*. London: Routledge and Kegan Paul.

Scott, J.C. (1985) *Weapons of the Weak*. New Haven: Yale University Press.

Seidensticker, E. (1983) *Low City, High City*. Tokyo: Tuttle.

Sheridan, K. (1993) *Governing the Japanese Economy*. Cambridge: Polity.

Sheridan, K. (ed.) (1998a) *Emerging Economic Systems in Asia*. St Leonards: Allen and Unwin.

Sheridan, K. (1998b) 'Japan's economic system', in K. Sheridan (ed.), *Emerging Economic Systems in Asia*. St Leonards: Allen and Unwin.

Shibusawa, M. (1992) *Pacific Asia in the 1990s*. London: Routledge.

Sinha, R. (1982) 'Japan and ASEAN: a special relationship', *The World Today*.

Skinner, Q. (ed.) (1985) *The Return of Grand Theory in the Human Sciences*. Cambridge: Cambridge University Press.

Sklair, L. (1991) *The Sociology of the Global System*. London: Harvester.

Stern, G. (1998) *The Structure of International Society*. London: Pinter.

Steven, R. (1990) *Japan's New Imperialism*. London: Macmillan.

Stockwin, A. (1999) *Governing Japan*. Oxford: Blackwell.

Strange, S. (1988) *States and Markets*. London: Pinter.

Streeten, P. (1972) *The Frontiers of Development Studies*. London: Macmillan.

Streeten, P. (1994) *The Role of Direct Foreign Investment in Developing Countries*. Tokyo: Sophia University.

Sugimoto, Y. (1997) *An Introduction to Japanese Society*. Cambridge: Cambridge University Press.

Swedberg, R. (1987) 'Economic sociology: past and present', *Current Sociology*.

Tanaka, S. (1993) *Japan's Orient: Rendering Pasts into History*. Berkeley: University of California Press.

Taylor, (1996) *Greater China and Japan: Prospects for Economic Partnership in East Asia*. London: Routledge.

Thorne, C. (1978) *Allies of a Kind*. Oxford: Oxford University Press.

Thorne, C. (1980) 'Racial aspects of the Far Eastern War of 1941–1945', from proceedings of the British Academy. Oxford: Oxford University Press.

Thorne, C. (1986) *The Far Eastern War: States and Societies 1941-1945*. London: Counterpoint.

Thurow, L. (1994) *Head to Head: The Coming Economic Battle Among Japan, Europe and America*. London: Nicholas Brearley.

Tivey, L. (ed.) (1981) *The Nation State*. Oxford: Martin Robertson.

Tsuru, S. (1993) *Japan's Capitalism: Creative Defeat and Beyond*. Cambridge: Cambridge University Press.

Tsurumi, S. (1987) *A Cultural History of Postwar Japan 1945–1980*. London: KPI.

Turnbull, M. (1977) *A History of Singapore*. Oxford: Oxford University Press.

Ueda, A. (1994) *The Electric Geisha*. Tokyo: Kondansha.

van Wolferen, K. (1989) *The Enigma of Japanese Power*. London: Macmillan.

Vogel, E. (1980) *Japan as Number One*. Tokyo: Tuttle.

Wade, R. (1996) 'Japan, the World Bank and the art of paradigm maintenance: the East Asian miracle in political perspective', *New Left Review*, 217.

Wade, R. and Veneroso, F. (1998) 'The Asian crisis: the high debt model versus the Wall Street–Treasury–IMF complex', *New Left Review*, 228.

Walter, J. (1992) 'Defining Australia', in G. Whitlock and D. Carter (eds), *Images of Australia*. Brisbane: University of Queensland Press.

Watson, M. (1999) 'Rethinking capital mobility, reregulating financial markets', *New Political Economy*, 4 (1).

Waswo, A. (1993) *Modern Japanese Society*. Oxford: Oxford University Press.

Waswo, A. (1996) *Modern Japanese Society 1968–1994*. Oxford: Oxford University Press.

White, R. (1992) 'Inventing Australia', in G. Whitlock and D. Carter (eds), *Inventing Australia*. Brisbane: University of Queensland Press.

Whitlock, G. and Carter, D. (eds) (1992) *Images of Australia*. Brisbane: University of Queensland Press.

Wilkinson, E. (1991) *Misunderstanding: Europe Versus Japan*. Harmondsworth: Penguin.

Williams, D. (1994) *Japan: Beyond the End of History*. London: Routledge.

Williams, D. (1996) *Japan and the Enemies of Open Political Science*. London: Routledge.

Winch, P. (1958) *The Idea of a Social Science and its Relation to Philosophy*. London: Routledge.

Woodiwiss, A. (1993) *Postmodernity USA*. London: Sage.

World Bank (1993) *The East Asian Miracle: Economic Growth and Public Policy.* Oxford: Oxford University Press.

Worsley, P. (1984) *The Three Worlds: Culture and World Development.* London: Weidenfeld.

Yamazaki, M., (1994) *Individualism and the Japanese.* Tokyo: Japan Echo.

Yasutomo, D.T. (1986) *The Manner of Giving.* Lexington: Heath.

Yoshihara, K. (1988) *The Rise of Ersatz Capitalism in Southeast Asia.* Oxford: Oxford University Press.

Yoshino, K. (1992) *Cultural Nationalism in Contemporary Japan.* London: Routledge.

Zhao, Quangsheng (1993) 'Japan's aid diplomacy with China', in B.M. Koppel and R.J. Orr (eds), *Japan's Foreign Aid: Power and Policy in a New Era.* Boulder, CO: Westview.

Zysman, J. (1996) 'The myth of a "global economy": enduring national foundations and emerging regional realities', *New Political Economy,* 1 (2).

INDEX

absentee landlords, 87
administrative guidance to firms, 93, 105, 108, 131, 181
aid programmes, 99–100, 147, 157–65, 169, 179, 183–5, 210
    rationale for, 152–3, 159–60, 183, 220–21
Ainu population, 121–2
America *see* United States
Anderson, B., 137
Anglo-Japanese Treaty (1902), 53, 56, 65, 70
Anti-Commintern Pact (1936), 57, 72
arts, the, 137–40
Asai, Ryoi, 139
Ashida, H., 86
Asia-Europe Meeting (ASEM), 14, 148, 167, 198
Asia-Pacific Economic Cooperation (APEC), 14, 17, 166, 174, 198, 201, 204
Asian financial crisis (1997–8), 110–12, 145, 151, 168, 192, 194–5, 198, 209, 224
'Asian ten', the, 148, 167
'Asian values', 111, 149, 201
Association of South East Asian Nations (ASEAN), 14, 79, 147, 157, 160–64, 167, 180, 187–8
atomic bombing of Japan, 74
Aung San, 76, 79, 156
Australia, 152, 162, 166, 174, 189–90

bad debt, 110, 168, 193
bakufu administration, 29
bakuhan system, 29
banking system, 40, 47, 49, 55, 92–3, 109, 193
Barraclough, G., 75
bathhouses, 139
Bauman, Z., 5–6
Beasley, W.G., 23, 29, 33, 64, 67, 69
Benedict, Ruth, 142
Bernard, M., 147–50, 200–201
Borthwick, M., 21, 68

Bose, Subbash Chandra, 76
Bowring, R., 21
Boxer Rebellion, 178
Brenner, R., 9
Britain *see* United Kingdom
bubble economy, 97, 100, 110, 133, 168, 192–4, 223
Buckley, B., 84, 115, 144, 181, 216, 222
Buddhism, 36, 135–6, 139, 142, 176
burakumin, 121–2
bureaucracy, the, 129–32, 159–60, 181, 216–17
bureaucratic decision-making, 27
Burma, 74, 76–7, 79, 155–6

cabinet government, 129
capital flows, 199
capital investment, 48–9, 57; *see also* foreign direct investment
capitalism, 9–10, 40, 92, 175
    different versions of, 16–17, 97, 202
caste system, 25–8, 30–31, 35, 41, 43, 117–18, 121–2
Chan, H.C., 206
Charter Oath, 36
Cherry, Kittredge, 124
Chiang Kai Shek, 178
children, attitudes to and upbringing of, 114–15, 122–3
China
    currency devaluation, 192
    four modernizations, 189
    historical relations with Western powers, 10, 32–3, 47, 51, 61, 153, 177–8
    imperial, 41, 176
    influence on Japan, 22, 25, 27–8, 31–2, 136
    Japanese military incursions into, 13, 56–9, 65, 72–6, 81, 154–6, 178
    Japanese relations with, 21, 54, 62–5, 70, 72, 80, 152, 161–2
    power and influence of, 14, 17, 146, 150–51, 171, 174, 195, 202

China (*cont.*)
   revolutions and civil war in, 70, 79, 83, 178
   tribute system, 52, 62
   see also overseas Chinese; Sino-Japanese War
Choshu, 35
Christianity, 137
civil code, 42, 47, 123
civil society, 149, 201
Clammer, J., 108, 119, 140–44, 214–15, 218–19
class structures *see* caste system
Clinton, Bill, 80, 156
coffee houses, 139
Cold War, 75, 78, 82, 84, 87, 89, 127, 130, 148, 166, 172, 180, 191, 195, 203–4, 207, 214, 222
colonialism, 10–13, 32, 51–2, 66–80 *passim*, 99, 146, 153–6, 161, 176–7, 181, 195; *see also* imperialism
'comprehensive security', 145, 220
conformity, culture of, 115, 133, 141, 182; *see also* obedience to authority
Confucianism, 25, 27–8, 35, 41, 66, 114, 135–6
constitution, Japanese, 36, 43, 54, 61, 71, 85, 128–9, 145
consumerism, 140–43, 181–2, 215
'continuing family', the, 114–19, 123
Control Faction, 72
core economy of Pacific-Asian region, Japan as, 12–14, 95, 98, 104, 146–52, 167–70, 174, 179–80, 183, 185, 191, 200, 202, 213, 220, 222, 224
corporatism, 97, 101, 104, 107–8, 116–17, 120, 128, 131, 144, 181–2, 214
corruption, 132, 216
credit facilities, 24, 49, 93
crime, 126
Cronin, R.P., 152, 161–2, 167, 183–5, 187, 220–21
crony capitalism, 111, 151, 156, 165
culture, 137–42, 201
   alternative approaches to, 134–5
   contentious issues of, 15
   diffusion of, 149, 221

daimyo, 22, 29–30, 35
decolonization, 75, 77–8, 153, 157–8, 195
democracy and democratization, 54–5, 70–71, 127, 130–31, 206, 214
Deng Xiaping, 174, 189, 195
deregulation, 101, 134, 168, 194, 198–9, 216, 224

determinism (geographical, ethnic, psychological, eugenic and cultural), 120, 127
'developmental' state and society, 108, 112, 118, 128, 144, 181–2, 186, 205, 211, 214, 222
Dobson, W., 160, 187
Dodge, Joseph, 88
Dore, Ronald, 107–8, 116, 211–12
Drifte, R., 210
Durkheim, Emile, 119
Dutch East Indies, 79, 155–6
Dutch influence on Japan, 28, 32, 66

East Asia Economic Caucus (EAEC), 166
East Asian Economic Group (EAEG), 14, 148
Eccleston, B., 121–2, 142, 181, 210–11
economic analysis, 15
economic planning, 92–4
Economic Stabilization Board (ESB), 86
economic success of Japanese economy, explanations for, 105–6
The Economist, 211
Edo, city of, 23–4, 29; *see also* Tokyo
Edo period, 26–8, 37–8, 139, 141
education, 42–3, 69, 85, 114–16, 125, 130–31, 182, 214
electoral system, 129–30, 133, 193
elite domination, 113, 169, 204, 218
elucidatory intention, 6
emancipatory engagement, 6
emperor system, 21–2, 26–9, 33, 35–6, 43, 48, 61, 80, 85, 158, 125, 128–9, 136
Enlightenment, the, 39, 66, 143, 202–6 *passim*, 208–9, 218–19
environmental concerns, 94–6, 215
Eurocentrism, 5–6
European economy, society and culture, key elements of, 173
European exchange rate mechanism (ERM), 198
European Union (EU), 14, 17, 34, 100, 111–12, 148, 165–7, 169, 172–3, 185, 190, 203–4, 214, 222
Evans, G., 205
expansionism, Japanese, 52–3, 56, 58, 63–4, 67, 70, 145, 150, 155, 218
   rationale for, 146
export-oriented development, 110, 164, 187–8, 192

fairness in society, 116, 120, 131
Fallows, James, 131

family relationships, 26–8, 41–3, 47–8,
    114–19, 123, 205
  within firms, 108, 116–17, 119
  within the national state, 118, 141
fascism, 57–8, 66, 75, 127, 154, 177–8
feudal system, 29, 37–41, 43, 66, 68, 117–18,
    144, 153, 177
financial systems, 39–40, 47, 49, 55, 93
'floating world', the, 138–9
'flying geese' metaphor, 148, 151, 162, 187,
    200
foreign direct investment (FDI), 100, 147,
    162–5, 169, 185, 221
Formosa, 76, 78; see also Taiwan
14th Year Incident, 39
France, 53–4, 58, 64, 76, 80, 128, 154–6, 178
'fukoku-kyohei', 38
Fukuzawa, Yukichi, 66

gender relations, 41, 115–16, 119, 122–4,
    182, 214
General Agreement on Tariffs and Trade
    (GATT), 112, 166–7
Genro, the, 128
Germany, 39, 53–4, 56, 64–72 passim, 77, 80,
    84, 104, 128, 154, 158, 178, 213
gift-giving, 141
global industrial-capitalist system, 165, 195,
    171–2, 175, 204, 222
globalization, 3, 7, 98, 111, 141, 167, 173, 184,
    197–8, 204, 221
gold standard, 40, 56
government, Japanese, role of, 40, 47–50, 57,
    90–99 passim, 106–9, 181–2, 205, 211,
    215
Gray, J., 197, 202–3, 205, 208
Great Depression, 56–7, 71, 81
Grimal, H., 77, 157
Group of Seven (G7) countries, 174, 204
groupism, 141–2
growth, 50–51, 90–98 passim, 104, 132, 206
Guadalcanal, 74
Gudeman, S., 107

Habermas, Jurgen, 4
Halliday, J., 186
Hamilton, C., 68–9, 164
harmony in Japanese society, 119–21, 127,
    141–4, 169, 175, 194, 204, 211, 213, 220
Hatta, M., 76
Held, D., 206
Henshall, K.G., 22, 24, 35, 55, 133, 193
hierarchical structures, 31, 42, 83, 117, 149,
    219
Hiroshima, 74

historical development experiences
  debates generated by, 15–16
  phases of and breaks in, 8–10, 20, 44,
    196–7
  understanding of, 18
history and pre-history of Japan (up to,
    1603), 21–3
Hitler, Adolf, 80, 158
Hobsbawm, H., 172, 222
Holding Company Liquidation
    Commission, 87
Hong Kong, 152, 160
Hosokawa, M., 129
Howe, C., 24
Huk rebellion, 79, 156
humanism, 215, 218–19
Hunter, J., 20, 23, 25–6, 31, 33–4, 36–7, 41–2,
    52–3, 62–3, 127
Huntingdon, S.P., 149
Hutton, W., 212

ideology, 3, 118–21, 127–8, 211
Ienaga, S., 73
Ikeda, H., 90, 94
Imperial Way Faction, 72
imperialism, Japanese, 154, 177
  'late', 54, 81, 144, 185
  phases of, 60–63
  see also colonialism
income and wealth, distribution of, 121,
    182
indicative planning, 92
individualism, 83, 119, 142–3, 174, 205, 219
Indo-China, 58, 76–7, 80, 155–7, 161, 174,
    176, 189
Indonesia, 188
industrialism, 3
industrialization, 39–41, 47–50, 59, 68–9, 80,
    94, 118, 140, 155–6, 164, 187–8
inequality in Japanese society, 120–21
inflation, 89, 96–7, 100, 133
Inoue, Kaoru, 35
institutional economic analysis, 107–8, 111
interest groups, 129–30
International Monetary Fund (IMF), 112,
    167, 173, 197, 202, 204
international relations, theories of, 148–9,
    200–201
Iriye, A., 70, 73, 146
Ito, Hirobumi, 35
Iwakura mission, 34

Japanese language, 120
Johnson, C., 131, 211, 213–14
Jomon period, 21

Kabo reform movement, 68
Kagoshima, 33
Kamakura period, 22
Kanagawa, Treaty of, 32
Karafuto, 67–8; *see also* Sakhalin island
Katayama, T., 86, 92
keiretsu, 105, 109
keisei-saimin, 50, 57
Keynes, J.M., 91
Khoo, K.J., 187
Kido, Koin, 35
Kim, H., 160
kokutai, 87
Kolko, G., 83
Korea, 17, 21, 44, 46, 52–4, 62–9 *passim*, 76,
    78, 152, 154–5, 160, 179, 185–6
Korean War, 78, 84, 88–92 *passim*, 109, 157,
    179
Koreans in Japan, 121–2, 186
Kornicki, P., 21
Krugman, P., 103, 204–5
Kuomintang (KMT), 75–6, 178
Kwantung, 67–8
Kyoto, 22

labour law, 87
land reform, 87
land values, 97, 110, 182, 193
leadership role for Japan, 210, 220
League of Nations, 44, 55–7, 60, 67, 72
learning from Japan, 210–11
leisure, 138–40, 182, 214
Lewis, Arthur, 40
Liaotung, 64, 154
Liberal Democratic Party (LDP), 82, 102,
    129, 132–3, 193, 217
liberalization for Japan, 182, 184, 198,
    214
lifetime employment, 105–6, 116, 182,
    212
Long, N., 165
Long Term Capital Management (LTCM),
    198

MacArthur, Douglas, 83
MacIntyre, A.J., 188
Macpherson, C.B., 206
Mahathir, M., 188
Malaysia, 14, 79, 148, 155–6, 166, 187–8
Manchukuo, 155–6; *see also* Manchuria
Manchuria, 53–4, 57, 63–8 *passim*, 72, 154,
    185
Mao Zedong, 76, 84, 87
March First Movement, 68–9
Marcos, Ferdinand, 79, 156

market liberalism, 106–8, 111, 113, 168,
    171–3, 193–7, 202–4, 209–13, 218–19,
    222
Marx, Karl, 18, 175
Matsukata, Masayashi, 35, 39, 47
Meiji Restoration and era, 9–13, 20, 29–44,
    60–63, 66–7, 70–71, 81, 104, 109, 114,
    118–19, 123–36 *passim*, 140, 144, 152–3,
    177, 181, 183, 213, 217
    later period (1894–1912), 46–55
    reforms of, 38, 43–4, 47
mercantilism, 104, 167, 171, 184, 213–14,
    218
merchants, status of, 26–7, 30–31, 38, 42,
    117
Midway Island, Battle of, 74
militarism, 46, 55–7, 59, 60, 67, 71–3, 77, 128,
    213
military production, 48–9, 109
Minamoto no Yoritomo, 22
Ministry of Foreign Affairs, 159, 161, 183
Ministry of Home Affairs, 38
Ministry of Industrial Development, 38
Ministry of International Trade and
    Industry (MITI), 58, 82, 90, 92, 94–6,
    102, 108, 159, 161, 181, 183
minority groups, 121–2, 127
model enterprises, 38, 49
modern world, the, Japanese responses to,
    46, 81, 83, 128, 144, 177
modernity and modernization, 3–5, 12, 34,
    67–8, 104, 128, 130, 175–6
Moise, E., 178
monetization, 24
'money politics', 129, 132
Moore, B., 58, 61, 153, 178
Morris-Suzuki, T., 62, 66
Mukden, 154
multinational corporations (MNCs), 163,
    167, 172, 185, 210, 222
Murasaki, Shikibu, 138
Muromachi period, 22

Nagasaki, 28, 32, 66, 74
Nakane, C., 41
Nara period, 22
National Income Doubling Plan, 90, 92–5
National Seclusion, policy of, 32
nationalism, 29, 33, 39, 44, 50, 54–6, 58,
    62–7, 70–71, 75–9, 125, 146, 154, 156,
    177, 179, 218
    cultural, 141
    economic, 102
nationstatehood, 11, 35, 38
new technologies, 98